Sharing in Christ's Virtues

∞

LIVIO MELINA

Sharing in Christ's Virtues

For a Renewal of Moral Theology
in Light of *Veritatis Splendor*

translated by
WILLIAM E. MAY

THE CATHOLIC UNIVERSITY
OF AMERICA PRESS
WASHINGTON, D.C.

The paper used in this publication meets the minimum requirements of American National Standards for Information Science—Permanence of Paper for Printed Library materials, ANSI Z39.48-1984.

∞

LIBRARY OF CONGRESS CATALOGING-IN-PUBLICATION DATA

Melina, Livio
    Sharing in Christ's virtues : for a renewal of moral theology in light of Veritatis splendor / Livio Melina ; translated by William E. May
      p. cm.
    Includes bibliographical references and index.
    ISBN 0-8132-0989-7 (cl. : alk. paper)
    ISBN 0-8132-0990-0 (pbk. : alk. paper)
      1. Christian ethics—Catholic authors. 2. Catholic Church—Doctrines.
  I. Catholic Church. Pope (1978– : John Paul II). Veritatis splendor.   II. Title.

BJ1249 .M34 2001
241'.042—dc21

                                99-087318

To Carl A. Anderson, William E. May,
and to the students of the Washington Session
of the Pontifical John Paul II Institute for
Studies on Marriage and Family

> *"Christ is the one who in this life gives us the virtues;*
> *and, in the place of all the virtues*
> *necessary in this valley of tears,*
> *he will give us one virtue only,*
> *himself."*

St. Augustine, *Enarrationes in Ps. 83, 11;* PL 33, 1065

Contents

∞

Foreword

∞

It is a pleasure to introduce this work of Rev. Msgr. Livio Melina. Msgr. Melina is professor of moral theology at the John Paul II Institute for Studies on Marriage and Family in Rome and editor of the Institiute's journal, *Anthropotes: Rivista di studi sulla Persona e la Famglia*. He is also the author of several Italian books in moral theology, of which some have been translated into Spanish and other languages, but not, unfortunately, into English.

I say "unfortunately" because I believe that Msgr. Melina is one of the most erudite and brilliant Catholic moral theologians of our time. And this is what makes introducing this book so joyful an occasion, because now readers of English will be able to profit from Msgr. Melina's thought-provoking and powerful presentation of key themes in moral theology "renewed" in the light of Vatican Council II and by the profound insights of Pope John Paul II.

The chapters in the first part ("Toward a Christocentrism of the Virtues: Lines of Renewal") were originally presented as a set of lectures to the students of the John Paul II Institute for Studies on Marriage and Family in Washington, D.C. in 1997. I had the pleasure of becoming a "student" myself for this week of lectures, and like my fellow students I was captivated by Msgr. Melina's wonderful presentation of the Christian moral life as essentially a following of Christ, one shaped inwardly by Christian virtues, gifts from God himself, enabling Jesus'disciples *to be* true to their vocation to holiness. I am confident that readers of this book will find that it opens their eyes to the beauty and depth of the Christian moral life as one enlivened by God's very own love. Although marked with the cross, for after all Jesus told us that to follow him we must take up our

cross daily, the Christian moral life is above all a pilgrimage to beatitude, to fulfillment in Christ, who will indeed be our "Simon of
Cyrene,"ready to help us bear any crosses he may give us.

The chapters in the second part "Ecclesial Sense and the Moral
Life: Perspectives and Developments"were originally published in
the journal *Communio* and have been revised for presentation here.
These chapters help us to understand more fully the significance of
our being members of Christ's body the Church, children of God
because we are the fruit of Christ's loving union with his bride, the
Church. Thus the Church is truly our Mother, and her teaching is
thus not an imposition of some alien doctrine but is rather a
reminder of truths we ought already to possess by virtue of our primordial act of faith, which makes us to be God's very own children,
and called, like Jesus our brother, to do only what is pleasing to the
Father. It is through our Mother the Church that Christ calls us to
holiness and through her that he gives us the ability to form, with
our brothers and sisters in him and with the Blessed Trinity itself, a
true *communio personarum,* a communion of persons.

Msgr. Melina's splendid book will find, I am sure, a warm wel-
come in the minds and hearts of men and women who seek sincerely to follow Christ and share in his virtues.

William E. May
Michael J. McGivney Professor of Moral Theology
John Paul II Institute for Studies on Marriage and Family,
Washington, D.C.

Sharing in Christ's Virtues

∞

Introduction

*I*t seems that with the encyclical *Veritatis splendor*, as with other magisterial interventions in the field of morality, many theologians reacted in a markedly critical way. Commentators centered attention principally on the second chapter of the encyclical, in which John Paul II proposes authoritative judgments sharply critical of positions affirming an autonomous morality; supporting the *creativity of conscience;* weakening or denying its dependence on truth; separating one's *fundamental option* from everyday, concrete actions; and denying the existence of absolutely binding moral norms on the basis of a *proportionalistic calculus* of goods and evils.[1]

There can be no doubt that in the theological discussions after Vatican Council II certain "interpretations of Christian morality incompatible with 'sound doctrine' (2 Tm 4.3)" (no. 29) were developed. Therefore the document, in carrying out the ministry of Peter's successor and with the authority of the ordinary magisterium proper to encyclicals, was intended to set forth clearly doctrinal aspects of critical significance in order to confront what the pope did not hesitate to call a "genuine crisis, since the difficulties which it engenders have most serious implications for the moral life of the

1. For an overview of the debates within Catholic moral theology on which the encylical *Veritatis splendor* seeks to shed light and to express an authoritative critical discernment, see the essays of William E. May, "Theologians and Theologies in the Encylical," *Anthropotes: Rivista di studi sulla persona e la famiglia* 10, no. 1 (1994): 39–59, and "John Paul II, Moral Theology, and Moral Theologians," in *Veritatis Splendor and the Renewal of Moral Theology,* ed. J. A. DiNoia, O.P., and Romanus Cessario, O.P. (Chicago: Midwest Theological Forum, 1999), 211–40.

faithful and for communion in the Church, as well as for a just and fraternal social life" (no. 5), so much so that "it is no longer a matter of limited and occasional dissent, but of an overall and systematic calling into question of traditional moral doctrine, on the basis of certain anthropological and ethical presuppositions" (no. 4).

The attention given to the technical descriptions and rational arguments of the second part of the encyclical has, however, resulted in overemphasizing the encyclical's "negative" criticisms and its philosophical dimension, obscuring its first part, devoted to the Christological foundation of Christian morality, and also its third part, concerned with the ecclesial and pastoral nature of the Christian moral life. These sections of the document, speaking broadly, have been considered as theoretically of little relevance, parenetic in nature and in any case somewhat peripheral to the heart of the teaching set forth. It has thus been somewhat easy to treat this encyclical very reductivistically. The encyclical nonetheless represents the first document of the magisterium devoted to the foundations of the Catholic moral life; but it is regarded as a simplistic and "repressive" document in comparison with true theology; it is dismissed as a document that simply failed to understand the positions it criticizes in their theological significance and that would like "to put theology aside" in the name of ecclesiastical discipline.[2]

But in truth, the encyclical *Veritatis splendor* (no. 29) explicitly invites moral theologians to deepen and perfect their labors in carrying out that renewal of moral theology called for by Vatican Council II in *Optatam totius* (no. 16). John Paul II's document, in fact, recognizes that this effort by theologians "has already borne fruit in inter-

---

2. This is the accusation leveled in the book *Moraltheologie im Abseits? Antwort auf die Enzyklika "Veritatis splendor,"* ed. Dietmar Mieth (Freiburg—Basel—Vienna: Herder, 1994). Similar charges are also made in the volume edited by J. Wilkins, *Understanding "Veritatis splendor"* (London: SPCK, 1994), which contains the essays that appeared in *The [London] Tablet.* One-sidedly negative and particularly harsh is the volume edited by Joseph Selling and Jan Jans, *The Splendor of Accuracy: An Examination of the Assertions Made by "Veritatis splendor"* (Kampen, The Netherlands, and Grand Rapids, Mich.: Kok Pharos/Eerdmans, 1994). For a critique of the Selling and Jans volume, see William E. May, *"The Splendor of Accuracy: How Accurate?,"* *The Thomist* 59 (1995): 465–84. For a critical overview of the first reactions to the encyclical, see A. Rodriguez Luño, *"'Veritatis splendor' un anno dopo. Appunti per un bilancio (1),"* *Acta Philosophica* 4, no. 2 (1995): 223–60.

esting and helpful reflections about the truths of faith to be believed and applied in life, reflections offered in a form better suited to the sensitivities and questions of our contemporaries" (no. 29). He likewise presents critical reservations and severe judgments for those theological positions not in conformity with "sound teaching" (see 2 Tm 4.3). The encyclical also offers positive directions for carrying on the work of renewing moral theology by exploring new paths that can overcome the limits found in the more recent tradition and in its insufficient revision. The encyclical, far from dispensing with moral theology or seeking to substitute for it, wants rather to stimulate the effort of renewal in the light of Vatican Council II. But to grasp this constructive perspective of the document and to perceive its "positive" directions, it is necessary to read it in its entirety: to give due consideration to the first and third chapters; above all, to read chapter two in the light of chapter one.

Now, several years after its publication, when the polemics characteristic of some immediate reactions to the encyclical have quieted down, I want to take up the invitation to develop the new directions of the encyclical and above all to take some steps of a positive nature, in the conviction that the crisis that theological-moral reflection still encounters can be overcome only if adequate answers are given to legitimate demands for renewal.

Beyond specific doctrinal points, *Veritatis splendor* focuses attention on two deep roots crucial in the widespread and systematic discussion of moral theology's heritage: the breaking of the bond between freedom and truth and of that between faith and morals (no. 4). The first factor is located above all on a philosophical level and reflects the crisis of postmodernity, which, because it does not maintain any possible link between reason and universal and permanent truth, abandons freedom to subjectivistic arbitrariness and ends up by proposing merely contractual procedures as the way to develop a public morality.[3]

The second factor, theological in origin, is found at an even deeper level and, as I will try to show, can be seen as the root cause of the

---

3. On this, see Carl Anderson, *"Veritatis splendor* and the New Evangelization," *Anthropotes: Rivista di studi sulla persona e famiglia* 10, no. 1 (1994): 61–73.

first rupture as well; because it unhinges the unity and totality of the act of faith, the rupture between faith and morality gives legitimacy to a pluralism of (contradictory) ethical views compatible, however, with membership in the Church. The result of these two ruptures is the loss of the intrinsic meaning of the human act and of its relationship with God.

If this analysis is correct, then the crisis of postconciliar moral theology can be interpreted, from a technical point of view, as the extreme crisis of the posttridentine manual tradition and its methodology. In it some problems were concealed in a merely casuistic debate, hidden in their deepest dimensions, but in turn exposed in bright light in the crisis following *Humanae vitae*. In the new context of secularization and of ethical pluralism, which demanded a more coherent foundation of norms, the inadequacy of the traditional way of imposing norms became unambiguously clear. Proportionalistic theories claimed, not without reason, to be the legitimate heirs of a certain kind of casuistic tradition, whose presuppositions they shared, seeking to remedy their lack of a rational foundation.[4]

The two principal deficiencies of the old and new manualist traditions can be described as "legalism" and "extrinsicism."[5] On the philosophical level, law was seen not as the expression of a truth about the Good, but as the principle of obligation deriving from the will of a lawgiver. On the theological level, the moral dimension was conceived as autonomous and extrinsic with respect to faith and grace. To avoid these inadequacies it is necessary to explore other perspectives and to find new philosophical and theological categories that will allow for restoring the bonds uniting freedom to truth and faith to morality.

4. The continuity of proportionalist views with the modern tradition of Catholic moral theology is defended by Bernard Hoose in his book *Proportionalism: The American Debate and Its European Roots* (Washington, D.C.: Georgetown University Press, 1987).

5. For a critical description of legalism, see Germain Grisez, "Legalism, Moral Truth, and Pastoral Practice," in *The Catholic Priest as Moral Teacher and Guide*, ed. Thomas J. Herron (San Francisco: Ignatius Press, 1990), 97–113; for extrinsicism, see Angelo Scola, *Questioni di antropologia teologica*, 2nd ed. (Rome: PUL/Mursia, 1997), 107–30.

The encyclical *Veritatis splendor* does not claim to be a systematic work in moral theology; however, it does not leave us without precious indications for deepening moral theology and giving it its theological and philosophical foundations. Two affirmations of the document seem to me especially fruitful for theological reflection: (1) "Love and life according to the Gospel cannot be thought of first and foremost as a kind of precept" (no. 29); (2) "Christian morality consists, in the simplicity of the Gospel, in *following Jesus Christ,* in abandoning oneself to him, in letting oneself be transformed by his grace and renewed by his mercy, gifts which come to us in the living communion of his Church" (no. 119).

The first assertion invites us to overcome a legalistic imposition of precepts—something that has characterized modern morality, as a "morality of law," a "morality of norms," or a "morality of duties." This is a morality elaborated from the perspective of the third person, that is, from the perspective of a judge who from outside offers criteria for assessing the conformity of action with moral rules. But it is not adequate to make decisions in conformity with legal norms. To be able to recognize the original perspective of morality, irreducible to a calculus of advantages or disadvantages flowing from an external act, it is necessary "to put oneself in the perspective of the acting person," who determines himself in and through his own freely chosen actions.[6] This is the direction in which one finds the "morality of the virtues," which has been rediscovered as representative of the stance of classical ethics (and, especially, the ethics of Saint Thomas Aquinas), as distinct from the stance of modern ethics.[7]

6. On this, see Martin Rhonheimer, "'Intrinsically Evil Acts' and the Moral Viewpoint: Clarifying a Central Teaching of *Veritatis splendor,*" *The Thomist* 58 (1994): 1–39, and "Intentional Actions and the Meaning of Object: A Reply to Richard McCormick," *The Thomist* 59 (1995): 279–311, which contains a sharp response to Richard McCormick's essay, "Some Early Reactions to *Veritatis splendor,*" *Theological Studies* 55 (1994): 481–506. Rhonheimer's essays are now available in the book *"Veritatis splendor" and the Renewal of Moral Theology,* 161–94, 241–69.

7. On this, see the valuable historical and theoretical studies of Giuseppe Abbà: *Lex et virtus: Studi sull'evoluzione della dottrina morale di San Tommaso d'Aquino* (Rome: LAS, 1983), *Felicità, vita buona e virtù: Saggio di filosofia morale* (Rome: LAS, 1989), and *Quale impostazione per la filosofia morale? Ricerche di filosofia morale,* vol. 1 (Rome: LAS, 1996). A very ample literature on virtues has developed in the United States, begin-

The second assertion permits us to recover the theological dimension of the Christian moral life, since it bears witness to the primacy of grace in our free response to God's initiative, to the Christological form of the gift that stands at the origin of every commitment and that shapes our every response, and to the ecclesial character of our new existence in Christ. Ecclesial incorporation into Christ through the means of grace is at the very heart of the moral dynamism of the faithful. Morality has need to be theologically "redimensionized": to find once more its specifically Christian links and dimensions, those that relate it tightly to dogmatic theology and, in particular, to theological anthropology.

But, as it has been said, the new wine of the Gospel cannot be contained within the bounds of a morality of precepts. Surely precepts, law, and norms can never be repudiated in morality, and no serious theological proposal can simply do away with them. But it is essential to relocate these factors within a new and more comprehensive perspective, one new and at the same time profoundly traditional.[8] This, then, is the hypothesis proposed in this volume for the theological understanding of Christian moral action: *participation in the virtues of Christ* by means of the grace of our ecclesial incorporation into him. A Christocentric theological perspective is associated with the standpoint of a morality of virtues, those dynamic dispositions of the subject toward new action, animated by charity or love.

The reflections to be proposed in this work, therefore, have a synthetic and programmatic character: they are, as it were, intuitions in

ning with the studies of Stanley Hauerwas, Alasdair MacIntyre, and Gilbert Meilaender, to mention only the more significant and better known authors. A survey of early discussions on virtue ethics is given by John Crossin, in his *What Are They Saying about Virtue?* (New York: Paulist Press, 1985).

8. The morality of Saint Thomas as a "morality of virtues" has been studied not only by Giuseppe Abbà (as already noted), but also by Jean Porter, *The Recovery of Virtue: The Relevance of Aquinas for Christian Ethics* (Louisville, Ky.: Westminster/John Knox Press, 1990); P. J. Wadell, *The Primacy of Love: An Introduction to the Ethics of Thomas Aquinas* (New York: Paulist Press, 1992); and Martin Rhonheimer, *Praktische Vernunft und Vernunftigkeit der Praxis: Handlungstheorie bei Thomas von Aquin in ihrer Entstehung aus dem Problemkontext der aristotelischen Ethik* (Berlin: Akademie Verlag, 1994). In the same vein of thought is my own work, *La conoscenza morale: Linee di riflessione sul commento di san Tommaso all'Etica Nicomachea* (Rome: Città Nuova Editrice, 1987).

need of verification and development; they do not provide a theory adequately and systematically based. They call for further work of criticism, of deepening, of discussion, and of argumentation. They are intended to suggest perspectives and not to put a close to inquiry. It is certainly not their intention to invoke John Paul II's encyclical for unwarranted support; they are intended, rather, to be of service to his school of thought, beginning that work of research that *Veritatis splendor* asked for.

The context serving as background to the present contributions further clarifies their limitations: the first part of the book consists of some lectures originally given to the students of the Washington Session of the John Paul II Institute for Studies on Marriage and Family in February 1997; the second part includes three articles on themes related to the ecclesial dimensions of morality; these essays have already appeared in English in the journal *Communio,* which has kindly granted permission for their inclusion here. Nonetheless, the occasional and surely not systematic character of the essays, which is shown in certain repetitions or lack of coherence—and for which I beg the reader's indulgence—does not deprive the work of a unitary thread of reflection, one running through all the meditations, and it will be useful to call attention to this unitary thread in this Introduction.

Part One of the work seeks to propose, in synthetic and programmatic terms, a theological hypothesis for organizing moral theology, one that is in harmony with the directions given in *Veritatis splendor* and one that likewise respects the requirements of both the "theological" and "scientific" character of the discipline, in accord with the views set forth by Vatican Council II (see *Optatam totius,* no. 16). This hypothesis can be described as a "Christocentrism of the virtues," which understands the moral life of the Christian as a participation in the virtues of Christ, by means of the grace of one's incorporation into the Church.

The starting point for Chapter One is furnished by a consideration of the challenges presented to Catholic moral theology in its efforts to preach morality within a context characterized by strong tendencies toward a radical subjectivization of conscience, which seeks to free itself from ecclesial communion. Overcoming this crisis requires taking into account the limits of the modern tradition and of the view that morality is "decision making according to legal norms" in order to rediscover both the breadth of the moral question as a quest for the true good of the person and the dimensions of Christian subjectivity, which springs from encountering the person of Christ and from the ecclesial participation in his grace.

Chapter Two has as its theme the originality of the moral perspective as the point of view of the first person or acting subject, who discovers in himself a desire for happiness, preceded by and animated by the experience of a love gratuitously offered, an anticipatory promise, as it were, of his fulfillment as a person. Human action, animated by the virtues, is an expression of freedom reaching out for the fullness of love, in which the person fulfills himself.

In Chapter Three the objective content of the moral good, which qualifies human acts, takes center stage. The moment of truth with regard to the good(s) of the person, by ordering us to the goods toward which human reason is naturally inclined, allows us to verify love and offers to the virtues their intrinsic rational measure. It is the truth that sets us free! The difficult question of the relationship between anthropology and ethics is confronted in the perspective of the recognition of the originality of moral knowledge, of practical knowledge. The singularity of the person and the universality of human nature are the undeniable poles for exercising Christian prudence, which, perfected by the gifts of the Spirit, guides one to fulfillment of one's own personal vocation in Christ.

At the heart of moral theology stands the problem of the saving significance of human action. Chapter Four is concerned with this issue, illuminating it by showing the nexus between faith, as the fundamental choice of the Christian, and the acts in which faith is called upon to express itself according to the dynamism of Christian freedom. The moral acts of the Christian, rooted in faith, reflect, according to an expression of Saint Bonaventure, that *splendor veritatis* which is Christ, in his filial obedience to his Father, through the Spirit.

Chapter Five focuses in a synthetic way on the proposal of a Christocentric ethics of virtue in accord with the indications suggested by the Seraphic Doctor. Christian life comes to birth in the encounter with Christ, who attracts and at the same time calls us to conversion. Ethics is born from aesthetics, from grasping the beauty of Christ, who provokes us to love, anticipating as a promise the fulfillment of self. The Christocentric perspective, in order not to remain inconclusive or reduced to conformity to precepts, can be expressed by means of the free or gratuitous participation in the virtues of Christ. The nexus between Christ and the Christian thus becomes richer and more intimate, paying respect to the wider and deeper dimensions of the moral question.

Part Two of this volume offers some applications, of a character above all ecclesiological. Morality has in truth need of a home: as Saint Augustine said, the Church is the *"morum regula,"* the place where the call to holiness is perceived, where the virtues of the Christian mature, where conscience is formed in the truth.

Chapter Six seeks to "reweave" the theological nexus between morality and ecclesiology. To end a sterile opposing of the magisterium and theology it is necessary to overcome the extrinsicism of an autonomous conscience and to rediscover the communal dimensions of our new existence in Christ. Our predestination in Christ, the eucharistic insertion into his gift of self, the priority of the Church as Mother—all these permit us to identify a more adequate figure of the Christian moral subject.

Chapter Seven examines the stance taken by the *Catechism of the Catholic Church* in its section on the moral life, which made the call to holiness the basis of the moral life. This allows us to show the deep unity of the moral and spiritual life, rediscovering the theological and communal dimensions of the call to perfection in love.

Finally, Chapter Eight takes up the theme of the communal form of the Christian moral conscience. In confronting the challenges of subjectivism, autonomism, and ethical pluralism, moral theology has the task of thinking deeply about the ecclesial dimension of the Christian subject. It is not sufficient to impose a merely extrinsic obedience to the magisterium: only by rooting obedience in ecclesial "communion" can those dispositions of thinking be formed that will allow, in docility to the Spirit, access to the truth that frees.

Before ending this Introduction I want to give a sincere word of thanks to those who have helped in the composition and publication of this little volume. I am first of all grateful to the students who followed my course in Washington, D.C., with sympathy, enthusiasm, and critical intelligence. Their questions and observations have made a great contribution and have been a decisive stimulus for publication. I also thank Professor Carl Anderson, vice president of the American campus of the Institute, who not only invited me but also welcomed me with great kindness. Above all I express my thanks to Professor William E. May, who welcomed me with an exquisite and fatherly willingness to make himself available; who helped me with his friendly, frank, and sharp observations in order to render some of my thoughts more precise; and who, *last but not least,* took on the task of preparing the translation, and honoring me by introducing me to the American public with his Foreword. I am also grateful to Samuel Martin, who generously offered to prepare the English typescript. Finally, I cannot pass in silence the intelligent aid that was given me, in preparing the final text, by Rev. Doctor Jose Noriega Bastos, my assistant at my chair of fundamental moral theology in Rome.

In dulcedine societatis, quaerere veritatem. As testimony of an initial experience and as a program of life and work, I want to make my own this well-known saying of Saint Albert the Great, in the hope that by means of this small book I may contribute to the common search for truth, the truth that both frees and renders work sweet.

Livio Melina
Rome, 29 June 1999
Solemnity of Saints Peter and Paul

PART ONE

∞

Toward a Christocentrism of the Virtues

LINES OF RENEWAL

∞

CHAPTER ONE

Between Crisis and Renewal

THE CULTURAL AND THEOLOGICAL
CONTEXT OF MORALITY TODAY

*I*n this chapter I want to offer some keys to the reading that will help us understand the fundamental framework within which the project of renewing moral theology is located according to John Paul II's encyclical *Veritatis splendor*. As is natural for a magisterial document, properly theological discourse is situated within the framework of pastoral concern. The first and third chapters of the encyclical in particular allow us to comprehend the *spirit* that inspired the Holy Father's intervention into the area of morality: faced with new challenges of history and of the restlessness of men in their search for the meaning of life, the pope's concern is to offer "everyone the answer which comes from the truth about Jesus Christ and his Gospel" (no. 2); he wants to make possible "this encounter with Christ" (no. 7), the encounter for which God has willed his Church (no. 7), and which alone can fully satisfy the desire of the human heart.

The question of morality is therefore situated within the framework of evangelization, which is "the most powerful and stirring challenge which the Church has been called to face from her very beginning" (no. 106). But at least for many peoples today the present time raises questions, including those concerned with the moral life, so much so that for the pope it constitutes "a formidable challenge to undertake a new evangelization" (no. 106).

The issue that can help us to better understand the profound significance of the encyclical is therefore that concerning the place morality holds at the heart of the new evangelization. And, with regard to this issue, we can immediately point out two contradictory tendencies presently operative in pastoral work. On the one hand, it seems that morality, at least in some of its traditional areas, such as sexual and conjugal life, and the defense of life, is seen as an obstacle to the acceptance of the Gospel because of its severe prohibitions in these areas. Consequently, there is a tendency to put morality on a secondary level or to keep quiet about it, in order to emphasize the *kerygma* in its purity and positivity. On the other hand, today there is a new demand for ethics within society, above all in relation to questions of public morality, social and international justice, bioethics, and social communications. There is talk of a "return of ethics," which is presented as a privileged and unexpected occasion for the Church to speak out. These are the horns of a dilemma: Are the ethical questions that today so disquiet man and challenge the Church the privileged occasion (the *kairos*) for a new evangelization or are they a snare that runs the risk of being transformed into a "moralistic putting to death of Christian truths?"[1]

To answer these questions it is first necessary to ask ourselves about the dimensions of what John Paul II calls "a true crisis" (no. 5) at the very heart of the moral teaching of the Church, one that derives from a more general "decline or obscuring of the moral sense" (no. 106). To point out the lines of an adequate response at the doctrinal and pastoral level, it will also be necessary to reflect deeply on the bond between the Gospel and morality.

I. A CRISIS OF MORAL PREACHING AND A CRISIS OF THE MORAL SUBJECT

To speak of a "crisis of morality" one risks a tedious, boring discussion. This can be easily seen by looking at two examples of exceedingly moralistic rhetoric: Cicero bewailed the moral decline of his day *("O tempora, o mores!")*, just as Bossuet, the great French

---

1. G. Angelini, "Ritorno all'etica? Tendenze e ambiguità di un fenomeno recente," *Il Regno/attualità* 14 (1990): 438–49.

preacher of the 1600s, denounced the decline of his day *("La morale se meurt, la morale est morte!")*. In order not to engage in a vague and rhetorical discourse, one "moralistic" in the pejorative sense of the term, it is necessary to grasp the specific elements of the present crisis and to discover its deepest roots. Moreover, it should be noted that for the Christian, above all, the word 'crisis' cannot have a meaning unequivocally negative in character: it refers to a "judgment," to a "putting to the test" on the part of God, that reveals the secrets of the heart and brings the truth to light. If a well-balanced paradigm (of crisis) is the subject of discussion, it amounts to a challenge for a purer perception of value, for the search for new and more adequate models.

Preaching and "the Subjectivization" of Morality

But what are the dimensions of the "crisis of morality," reflected in a crisis of moral preaching? Obviously, we are not talking only of the discrepancy between theory and practice, between what is affirmed in theory and the conduct of one's life: the problem of inconsistency is neither new nor surprising; sad to say, this problem will always accompany the history of the Church and of humanity, for it is a sign of man's fragility and of his mysterious inclination to sin. The specific characteristic of the present crisis must therefore be sought elsewhere.

Some years ago Cardinal Paul Poupard published the results of an investigation of the moral situation, in which he enlisted the help of 220 correspondents from all over the world.[2] In the conclusion of this comprehensive, well-documented analysis he speaks of two dimensions of the "crisis": on the one hand, the calling into question of a certain system of traditional values; on the other hand and more radically, the rejection of an ethical code having an external reference point in favor of *a radical subjectivization of morality*. Thus the specific trait of the present situation insofar as it regards the ecclesial community is not simply the repudiation of some moral norms taught by the magisterium that are no longer observed and shared, but is rather *the imperviousness of the conscience of so many of*

2. P. Poupard, *La morale chrétienne demain* (Paris: Desclée, 1985).

the faithful to the moral teaching of the Church as such. This teaching is
no longer taken for granted as the authoritative point of reference
for making judgments about good and evil. The crisis is not so much
a crisis of "practice," but of the "judgment" about good and evil. It
claims for the conscience of the individual the authority of
autonomously deciding what is good and what is evil (*Veritatis splendor,* no. 55). Every intervention of the magisterium is seen as an arbitrary intrusion; at least it ought to modify its claims and accept the
fact that it can only modestly propose its teaching as a mere suggestion, with no obligatory value, regarding matters that should "be
taken into account."

Some have spoken of a latent, but nonetheless real, "moral
schism," through which an ever-increasing number of the faithful
and of pastors, while not openly contesting "official" teaching, keep
their distance from it, no longer granting it the value of a criterion
decisive for Church membership.[3] Thus a diffuse resignation prevails, as it were, in preaching: it is better not to preach morality,
above all morality in regard to certain hot topics, so as not to disturb
the consciences of the faithful. Refuge is sought in the *kerygma,* or
talk is limited to vague exhortations regarding love, delegating to
each of the faithful moral judgments about their own concrete
behavior. The entrusting of things to personal conscience, a conscience that is exalted as the unique and supreme judge of the moral
value of an act, but that is left without authoritative statements that
could enlighten it, thus becomes the sole content of moral preaching or of pastoral advice.

So runs the theory regarding the compatibility of *"ethical pluralism"* with the unity of the Church.[4] Christian identity would be safeguarded by an act of faith and of adhesion to specifically Christian
transcendental attitudes, that is, relating to that intentional interiori-

3. See F. Boeckle, "Humanae vitae als Pruefstein des wahren Glaubens? Zur
kirchenpolitischen Dimensionen moraltheologischer Fragen," *Stimmen der Zeit* 115
(1990): 3–16.

4. See, for instance, the contribution of J. Fuchs, "Moral Truths—Truths of Salvation?," in his book *Christian Ethics in a Secular Arena* (Washington, D.C.: Georgetown University Press, 1984), 48–67, and that of P. Schmitz, "Ein Glaube-kontroverse
Gewissensentscheidung," in *Gewissen: Aspekte eine vieldiskutierten Sachverhaltes,* ed. J.
Horstmann (Schwerte: Katholische Akademie, 1983), 60–76.

ty that "transcends" every particular "categorical" act, for example, an attitude of "openness" to God and to others. Operative moral norms, for instance, those regulating sexual behavior or the killing of human persons, on the other hand, would be relevant only to a right worldly order and not to salvation. But the magisterium could not claim, in regard to conduct in this world, a competence specifically different from that depending on the reasonableness of its arguments, because even Revelation, being limited to "truths of salvation," could not give binding directives in this area.[5] Therefore, in the Church there can exist a pluralism of moralities, relative not only to different cultures but also to individual persons. Thus, for instance, African Christians should be allowed to practice polygamy, and all believers ought to be granted the faculty of deciding autonomously whether something is ethically "right" for their particular situation.

The individual moral conscience is therefore emancipated from ecclesial "communion." But this is possible only if one can first of all justify the claim that morality (or at least a certain level of morality or certain spheres of morality) is irrelevant for the life of faith and for salvation. When viewed properly, the real problem that these positions—practical or theoretical, theological or pastoral—bring to the fore is that of the identity of the Christian faith and of its connection with the moral life (see *Veritatis splendor,* no. 3).

Viewed from this perspective, the phenomenon previously noted of the "return to the ethical" turns out to be very ambiguous. Troubled by macroeconomic and financial systems, by the newly acquired human powers over biomedical sciences, technical information, and communication, and so on, more and more some people turn to the Church because they feel ill- prepared to cope with the ethical challenges that all this entails and because they recognize in the Church a great moral tradition. But while they want rules to discipline behavior, they refuse to listen to the whole meaningful context that justifies these rules and makes them understandable. They ask the Church for a normative ethics for certain areas of

5. See J. Fuchs, "Christian Morality: Biblical Orientation and Human Evaluation," *Gregorianum* 67 (1986): 745–63.

social life, but reject its normative rules for certain areas of personal life, and above all they avoid any confrontation with a metaethics, which could provide the foundation for and give meaning to moral norms, because this involves the fundamental question of the meaning of human freedom and its ultimate end.

The Crisis of Modern Subjectivity

It is paradoxical above all that within the ambit of Catholic theology there should arise proposals concerning the complete subjectivization of morality, especially at a time when the crisis of the subject is fully evident. Individualistic modern thought is not a solution to the problem precisely because what is in crisis is the subject himself, as the indispensable reference point for moral responsibility. We are confronted with a *crisis of modern subjectivity,* which in the West is the end result of bourgeois society.[6] The exclusive reference to the subject's autonomous conscience is not only an inadequate foundation for morality but one that is also historically debatable.

Modern subjectivism, in fact, is only apparently an exaltation of the *subject;* in reality, it is the absolutization of the *individual,* isolated in himself and in competition with all others in affirming his own desires and exercising his own freedom. But in truth the condition making it possible for a subject to exist is the capacity of deliberately and freely initiating action with a view toward some ideal; but this requires a transcendence of freedom over one's own desires, the rejection of internal and external mechanisms that subject the individual to extrinsic forces. What modern mass society threatens is the inner unity of the individual, the unity permitting one to overcome fragmentary and ever-changing desires and making one truly a subject. For this the essential task of law is to moderate desire.[7] Saint Paul acknowledged that he "would never have known what evil desire was unless the law had said, 'You shall not desire'" (Rom 7.7). Temperance, by moderating the instinctive impulse of eager desire, which tends to devour everything immediately, makes room for lis-

6. I am summarizing some illuminating analyses provided by R. Buttiglione, in *La crisi della morale* (Rome: Dino, 1991).

7. See the reflections of G. Angelini, *Le virtù e la fede* (Milan: Glossa, 1994), 100–106.

tening and for hearing the word: "Not by bread alone does man live, but by every word . . ." (Deut 8.3). One cannot speak with a full mouth; temperance allows dialogue with the other. The rational will surge up only when the immediacy of desire and the instability of its wishes are controlled and referred to a meaning that over-comes the partiality of the object on which desire bears.

When "reason is silent about values," the individual is left to the emotion of the moment, which he succeeds in surpassing through means of a free self-determination.[8] The "I" is fragmented into moments and areas of life each quite distinct from the other; it becomes a fragile "I," easily dominated by different and opposed laws that are imposed on it from time to time by the social organiza-tion. The individual is reduced to playing different characters in dif-ferent scenes, with different roles and rules: one sphere is econom-ics, another that of the family, another politics, another concerned with leisure time. The fragmented and individualistic "I," unable to become a free subject of action, is the victim desired by every bureaucratic power.

2. THE ROOTS OF THE CRISIS

John Paul II, in his encyclical *Veritatis splendor,* shows that he is ful-ly aware of the dimensions of the moral crisis as a crisis of the sub-ject. He points out two deep roots of this crisis: on the philosophical plane, the rupture of the bond between freedom and truth, and, on the theological plane, the rupture of the nexus between faith and morality. In developing our analysis along this path, in the light of the directions given in the papal document, we will also be prepar-ing ourselves to bring together positive indications for an adequate answer to the crisis.

The Rupture of the Bond between Freedom and the Truth

A prime root of the crisis is widespread in contemporary society and shows itself as the complete disappearance or negation of the idea of moral truth, which is meant to guide freedom. In the back-

8. See A. MacIntyre, *After Virtue: A Study in Moral Theory* (Notre Dame, Ind.: Uni-versity of Notre Dame Press, 1985).

ground looms the tragedy of a culture in which the idea of truth no longer finds a home.

The German philosopher Martin Heidegger was one of the first to describe what was happening: technological thought, so powerful and effective in the discovery of means, is in no way neutral, but implies a very precise vision of reality and a correlative conception of human liberty (see *Veritatis splendor,* no. 46).[9] The technical or instrumental aspect of reason has overwhelmed its philosophical and sapiential aspect. A prevailing element of this kind of rationality is *the negation of the idea that there is any truth about a created thing that is to be respected* and the related concept that everything can thus be manipulated without limits, save those pertaining to the calculus of one's own advantage. If the being of the world does not come from a creative act of God, if it does not express his wise plan, but derives from chance, then everything can be changed and everything is open to manipulation.

The emergence of the ecological crisis has dramatically cast light on the insufficiency, so self-destructive, of this way of conceiving things. Long ago Rabelais admonished that "science without conscience is nothing but the ruin of the soul." But where can conscience find adequate reference points for assenting to a truth that can enlighten it?

The crisis of truth in ethics is called "noncognitivism": moral values are not the fruit of knowledge, but of subjective feelings/emotions or arbitrary choices. The judgments that we give about the good are not rooted in any knowledge, in principle accessible to all, but are the expression of subjective taste, and it makes no sense to debate about such tastes, or else they are the fruit of an arbitrary choice. An "ethics without truth"[10] must dig its roots deep into the irrational and search for rules of formal tolerance in order to allow in some way for a kind of civil coexistence. The moral question is reduced to a procedural problem: ethics must be limited to estab-

---

9. M. Heidegger, "Die Frage nach der Technik," in *Vortraege und Aufsaetze* (Pfullingen: Neske, 1954), 29–31.

10. This is the title of a book by the Italian philosopher U. Scarpelli, recently deceased, which supports the arbitrariness of the choice establishing the bounds of good and evil: *Etica senza verità* (Bologna: Mulino, 1982).

lish the rules of an impartial discussion among participants, without being able to investigate the rational foundations of their positions.[11]

The Rupture of the Nexus between Faith and Morality

The second root of the crisis concerns Christian subjectivism, but also the shaping of post-Christian moral subjectivism in the Western world. The Protestant theologian Wolfhart Pannenberg has singled out the critical role played by confessional differences and the wars of religion that troubled Europe between the second half of the sixteenth century and the first half of the seventeenth century.[12] Faced with the fragmentation of the Christian universe and the subsequent impossibility of continuing to base social coexistence on a common religious basis, humanists and rationalists of the modern period turned to reason as the sole source of universal moral evidence. Reworking the theses of a decadent medieval Scholasticism (Gregory of Rimini) and also the rich patrimony of the Second Spanish Scholasticism, the Dutch jurist Grotius proposed a theory of natural law valid "even if it were granted that God does not exist."[13]

The high point of the secularization of morality completely loosed from every reference not only to the Christian faith but to any religious belief came with Immanuel Kant. In his opusculum *Religion within the Limits of Reason* (1793) he asked what of Christianity was still valid for modern man, who, having dared to subject himself to reason, has become adult and emancipated from every external authority. His answer is that the moral part of Christianity has permanent value: Christian morality in fact is the expression of truly universal ethical demands, valid for *all* men of *all* times. But it is necessary to detach it from every historical reference to and from faith in the person of Jesus (in fact, "an individual historical fact can never found a universal truth," according to the famous postulate formulated by G. E. Lessing), and from every relationship to the doctrines of sin and of grace. The elements of the permanent validity of

11. This procedural ethics is the theme of J. Habermas, *The Theory of Communicative Action* (New York: Oxford University Press, 1986).

12. See Wolfhart Pannenberg, *Ethik und Ekklesiologie: Gesammelte Aufsaetze* (Göttingen: Vandenhoeck & Ruprecht, 1977), 55–69.

13. H. Grotius, *De iure belli ac pacis,* Proleg. #11: "etsi daretur Deum non esse."

Christianity would consist in its reduction to a secularized, internal ethic.

This way of thinking about Christianity, in addition to its acceptance in the world of culture and among philosophers, is now widely diffused among the common people. How often do we hear it said that to be a Christian it is enough to live honestly and to follow one's own conscience! It is thought that the nucleus of Christianity that counts is that constituted by its moral precepts, and that to live in fidelity to these precepts means to follow one's own conscience. Thus has been elaborated an ethics of absolute imperatives, characterized by a great rigor and by very severe demands put on persons. An interior ethic, a lay ethic, an ethic of obligation. An individualistic ethic.

The "Shipwreck" of Modern Ethics

Evaluating this historical process in the light of its contemporary results, Romano Guardini has spoken of the betrayal of the modern epoch in its confrontation with Christianity.[14] It, the modern epoch, was shaped as a parasite on Christianity, living off the interest of the moral values discovered and accumulated during the Age of Faith and exchanging them for neutral values, values even possible outside the context of Christian faith. But, says Guardini, this betrayal has now attained its end: in our age it has been and is being made manifest with ever- growing evidence that *outside of Christianity and faith it is humanly impossible to live Christian values.* In our day is being revealed more and more the face of a non-Christian existence, and the emptiness and fear that this portends. Faith in the progress of science has long since disappeared, to be replaced by an anxious search for ethical points of reference to keep man from destroying himself and his world with the powerful technological tools he has developed. "The time of a terrible but salutary clarification will come," says Guardini. "No Christian can find cause for celebrating the radical denial of Christianity. . . . But it is good that this betrayal has been put into the open. For now can be seen what reality effec-

14. R. Guardini, *The End of the Modern World* (Chicago: Regnery, 1984).

tively is when man is disconnected from revelation and its fruits begin to vanish."[15]

From the perspective of moral theories, it seems that some clear symptoms of the end of this phase can already be seen and that one can give a "theological" reading of the overcoming of contemporary ethics. The Kantian claim was in fact that of guaranteeing the absoluteness of morality, detaching it from the context of faith. The ethic of autonomous reason was presented as a rigorous ethics of duties, so as to guarantee the greatest moral requirement, that of respecting the person. But if man, of himself, cannot succeed in observing the law and if he does not want to feel continually accused by it, and if he cannot in some way find pardon for his deficiencies, then there remains only one route open: since man is not able to conform himself to the law, *he must conform the law to himself and his possibilities.* The definition of *the human* will not be in conformity with the ideal revealed by Christ nor with the absolute demands of that truth that sounds within the depths of every man but will be measured on the basis of each one's possibilities, his own limits, the circumstances in which he comes to find himself.

To remedy this tragic situation, which the Scottish philosopher Alasdair MacIntyre describes, in his fine volume, as a "shipwreck," it is necessary *to rediscover the full dimensions of the moral question,* to rediscover an "ethic of virtue" along the lines of the classical tradition.[16] Instead of asking only "What must I do?," morality has the task of inquiring into three very radical questions: (1) Who am I? Who ought I to become? (2) What kind of attitudes and what kind of actions can lead me to what I ought to become? (3) What kind of community can help me attain the ideal to which I am called? These are the paths along which the task of reconstructing the moral subject can be directed.

In fact, it is possible for a free subjectivity to emerge only where, on the ultimate horizon of willing, there appears an ideal capable of measuring aspirations against real goods. Only when the will is recognized in its opening to what is good according to reason does the

---

15. Ibid., 101.
16. See MacIntyre, *After Virtue,* 204–25.

desire for immediate gratification become disciplined; only then can arise that true freedom on which morality is based: *iudicium rationis radix libertatis,* the root of freedom is the judgment of reason.

And the promising experience of an ideal is not born in an individualistic isolation, but is anticipated in the interpersonal encounter of love. The communal dimension thus is incompatible with every utilitarian attitude toward the individual; it is a founding experience of subjectivity itself. In this sense MacIntyre's questions can and must be reformulated: (1) Who do I truly want to be? And, if the ultimately adequate answer is given to me in the encounter with Christ, in the Church, it then follows: (2) How ought I to live in order to realize communion in love?

3. RECONSTRUCTING THE CHRISTIAN MORAL SUBJECT

The dimensions of the crisis of morality and of its proclamation call urgently for a new and radical pastoral responsibility: the reconstruction of the Christian moral subject. Faced with the difficulties against which moral proclamation bangs its head, a mere reproposing of the norms will not suffice, nor can we bracket morality, which is an integral part of the Christian proposal (see *Veritatis splendor,* no. 107). The affirmative task that the encyclical *Veritatis splendor* points out and whose fundamental lines of thought it traces is that of relocating morality in its theological context, within the horizon of an evangelization that must be "new in its ardor, its methods, and in its expression"[17] and that must have as its objective the building up and education of the new man, who is born from an encounter with the Gospel.

It seems to me that John Paul II suggests three directives for the reconstruction of the Christian moral subject: to rediscover the nexus between freedom and truth, to rediscover that between faith and morality, and to offer moral life a home. We will examine these successively, seeking to understand the implications for a new start for moral theology and for showing how they are of value in

17. John Paul II, "Address to the Bishops of Celam," 9 March 1983; *Insegnamenti di Giovanni Paolo II,* 6, no. 1 (1983): 698, cited in *Veritatis splendor,* no. 106.

responding to the needs that we have been exploring in the previous analysis and what the moral question poses to evangelization today.

To Rediscover the Nexus between Freedom and Truth

Before developing the theoretical reflection of chapter two of his encyclical, the pope allowed himself to meditate at length on the Gospel passage narrating the encounter of the rich young man with Jesus (Mt 19.16–22). That meditation was not casual or merely extrinsic to the whole structure of the discourse of the encyclical. It is in the light of the Gospel that John Paul II examines the nature of human freedom. Thus his is not an abstract formalization of concepts; before every theoretical reflection his thought springs from a consideration of the dramatic character of freedom, which gives evidence of itself in that encounter. This encounter is at least provisionally unsuccessful for the young man, who is nonetheless awakened by a question that stands at the heart of every moral task: "Master, what good must I do to have eternal life?"

Jesus' answer is an invitation to the young man to discover the deepest roots of his question. "Why do you ask me about what is good? There is only one who is good." The question of morality, before being a request for norms, for rules to establish what is allowed or not allowed, permitted or not permitted, is a yearning for the Absolute Good, it is a desire and a demand for life. The good to which man aspires in the depths of his heart is always something more than he can "do": there is never an end to his "doing." The question about the good, therefore, has a religious character and not merely a moral one: it is the problem of salvation and not one of consistency. And the response cannot be brought about by man but only accepted as a gift. Nevertheless, action is not extrinsic to the religious tension of the human spirit confronted with the Absolute Good, which man cannot attain. Action bears witness to this longing for the infinite and is called to realize it symbolically.

This understanding allows us to overcome the narrowness of a "morality of duties" or "a morality of laws" and to rediscover the inspiration that for so many centuries had been classic. For this great tradition, in fact, the first and basic moral question is the question of happiness, of blessed fulfillment. In one of the first systematic treatises of Catholic moral theology, Saint Augustine's *De moribus ecclesiae catholicae,* the saint begins precisely with this question: "What therefore must be our point of departure? . . . Let us seek with the help of reason how a man ought to live. Certainly, we all want to live happily and in the entire genus of man there is no one who does not assent to this affirmation even before it has been fully enunciated."[18] Morality comes to birth as an answer to the question of *true* happiness, understood in all its breadth and seriousness: the question, that is, of the true last end that man seeks in every one of his deeds; the question of a love objectively good, which qualifies the whole of life because it impresses on life a decisive orientation toward the end that in truth merits being pursued.

Kant's critique founders on this concept, for he had denied the possibility of grounding morality in a truly objective and unconditioned way on a eudaimonistic basis;[19] according to Kant, eudaimonism would introduce a subjectivistic principle and interest that would destroy every noble movement deriving from virtue. But this critique is valid only within an empiricist perspective on the raising of the question of happiness: in reality there is a true Absolute Good that responds to man's desire for happiness. This desire is not necessarily egoistic; on the contrary, true love of self has an ecstatic character: it comes to birth as a spontaneous inclination to love one's own natural good, but then it puts the subject before a choice within which, with the help of divine grace, love of God for his own sake and above all else can be affirmed, as the authentic content of a spontaneous tendency for love of one's self.[20]

Therefore there is a first fundamental internal reference for the reconstruction of the moral subject: that truth about the Good, which from within calls man to overcome constantly every narrow

18. Saint Augustine, *De moribus ecclesiae catholicae,* I, II, 3, and III, 4 (Ed. Benedictine; Paris: R. Roland-Gosselin, 1949).

19. I. Kant, *Foundations for a Metaphysics of Morals,* II.

20. See A. Scola, *Identidad y diferencia. La relacion hombre-mujer* (Madrid: Encuentro, 1989), 24–34, in which Scola provides a critical exposition of the classical debate over the Thomistic concept of love, that is, between the "physical" conception (P. Rousselot) and the "ecstatic" conception (L. B. Geiger). Scola proposes a middle route and solution, which I follow.

and egoistic answer, to open himself up to the dimensions of the Absolute Good. The human person, created in the image of God, has impressed originally within himself, in his own reason and will, an orientation toward the Good. In the light of that first truth, which makes up part of his creaturely image, reason spontaneously discovers that originating law of being, which is the natural law, the participation of human reason in the creative Wisdom of God (see *Veritatis splendor,* no. 43).[21] Bound up with the very structure of the person in his constitutive inclination toward the Good, the natural law is not opposed to freedom but in fact points out the path for it to follow: it is the true law of freedom. In this sense Pope John Paul II, in *Veritatis splendor,* with reference to the natural law, proposes anew the Gospel phrase of John: "You will know the truth and the truth will set you free" (Jn 8.32).

Rediscovering the Bond between Faith and Morality

It has already been said that the moral question today is posed with a new radicality and that the real problem standing in the way of evangelization is the rise of a new subject. But how does the Christian moral subject come to birth? The answer that John Paul II gives is simple: he comes to birth from an encounter (*Veritatis splendor,* nos. 7–8), from the encounter, namely, between the quest for happiness or blessed fulfillment, which dwells in the human heart and motivates every initiative of his freedom, and the person of Jesus, the one whose charm has awakened even in the young rich man the promise of an unexpected fulfillment of his own destiny.

In his *Life of Christ* the French writer François Mauriac reports compellingly the impact that the person and teaching of Jesus must have had on the people who followed him. Imagining the scene of the Sermon on the Mount, he describes the thronging of the crowd around the heights of the mountain, until there was no more room and some had to stand in a place where they could not hear very well what the Lord was saying. Only now and then the wind carried a word to them, repeated with an accent and compelling power, a

---

21. See A. Scola, *La fondazione teologica della legge naturale nello Scriptum supra Sententiis di San Tommaso d'Aquino* (Freiburg im Schweiz: Universitaetsverlag, 1982).

word that brought meaning to their struggle to follow him and to their difficulty in hearing him: "Blessed . . . Blessed . . . Blessed . . ." They understood that that word was spoken for them, that they were there precisely for that reason: for the promise of happiness, of blessedness that Jesus had stirred in their hearts with his words, his gestures, his person.

In this sense one can say that ethics is born of aesthetics, that is, of the fascinating encounter in which one perceives that the promise of blessed self-fulfillment is realized in a human way. If moral dynamism is the dynamism of love, love is provoked by beauty. Ethics is born from an encounter in which the communion of persons is anticipated. The desire for happiness, now confused and restless, finds in this encounter its fulfilling hermeneutic: love precedes desire[22] and reveals the true dynamic of the gift of self.

The Gospel therefore is the answer freely, surprisingly, and superabundantly responding to the demand for happiness that is in the heart of man. In this sense, as Vatican Council II affirms, Christian morality finds its source in the Gospel (Dei Verbum, 7). Here we are at one of the key points of our discourse, that which concerns the nexus between morality and the Gospel.

There has been a consistent Protestant tradition, one not without influence on Catholic theology, that systematically opposes the Gospel and morality. The evangelical moral theologian Roger Mehl expresses this opposition in this way: "The Gospel is not a morality, but belongs to another order of reality. The question which the Gospel poses is that of faith and not that of morality."[23] Similarly Emil Brunner dialectically opposes the order of morality, which has only profane value and refers only to duties, and the order of faith, which is pure grace, without entangling human freedom.[24] There are two possible ways of escaping this radical opposition: either a Gospel without morality or a morality without the Gospel. The first

22. Saint Thomas Aquinas, *Summa theologiae*, I–II, q. 25, a. 2: "amor praecedit desiderium."

23. Roger Mehl, *Catholic Ethics and Protestant Ethics* (Philadelphia: Westminster Press, 1971).

24. See Emil Brunner, *The Divine Imperative* (New York: Harper & Row, 1953); German original, *Das Gebot und die Ordnungen* (Tubingen: 1932).

is the Barthian solution, which, in order to affirm the absolute gratuity of God's intervention in human history, has to deny every contribution of human freedom. The second is that typical of pietism, which, abandoning dogma as arid and divorced from life, substitutes for it as its own proper content the Christian relevance of a pragmatic moralism.

On the other hand, the position of Catholicism can be summed up in the formula, now classical in the magisterium from the time of the Council of Trent: *"fides et mores"* (faith and morals).[25] There is surely a primacy of faith and of grace, that is, a primacy of the divine initiative. But this is not in opposition to a human response, which this initiative arouses and demands. Christian faith, in fact, as *Veritatis splendor* says at no. 88, "is not simply a set of propositions to be accepted with intellectual assent," but rather *"a truth to be lived out,"* "a decision involving one's whole life," "a new and original criterion for thinking and acting." Joseph Cardinal Ratzinger, in his presentation of the encyclical to the press, recalled that the first name that the Christian religion recognized as fitting for defining itself and that was frequently used in the Acts of the Apostles (see, for instance, Acts 22.4) is "the way."[26]

Christianity is first of all a concrete way of living, a praxis that is born of faith: it is not a vague gathering of ideals that can be interpreted in different and contradictory ways, according to subjective tastes, but is rather a precise and recognizable form of life. Every separation between the confession of faith and the moral life in truth would constitute, according to the First Epistle of John, a denial of the logic of the Incarnation, a refusal to believe that Christ has come in the flesh.[27]

To resume the thread of our discourse: if it is necessary, in order to reconstruct the moral subject, to reestablish the nexus between freedom and the truth, the Christian is the one who has encountered

25. On this matter, see M. Bevenot "Faith and Morals in Vatican I and the Council of Trent," *Heythrop Journal* 3 (1962): 15–30; and T. Lopez Rodriguez, "Fides et mores en Trento," *Scripta theologica* 5, no. 1 (1973): 175–221.

26. In *L'Osservatore Romano*, 6 October 1993.

27. On this, see Raymond E. Brown, *The Epistles of John* (New York: Doubleday Anchor, 1982), 128–36.

and recognized this truth in the encounter with the person of Jesus. He who said "I am the way, the truth, and the life" is the "living and personal law" (*Veritatis splendor,* no. 15) of existence. For the Christian, the truth is not an abstract concept but a person: it is Christ who reveals in truth the heart of man, who reveals to man his highest vocation (*Gaudium et spes,* 22). Man in fact has been created "in Christ," and the natural law is part of the creaturely image, which shines forth in full light in the incarnate Son, the perfect image of the Father (Col 11.15). In this sense *Veritatis splendor,* in a passage packed with theological content, casts light on the Christological foundation of the natural law: "Christ is the 'Beginning' who, having taken on human nature, definitively illumines it in its constitutive elements and in its dynamism of charity toward God and neighbor" (no. 53). The dialogue with all men on the requirements of the good of the person (natural law) does not therefore have need to put faith aside. Faith does not *exclude* but rather *includes* human morality, showing the ultimate meaning of the requirements that reason also can discover on its own.

In the encounter with Christ the drama that every serious moral duty connotes also finds its answer: the sad discovery of its own inconsistency, of its own fragility, of the continual betrayal of the good that has been recognized as obligatory. It is a drama that from its very beginning the encyclical recognizes and poses at the heart of its reflection (no. 1) and which finds its solution in the offer of the mercy that pardons sin and of the grace that sustains the path of freedom (nos. 101–5). Against the temptation to reduce the measure of moral exigencies to what seems possible for a fragile freedom marked by sin, John Paul II reaffirms the great hope deriving from the saving presence of the Lord: *"only in the mystery of Christ's redemption do we discover the 'concrete' possibilities of man"* (no. 103). Because of this mystery the keeping of the commandments, which "can be difficult, extremely difficult . . . is never impossible" (no. 102). It is here, in these very difficult situations, that there comes into play the grandeur of the vocation of man and the reality of the Redemption: "so that the cross of Christ might not be voided" (1 Cor 1.17).

A Home for Morality

But how can this presence of the mystery of the Redemption be realized in the concreteness of moral existence, this contemporaneity and companionship of Christ with man, which makes possible man's rebirth as a new subject?[28] We are concerned here with the third direction qualifying the Christian moral proposal and which connotes its "extraordinary simplicity": contrary to all appearances, this—the Christian moral life—is not "too demanding, difficult to understand, and almost impossible to practice." To the contrary, "Christian morality consists, in the simplicity of the Gospel, in *following Jesus Christ,* in abandoning oneself to him, in letting oneself be transformed by his grace and renewed by his mercy, gifts which come to us in the living communion of his Church" (*Veritatis splendor,* no. 119). The Church, therefore, is the "home" that morality needs.

In his *Nicomachean Ethics* Aristotle already noted the importance of a community, of a company of friends, for forming the moral subject. Commentators have noted that, at the beginning of book 8 one can see a turn in the thought of the Stagirite:[29] he claims that the "polis" is no longer the place of that political friendship capable of providing an education for the good life. It lacks fundamental agreement on the Good: each one lives in accord with what appears to himself and pleases himself. Aristotle therefore looks for a new home for ethics, and he finds it in the friendship with those who love the true Good and who support one another in struggling for it. We cannot become good without friends; indeed, the first and fundamental moral choice is the choice of friends.

Truly, in this choice of friends one ultimately and implicitly chooses also the good that unites persons in friendship and that gives to the friendship its content. In fact, friendship is constituted

---

28. On this, see the essays by José L. Illanes and Jean Laffitte in *Gesù Cristo, legge vivente e personale della Santa Chiesa,* ed. G. Borgonovo (Casale Monferrato: Piemme, 1996), 172–223. This volume also contains the Atti del IX Colloquio Internazionale di Teologia di Lugano sul primo capitolo dell'Enciclica *Veritatis splendor,* held at the Facoltà Teologica di Lugano, Lugano, 15–17 June 1995.

29. See P. J. Wadell, *Friendship and the Moral Life* (Notre Dame, Ind.: University of Notre Dame Press, 1989), 43–68.

through the experience of an encounter in which one catches a glimpse of the promise of fulfillment. Friends, before they even begin to see one another, have a will to glimpse that fullness and ask themselves in awe and gratitude, "What! You too? I thought that no one but myself. . . ."[30] The Christian has glimpsed in faith a singular fullness: to be loved by God the Father as he loves Christ, the Son, and to love as Christ himself loves. He has glimpsed this in the encounter with a human reality, normally by discovering Christ in a communion experienced among Christians, in the encounter with the Church, Christ with us today.

The true homeland of the Christian is not in this world, among earthly ordinances and institutions. The Christian is a pilgrim and guest, on the road to his heavenly home. But already on this earth he lives "in Christ." Saint Paul frequently used this expression to indicate the new condition of the believer: he has been sacramentally transfigured "into the Son." And, as this membership is not realized in an individualistic way, but in a communitarian way and in communion, this gives rise to the new body of the Son: the Church. This, the Church, is the home, the house, the family in which the Christian lives and in which his freedom as a son can grow. The Church, as *Veritatis splendor* says, is *"Christ's relevance for people of all times"* (no. 25).

From the pastoral point of view, a clear directive flows from this: in order for the new Christian moral subject to emerge, it is necessary that the Church be really a habitable "home," a place of visible and encounterable communion in which fraternity and fellowship can be experienced. To make the Church present as an effective community is therefore a pressing need for seeing to it that the beautiful expression of Saint Augustine, cited by Pope John Paul II in no. 119 of his encyclical, may be realized fully: "he who would live has a place to live, and has everything needed to live. Let him draw near, let him believe, let him become part of the body, that he may have life. Let him not shrink from the unity of the members."[31]

---

30. C. S. Lewis, *The Four Loves* (New York: Harcourt, Brace, & World, 1960), 113.
31. Saint Augustine, *In Ioannis Evangelium Tractatus*, 26, 13: CCL, 36, 266.

CONCLUSION

We have asked ourselves about the place that morality ought to have in the context of evangelization today. We are now ready to understand the answer of the encyclical: "Evangelization also involves the presentation and proclamation of morality" (no. 107). A little later it is added that the life of holiness is a very powerful and fascinating way of evangelization, because in the life of saints the glory of God, which makes man live, shines forth. And thus the theme of morality is coupled with that of the beauty and glory of God.

The first word of the encyclical, that which gives it the title "the splendor of truth," is the classic definition, of Platonic origin, of beauty: beauty is the splendor of truth. The last word, which brings the final prayer to conclusion, invokes Mary's intercession that all our life might be "for the praise of God's glory" (no. 120). The theme of man's happiness (no. 9) is set within the perspective made possible by God's gratuitous intervention of life's ultimate purpose as being "for the praise of God's glory" (no. 10) and of the fascination aroused by encountering Jesus (no. 8).

The profound movement of the spirit of the pope, to which each of us is invited, is therefore that of turning to the face of Christ, to let oneself be conquered and charmed by his beauty. In truth, the Church, as the faithful spouse of Christ, cannot stop looking with love on that face, the face of "the most beautiful of the children of man" (see no. 85). The glory of the Father above all shines on the face of the Crucified One, where the love that gives itself from its depths is revealed and in this love is also revealed the deepest meaning of human freedom.

Here is the answer to our initial question: faced with the dimensions and challenges of the moral crisis, evangelization today will succeed not by accepting subjectivization or by leaving moral themes aside but only if, surpassing moralism, it knows how to present the beauty of the Face of Christ, the face that attracts, with word and above all with a life of holiness. This is the framework also for the hoped-for renewal of moral theology, a renewal whose most important features, present in the encyclical, we will seek to develop and to support with evidence.

CHAPTER TWO

∞

An Ethics of the Good Life
and of Virtue

*H*ere our central interest is the possibility of the foundation at a
truly scientific and theological moment of a moral theology,
within the framework indicated by Vatican Council II and, in a way
wholly unique, by the encyclical *Veritatis splendor.* In a well-known
directive, *Optatam totius,* the Council's document on the theological
formation of priests, it had affirmed: "Particular care is to be taken
in perfecting moral theology in a way that its scientific explanation,
better founded on Sacred Scripture, might illustrate the nobility of
the vocation of the faithful in Christ and their obligation to bear
fruit in charity for the life of the world" (no. 16).

I. FACTORS FOR ELABORATING MORAL THEOLOGY IN THE SPIRIT OF VATICAN COUNCIL II AND OF "VERITATIS SPLENDOR"

These words of the Council alert us to two elements constitutive
of a projected moral theology that are also the two necessary factors
for its elaboration as a systematic and critical reflection on the life of
the Christian in the light of Revelation. On the one hand, and first of
all, there is the need of a *theological foundation* for moral discourse.
From this perspective, a theology truly nourished by Scripture must
be placed within the horizon of the most exalted vocation that the
Christian receives "in Christ": the horizon of a supernatural final
end that gratuitously fulfills, beyond every expectation and creaturely possibility, the human desire for happiness. On the other hand,

there is need for the necessary *scientific character* of theological reflection, which must organically and critically develop its inquiry in the light of Revelation, by means of arguments—and therefore also by making use of philosophical concepts—that can adequately interpret moral experience in harmony with its theological foundation. If Revelation offers the principle or starting point for moral theology, it is up to reason to determine its concrete meaning, applying it to the varied situations of life and systematically organizing its understanding in detail.[1]

The presupposition implied by the Council's affirmations and by our research is a restlessness over and a dissatisfaction with the situation of moral theology, which needs renewal both from the viewpoint of its theological foundation and from that of its scientific grounding. There is dissatisfaction with both the preconciliar manualist tradition and with postconciliar efforts at renewal.

a. With regard to the *theological foundation,* it has been observed that in general the preconciliar manualist tradition (a specific and varied literary genre common from about 1600 immediately after the Council of Trent up to Vatican Council II)[2] did not give much attention to the theological foundation of morality. The neat division of the tracts between morality and spirituality attributed only to the second specifically Christian theological elements, leaving to morals the study of the minimal obligations based on natural law. Moreover, a legalistic undergirding was prevalent in which the obligatoriness of the law was founded on the will of the legislator and on his authority (in the words of William of Ockham, *"bonum quia iussum, malum quia prohibitum,"* good because commanded, evil because forbidden); this legalistic emphasis diverted attention from investigating the reasons of the truth of norms and their theological rooting.

On the other hand, in the postconciliar period, after a first phase of a one-sided and unbalanced biblicism, things remained disap-

1. See G. Perini, "Il 'trattato' di teologia morale fondamentale," *Divus Thomas* 14 (Bologna: Ed. Studio Domenicano, 1996).

2. Cf. Louis Vereecke, C.Ss.R., *Da Guglielmo d'Ockham a Sant'Alfonso de Liguori: Saggi di storia della teologia morale moderna (1300–1787)* (Rome: Alfonsiana, 1990), and Servais Pinckaers, O.P., *The Sources of Christian Ethics,* trans. Sr. Mary T. Noble, O.P. (Washington, D.C.: The Catholic University of America Press, 1995), 254–79.

pointing, oscillating between leitmotifs that were attractive but too vague for guiding action and norms historically dated. There was talk about "the limits of biblical morality" (W. Kerber), of its "insufficiency" (J. Endres), of its contribution only at the level of "general orientations" (J. Fuchs). And, instead of a moral theology, talk began of a "theological ethic," in which Scripture would offer only parenetic suggestions while autonomous reason determined concretely the norms of action. In a highly diversified movement there was a search for developing a foundation that would be not only biblical but theological and indeed Christological. The theme "Christology and morality" was put at the center of the debate, and moral theologians and dogmatic theologians alike occupied themselves with it. The latter came to the help of the former after the disappointment experienced with biblicists. But here too they were confronted ultimately with dissatisfaction because they concurred that the Christological foundation by itself was not enough. Some, after an initial enthusiasm over a dogmatic moment, ended up by abandoning particular normative directives for a subjective intuition of conscience. Not without reason was there talk of an "inconclusive Christocentric morality."

b. The second problem, that of the *scientific character* of moral theology, is inescapable. This requires philosophical reflection and the rational elaboration of concepts that can serve to develop and determine the fundamental theological perspective and the principles of Revelation. *Veritatis splendor* speaks explicitly of this need. At no. 82 it says that the biblical morality of the Covenant and of the commandments, of charity and of the virtues, has need of a doctrinal explanation by way of the doctrine of the moral object. In fact, "without this rational determination of the morality of human action, it would be impossible to affirm an 'objective moral order' and to establish any determinate norm from the viewpoint of its content that would oblige without any exception." Moral theology, therefore, is properly constituted in the encounter between revealed truth and the exercise of reason so far as its scientific character is concerned.

The manualist tradition was not very concerned with the scientific character of its presentation. It adopted, after all, the perspective common to "modern" morality: that of the external normative regulation of acts, assuming that this was the only possible type of ethics and failing to recognize that it was only one of those possible; it was therefore a form of ethics profoundly different from the classic form not only of Saint Augustine, but also of Thomas Aquinas, from whom it pretended to take inspiration.[3]

Morality was thus undertaken focusing on two elements, the law and conscience: the objective criterion for regulating acts and the subjective criterion. Thus Saint Alphonus Maria de Ligouri begins his *Theologia moralis,* which became the magisterial reference consulted by later works, in this way: *"Duplex est regula actuum humanorum: una dicitur remota, altera proxima. Remota, sive materialis, est lex divina, proxima vero, sive formalis, est conscientia"* (The rule of human acts is twofold: one is called remote, the other proximate. The remote or material rule is the divine law; but the proximate or formal rule is conscience). The two elements, law and conscience, are conceived as being in potential conflict with each other: the one who takes his stand with conscience is only defending the subject and his freedom in face of the exorbitant claims of the law, which is the expression of some external will. L. Lehu, a moralist of the first half of this century, went so far as to say that human acts, the object of moral theology, were the battlefield contested by two adversaries: law and conscience.

Dissatisfaction with the legalism and the presumed authoritarianism of traditional moral theology led the "new" moral theology to two opposing solutions: on the one hand, an overemphasis on conscience and therefore on the subjective element, to which was attributed a power "creative" of norms or at least an ample capacity to reshape them and to interpret their demands; on the other hand, a different founding of the objective norm within the perspective of teleologism, of consequentialism or proportionalism: ethical theories that base the moral norm on a calculus of proportionality and a weighing of the consequences of an act, its capacity to promote a

3. See G. Abbà, *Quale impostazione per la filosofia morale? Ricerche di filosofia morale* (Roma: LAS, 1996), vol. I, 53–74.

better state of affairs at the level of premoral goods and evils. Both these tendencies were repudiated by *Veritatis splendor* as contrary to Christian morality and inadequate for expressing the requirements of absoluteness and of objectivity (nos. 54–64; 71–81).

2. FROM THE "ETHICS OF THE THIRD PERSON" TO THE "ETHICS OF THE FIRST PERSON"

But in philosophical circles, particularly Anglo-American ones (at first in England and then above all in the United States), there has been from around the beginning of the 1960s, but more widely and vigorously since the 1980s, a radical questioning of the modern ethic of the norm. The most notable work here is surely that of Alasdair MacIntyre: *After Virtue: A Study in Moral Theory* (Notre Dame, Ind.: University of Notre Dame Press, 1987), which speaks of a veritable "shipwreck" affecting modern ethics.[4]

Elisabeth Anscombe, in a famous article in 1958, was the first to decry the fallaciousness of this "modern" posing of the moral question, even within the horizons of secular philosophy.[5] No longer acknowledging God as lawgiver, this modern way of conceiving morality empties the concepts of duty and of obligation of meaning. The principal element completely missing in this way of framing the moral problem is the absence of a psychology of action that could clarify the role of intention in action. Already Stuart Hampshire, in an article in 1949,[6] had noted the deep roots of the changed perspective that put modern morality at odds with classical morality. He noted how decisive for ethics is the shift of the principal point of

4. By "modern ethics" is meant that way of elaborating moral theory begun during the seventeenth century—the view that saw the ethical problem as one of identifying just action and its rules (on this, see Giuseppe Abbà's *Felicità, vita buona e virtù: Saggio di filosofia morale* [Rome: LAS, 1989], 87–107). Early advocates included the Spanish theologian Francis Suarez (1548–1617), S.J., and the English philosopher Thomas Hobbes (1588–1679); the first considered the moral problem from the viewpoint of the divine Lawgiver and his laws, with the consequent demand of obedience on the part of human creatures subject to his laws; the latter reduced the moral problem to the need of identifying rules for social collaboration.

5. G. E. M. Anscombe, "Modern Moral Philosophy," *Philosophy* 33 (1958): 1–19.

6. S. Hampshire, in *Revisions: Changing Perspectives in Moral Philosophy,* ed. A. MacIntyre and S. Hauerwas (Notre Dame, Ind.: University of Notre Dame Press, 1983).

view under which the moral problem is posed: the substitution of the ancient perspective of the first person or the acting subject by the modern perspective of a third person or of the external observer of the act.

What is designated here as the "ethics of the first person" is rooted within the perspective of the subject, who in his acting is called upon to realize acts that are excellent, that direct him to his own fulfillment. In this perspective the intrinsic finality of the act of the person is a privileged dimension, and virtues enter as decisive factors and essential principles of the good act precisely because they bear directly on the "teleological" or finalistic dimension of acting.

The "ethics of the third person," on the other hand, is situated within the perspective of the observer (a judge or confessor), who evaluates the external act according to its conformity to the rule; only by beginning with that element does the ethics of the third person consider the internal act and the factors concerning its moral imputability. The human act is here considered as an event that happens and provokes a certain state of affairs, which is in conformity with or not in conformity with a legal rule. Virtues are of completely secondary and negligible consideration: they only concern the executive facility of producing certain kinds of acts.

It is clear, therefore, that the viewpoint of the third person is in harmony with the limited scope and perspective within which the posttridentine manuals of Catholic moral theology operated: they were fundamentally designed for the formation of confessors and were meant to help them to judge with certainty the acts confessed by penitents in the light of the commandments. In this perspective D. M. Pruemmer distinguishes within the human act its *"esse physicum"* (the external element of the event) and its *"esse morale,"* which is a quality accidental to the first, obtained by considering the transcendental relationship of the physical act with the law.[7] Proportionalism, while proposing different criteria for determining the morality of acts, shares the same extrinsicist starting point with

7. D. M. Pruemmer, *Manuale Theologiae Moralis secundum principia S. Thomae Aquinatis* (Freiburg im Breisgau: Herder, 1935), nos. 99 and 111.

respect to action theory: for proportionalists, the human act is first of all an external event that happens and produces a change in the state of affairs. Its morality is dependent no longer on its conformity with a law fixed once and for all times, but on the preponderance, rationally determined, of premoral goods over evils that the act effects.

We can now grasp the truly innovative significance of a passage in _Veritatis splendor,_ a passage situated within the decisive context of the identification and moral qualification of acts: "In order to be able to grasp the object of an act which specifies that act morally, it is therefore necessary to place oneself in the perspective of the acting person. . . . By the object of a given moral act, then, one cannot mean a process or an event of the merely physical order, to be assessed on the basis of its ability to bring about a given state of affairs in the outside world. Rather, that object is the proximate end of a deliberate decision which determines the act of willing on the part of the acting person" (no. 78). At the heart of the encyclical's ethical argument, therefore, we find an invitation to change the perspective within which action is to be considered, a change that is decisive for the solution of the ethical question about the morality of human acts. The change of perspective consists in putting oneself "in the perspective of the acting person," who chooses and orders himself to a determinate end and in this way shapes his own life as good or bad.

See now how the question guiding our search for an adequate theological and scientific foundation of moral theology has been made more definite and precise. It is a question that is also a hypothesis to be tested: the conception of an ethics of the first person, which has, as its central concepts, those of finality, of the good life, and of virtue. Is this a more adequate foundation for a moral theology than the ethics of the norm? Can it constitute an adequate basis for renewing moral theology, a basis that overcomes the limits and aporias of the older and more recent past? And if so, under what conditions?

3. THE "ORIGINAL" MORAL SITUATION AND THE DESIRE FOR HAPPINESS

To put oneself within the perspective of the acting person means to identify the characteristics of the "original" or "originating" moral situation—that is, the situation that gives rise to morality—that in which the human person finds himself exercising his freedom in and through choices that shape his freedom in a unique way.

In this original situation the subject also has an initial and singular experience of fulfillment that precedes desire and explains it. This experience is utterly singular because it is given to him prior to any deliberate intention as a foretaste or promise more primitive and greater than his own will and the will of others.[8]

One can understand this by reflecting on the experience of friendship. At the origin of the bonds of interpersonal proximity and reciprocity, prior to the decisions of the subjects, is a more radical bond that contains in itself the germ and hope of a fullness in the communion of persons. Freedom, in this original experience, manifests itself more as an assent to a promise gratuitously given and as an encounter with the other than as a choice. It is as it were a call to us to transcend ourselves, to attain the good that is anticipated and promised.

Moreover, the desire that moves one to act is not first of all the expression of a lack but is preceded by an initial gift that serves as a foretaste or promise of a dimly seen fullness. Desire finds its origin in love,[9] and love its origin in an experience of particular fullness, in the promise of a personal communion, granted at the very dawn of the moral life. This is even more clearly so in the experience of grace, where the desire to love God is aroused by the encounter with him and by his gratuitous gift of himself; an anticipatory sign of this love, and one with great metaphysical and ethical meaning, is a mother's loving glance at her child.[10]

---

8. On this, see G. Angelini, *Le virtù e la fede* (Milan: Glossa, 1994), 85.

9. Saint Thomas Aquinas, *Summa theologiae*, I–II, q. 25, a. 2: "amor praecedit desiderium."

10. The metaphysical value of this originary "glance" of a mother toward her child is indicated by Hans Urs von Balthasar in his very last writing, which has as it

In the particular and concrete goods that attract his attention, man somehow perceives with his reason the fullness of a good in which all other goods find their ultimate meaning. It is precisely this experience of anticipated fullness that allows man to go beyond the immediate empirical dimension of an attraction toward concrete goods, giving his desire a truly human and personal dimension. Thus, at the origin of our acting is encountered the desire awakened by love in such wise that the will tends toward the realization of the promised fullness by means of the concrete act.

The dimension of moral action precisely as moral is revealed in man when he becomes aware of the close bond between the experience of an anticipated fullness in the encounter with the Good and its realization or actualization in and through his free action; it is through freely chosen acts that man gives himself his own moral being according to the fullness promised him and by which he is attracted. Thus is born the practical ideal of a good and happy life, one based on acts that contribute to its realization: good, excellent acts full of meaning insofar as they are, in the ultimate analysis, efforts to realize a fullness of life. Our acts not only concern the realization of goods external to us—they not only change the external state of affairs by effecting advantages or disadvantages—but they give us our very own identity. The choices made by the acting person can be worthy or unworthy of him. In free action the author of the action puts his own identity into play. This is the original meaning of 'praxis' (Gk: *praxis*), which qualifies morality as a wisdom with respect to acting or "doing" *(agere)* and distinguishes it from "making" (Gk: *poiesis*; Lt: *facere*) or the merely "technical" aspect of action ("doing" [*agere*] is not to be identified with "making" [*facere*]).[11] Only in the light of this distinction can we make sense of the affirmation of the ancient philosopher Democritus, according to

---

were the value of a spiritual and theological last will and testament; see "A Resume of My Thought," *Communio* 15, no. 4 (1988): 468–73.

11. For a recovery of the classical distinction between "doing" (praxis) and "making" (production) in an adequate action theory—a distinction missing in the perspective of the modern ethics "of the third person"—see R. Bubner, *Handlung, Sprache, und Vernunft: Grundbegriffe praktischer Philosophie. Neuausgabe mit einem Anhang* (Frankfurt am Main: Suhrkamp, 1982), 55–109.

whom the person who does an injustice is more unfortunate than the one who suffers it.[12] This statement bears witness to the discovery of the moral dimension of action, that, namely, concerned not with the change realized in the state of external affairs by an event that is independent of the one who acts, but rather with the change that the choice brings about in the one who acts: he in fact becomes good or evil, just or unjust, as a result of something that depends solely upon his freedom. The really "infinite" difference between these two levels of consideration is what verifies an affirmation—in other respects repugnant and upsetting—of Cardinal Newman, according to whom "it is preferable that the whole world die in the midst of atrocious sorrows brought on by excruciating agony than that the smallest act of injustice be committed."

When one speaks of the "moral good" one understands, first of all, the moral good that is the very person who chooses, that is, it is the "good of the person"—what makes the *person* good—insofar as he becomes good by means of his choices. This is possible only because his will has the unique characteristic of being "sealed" by the way in which the subject freely realizes himself with respect to different intelligible human goods (for example, life itself, knowledge of the truth). The latter are in this sense goods "for the person"; they form the object of different choices. Thus, as we will see more clearly in Chapter Three, the moral goodness of the person is determined not only by the subjective intentionality of "willing the good" but also by the adequate relationship that the will establishes regarding these concrete good objects of choices, on the basis of a rational knowledge that has a connotation specifically practical.[13]

12. See Diels/Kranz, *Die Fragmente der Vorsokratiker* B 45.

13. The moral good or the good that makes the *person* unqualifiedly good, is thus preeminently the *good of the person*. Various intelligible human goods, for instance, life itself and knowledge of the truth, are not "goods *of* the person" in this preeminent sense. After all, one can be alive, enjoy good health, and be extremely erudite and intellectually brilliant and still not be a morally good person, a person who is good without qualification. But intelligible human goods such as bodily life itself, health, knowledge of the truth, etc., are "goods *of* the person" in the sense that they are goods intrinsically perfecting the person: they are "noble goods" *(bona honesta)*, not mere "useful goods" *(bona utilia)*, i.e., merely instrumental goods extrinsic to the person. [Translator's note: On this, see the more extensive discussion of this matter by Professor Melina below, in Chapter Three.]

The good to which the appetitive and willed inclination of the acting subject is related must be in fact the "true" Good and not merely a good "apparent" for me. It is the object, that is, of a rational judgment, based on objective truth, and not merely the expression of a subjective and arbitrary preference. The recognition of what is in truth good, in place of the merely apparent good, is the central problem of morality. To attain the truth of moral action does not mean eliminating the subject with all his dynamism, but instead means establishing the conditions for the grasp of the true Good, and these conditions are by nature not merely rational but also affective. The original or originating practical situation calls out not only for reason but also for affectivity and desire; thus it is that the grasp of the Good depends on the dispositions of the subject: *"Qualis unusquisque est, talis finis videtur ei"* (to each one that appears desirable as an end, that is, as a good, which corresponds to his dispositions). Of concern here is a perception of the Good that takes place in one's affective reaction, in the emotions. Emotion is a foretaste or herald of meaning that reason can then bring to light.[14] It is precisely here that the decisive contribution of the virtues enters in: by means of a connaturality of the subject with the true Good, they make it possible for what really is good in itself and in accordance with the truth also to appear good to the virtuous person. By means of a virtuous connaturality, that which is good "in itself" *(bonum simpliciter)* is perceived also as good "for me" *(bonum conveniens).*[15] Thus, as Aristotle and Saint Thomas both teach, "the virtuous person is the living measure of the good, because for him the apparent good is also the good in truth and in itself."[16] The reason for this is found in the fact that human affectivity, thanks to the virtues, is impregnated with reason and thus reacts to concrete goods in accord with the order human reason impresses on it in the experience of the fullness of the Good that has been promised it.

14. See G. Angelini, *Le virtù . . .* , 86–89.

15. On this, see the following passages of Saint Thomas Aquinas: *Summa theologiae,* I–II, q. 9, a. 2; *De Malo,* q. 6c; *Sententia Libri Ethicorum,* III, 13.

16. Aristotle, *Ethica Nicomachea,* III, 4, 113a 29–34; Saint Thomas Aquinas, *Sententia Libri Ethicorum,* III, 10, 88–90. See L. Melina, *La conoscenza morale: Linee di riflessione sul Commento di san Tommaso all'Etica Nicomachea* (Rome: Città Nuova, 1987), III–12.

Therefore the goods, in the original practical situation, are also reasons for acting: they represent goods for the human subject as such, those virtuous ends that make human life as such good, constituting for it a *telos* (end) having normative value, which imposes itself as an obligatory ordering in the movements of desire and in the choices of the will.[17] Morality is therefore that ordering of desire and of will required for a good life: this ordering is not an external regulation of acts because they are in harmony with law or because they produce better results in the world; it is rather that interior harmony that reason introduces into our passions and choices precisely so that man might *be* himself. It is a harmony, an order that is not only a subjectivistic psychological expression but the reflection of the truth about the Good that fulfills man's desire.

The aspiration for individual goods is rooted in the desire of a full and complete Good; thus the pursuit of particular goods necessarily refers to the pursuit of an ultimate end. Recovering finality as a constitutive dimension of moral action helps us grasp the correspondence between the moral good and the fulfillment of one's own destiny, as *Veritatis splendor* affirms (no. 8). This puts the question of the desire for happiness at the foundation of morality.[18] The "classical" ethics of the first person, which has as its theme the question of the good life, is a morality rooted in happiness. Happiness is, in fact, as has been said, the only thing to which we can reasonably aspire as an end in itself.[19]

W. Tatarkiewicz, in a classical study on the term,[20] showed its extreme semantic complexity. However, there appear to be two principal concepts of happiness: (1) There is the modern concept ('happiness'), which understands it as the satisfaction of one's own life understood as a whole. This is a subjective perspective in which the

17. On this, see G. Abbà, *Quale impostazione . . .* , 245–47.

18. Here allow me to refer to my essay, "Desire for Happiness and Commandments in the First Chapter of *Veritatis splendor,*" *The Thomist* 60, no. 3 (1996): 341–59. This essay is now found in *"Veritatis splendor" and the Renewal of Moral Theology,* ed. J. A. DiNoia, O.P., and Romanus Cessario, O.P. (Chicago: Midwest Theological Forum, 1999), 143–60.

19. Here see M. Rhonheimer, *La prospettiva della morale: Fondamenti dell'etica filosofica* (Rome: Armando, 1994), 31–78.

20. W. Tatarkiewicz, *Analysis of Happiness* (The Hague and Warsaw: 1976), 1–36.

only indisputable criterion of happiness is the subject's judgment; it therefore lacks the capacity of distinguishing between true and false happiness. (2) And there is the classical concept (Gk: *eudaimonia,* Lt: *beatitudo*), which conceives of it as the perfection of life according to an ideal of fullness and of the "good" life corresponding to reason and therefore based on the nature of the human person. In this later vision, therefore, it is not only possible but necessary to refer to objective, reasonable criteria in order to establish what true happiness is.

Saint Augustine, in his *De Trinitate,* offers a definition of what constitutes happiness in an objective sense: "Happy is he who at the same time has everything that he wants and does not want anything evil."[21] For happiness, subjective satisfaction (to have everything one wants) is not enough; it is also necessary that there be rectitude of the will (not to want anything evil). And here the object wanted makes the difference: "what causes the happiness of the happy man is the good." For the Doctor of Hippo happiness has therefore an objective character: one can distinguish between true and false happiness by reason of the object of the will, the Good.

Saint Thomas Aquinas in his *Summa theologiae* brings the criterion for identifying true happiness back to the interior of the subject: "To desire happiness is nothing other than to desire the satisfaction of the will,"[22] but then he affirms that only the true Good can *fully* satisfy the will. Here we see the recovery of the totality of the horizon of desire, linked to the will, that is, to appetite guided by reason, which preserves the opening to the infinite.

To every attempt to found morality on the desire for happiness it seems possible to oppose as insuperable the Kantian objection that sees the absoluteness and disinterestedness of the moral imperative threatened by the bond linking morality to such a subjective and empirical element, one also in the subject's own self-interest.[23] Furthermore, from the theological perspective, founding morality on

21. Saint Augustine, *De Trinitate,* XIII, 4, 7–9, 12, "Nuova Bibliotheca Agostiniana" (Rome: Città Nuova, 1973), vol. 4, 514–29.

22. Saint Thomas Aquinas, *Summa theologiae,* I–II, q. 5, a. 8.

23. I. Kant, *Foundation of the Metaphysics of Morals* (Italian translation by R. Assunto, *Fondazioni della metafisica dei costumi* [Bari: 1980], 39–49).

the desire for happiness seems to run the risk of unexpectedly changing God from an end that must be loved and willed for itself above everything, into a mere means for "my" self-realization.[24] And, in truth, there is always the possibility of distorting the natural aspiration for happiness, a perversion in the form of a search for one's own subjective self-realization.

Nonetheless, the question of happiness has a much different configuration within Christian theology, in particular in the thought of Saint Augustine and Saint Thomas.[25] Not only was the matter formulated in objective terms and therefore provides room for the moment of truth—which enables us to distinguish between true and false happiness—but above all there was the recognition that complete happiness is not possible on this earth. Thus the search for the Good was freed from a too narrow connection with the happiness that one can hope to obtain, and the primacy of the good over pleasure was assured. Only in God can one find true and complete happiness, and only toward him ought the love of man be directed. Thus the limits of philosophical eudaimonism were overcome and likewise the danger of making God a means to one's own happiness—which for Saint Augustine is precisely what constitutes the essence of sin.

4. HUMAN ACTS AS IMPERFECT ACTUATIONS PREPARING FOR AND ANTICIPATING HAPPINESS

In the perspective of an ethics of the first person, therefore, there is a distinction between the Supreme or Sovereign Good that constitutes man's beatitude and the act by means of which he attains that beatitude.[26] If God is the ultimate end, the only reality that can satisfy the human desire for happiness, beatitude consists subjectively in that perfect act in which man's being is fulfilled: the loving vision of

---

24. H. U. von Balthasar, "Homo creatus est," *Saggi teologici* (Brescia: Morcelliane, 1991), vol. 5, 9–26.

25. See W. Pannenberg, *Grundlagen der Ethik: Philosophisch-theologische Perspektiven* (Göttingen: Vanderhoeck & Ruprecht, 1996), 27–36.

26. Saint Thomas Aquinas speaks of the *finis cuius* (God as the object in which man's beatitude lies) and the *finis quo* (the subjective attainment and enjoyment of that supreme Good); see *Summa theologiae*, I–II, q. 1, a. 8.

God. We have been made for this perfect act, and the acts that we do on this earth are in a certain sense nothing more than imperfect actualizations preparatory to this supreme act.

See now the significance of time and of human freedom, which determines itself within history through individual choices: we are talking about the movement of the creature who tends to God as the Supreme Good for which he has been made. Saint Thomas calls this the *"motus rationalis creaturae in Deum"* (the movement of the rational creature toward God), and sums up man's moral life in this perspective.[27] In contrast to angels, who determine themselves through one act outside of time, humans express their freedom in a multitude of acts through which the discursiveness, the fragmentariness, and the revocability of choices make the road to happiness difficult and dangerous.

On the one hand, the perfect and beatifying act exceeds the natural capacity of man and can only be a gift from God, who calls the rational creature to share in his own divine life with a gesture of absolutely gratuitous love. On the other hand, this act demands that one prepare oneself for it and receive it through a freely given consent. Therefore the truly theological perspective on human acts within time now appears: historical human acts of freedom within time prepare us for the ultimate and definitive act outside of time: by means of free consent to divine grace they "merit" and anticipate eternal beatitude.

Undergirding this conception stands a metaphysics of action and an eminently dynamic ontology of created being.[28] The being of man is given as *actus primus* that tends toward its completion by means of the activity of freedom, *actus secundus*. The substantial form received in creation is imperfect and exists only in tension with what is other than itself: it is proper to the human dignity of the free and rational creature to be able to establish its orientation toward its own proper perfection by means of free choices. The action of a

27. *Summa theologiae*, I, q. 2, Prologus; cf. G. Abbà, *Lex et virtus: Studi sul-l'evoluzione della dottrina morale di san Tommaso d'Aquino* (Rome: LAS, 1983), 160–65.

28. On this, see J. de Finance, *Etre et agir dans la philosophie de Saint Thomas*, 3rd ed. (Rome: Pontifical Gregorian University, 1965), 214–53.

man is therefore at the same time an expression of the riches of a being who expands and embraces reality, and an expression of a constitutive poverty, insofar as, having experienced the fullness of the Good anticipatorily in the experience of friendship, he also discovers that of himself he can never attain this fullness.

The formal and unitary perspective within which human acts can be understood is that of "merit": of the collaboration of freedom with the grace of God, who calls us to share in a supernatural beatitude. The meritorious act of the Christian carries in itself an anticipation of future happiness. God is present in meritorious actions working in synergy with us by way of faith. Aquinas always spoke in this way in his Commentary on the Sixth Chapter of John's Gospel: "In truth, faith is the principle of all good actions; and therefore faith itself is said to be a work of God. But if faith is a work of God, in what way can men complete God's work? The question finds its resolution in Isaiah 26.12, which says: '*He has worked our works in us!*' In truth, the very fact that we believe and whatever good we do is in us a work of God; the same is said in Philippians 2.13: '*it is He who works in us both the willing and the doing!*'"[29]

What is presupposed on man's part for the meritorious worth of an act—free collaboration with grace—is made up of two elements: the voluntariness of the act and its moral value. A human act can be meritorious only if it is truly free and in conformity with the true good of the person. And here, once more, the ethical point of view of the first person comes into play: the act is moral insofar as it expresses the person's movement toward his fulfillment. The moral agent is truly identified morally by his choices, which shape him and perfect him, if they are good, and direct him toward the end for which he is destined.

In this perspective, the action that prepares for the attainment of happiness is included in its intrinsic objective intentionality. Thus one can speak of *intentional action at its root,*[30] indicating thereby the

29. Saint Thomas Aquinas, *In Joannem Lectura,* VI, lect. III, nos. 901–2.

30. Cf. M. Rhonheimer, *La prospettiva della morale,* 85–89, which coins this decisive concept of action theory from the analysis of G. E. M. Anscombe, *Intention,* 2nd ed. (Oxford: Blackwell, 1963), and A. C. Danto, *Basis Handlungen,* in *Analytische Handlungstheorie,* ed. G. Meggle (Frankfurt am Main: 1985), vol. 1, 89–101.

objective intentional content of the action seen as a choice in which the human will determines itself in its confrontation with an intelligible good. Here we are dealing with a decisive precision from the moral point of view that allows us to avoid two limiting and extrinsicizing conceptions: that of an objectivistic materialism, which considers only the physical and external aspect of the act and describes it as a natural event and not as a choice; and that of subjectivism, which attributes to intention, disconnected from choice and its rational content, the capacity to determine exhaustively the meaning of what is being done.

To make this matter more easily understood we can introduce an example. If a contractor in grave economic difficulties, in order to maintain his business of building public works, agrees to corrupt a public official so as to obtain labor contracts, the deed he does (to leave a check made out in the official's name as a "share") cannot be described either materially as "signing his own name to a piece of paper," or subjectively as "saving jobs for those dependent on me." The first description does not define a human action, but only an event that happens. The second identifies the further or ulterior subjective intention for whose sake one does something, but it does not express the objective intentional content of the act as chosen: "that which I do" *(what)* in the perspective of the "why" or "because" intrinsic to the choice and which makes it understandable. And in truth the object of choice is precisely "to corrupt a public official."

5. VIRTUES AS WAYS TO FULFILLMENT

If we put ourselves in the perspective of the acting person at the interior of the originating moral situation and understand human acts as imperfect actuations that prepare for the attainment of the final end of beatitude, which can be granted only by God, then we cannot fail to perceive the enormous difficulties that need to be overcome. We have already referred to the theologically decisive question that it is only by means of the intervention of divine grace that the person can act in a manner worthy of the supernatural end to which he is called. But serious difficulties arise even from the perspective of the human presuppositions for moral action. The gap between the historical and the existential condition of the human subject for performing by himself an excellent act and performing the perfect act is enormous. How is it possible to confer on the manifold, varied, fragmented, unstable movement of our acts that unity that permits us to anticipate and prepare for the perfect act? Human freedom clamors for order, direction, stability, without at the same time losing itself in rigid and mechanistic behavior.[31] On the part of practical reason, which contains in itself the principles of the moral evaluation of human acts, there is nonetheless difficulty in directing man's concrete and daily acts toward God because of the extremely variegated and complex situations in which man finds himself. The generic orientation to the Good, which belongs to the rational nature of the will, is not enough to determine itself in the case of particular goods. For a particular good to be recognized and chosen, it must be grasped not only as good in itself but also as a good fitting "for me," corresponding to my affections, to my sentiments, to my desires, as has been noted already.

The theory of the virtues is the answer to all these difficulties— virtues understood as principles of good action. Virtues are modes of the subject's being through which his interior dynamisms, both affective and intellectual, are integrated and disposed to act fittingly for the Good. We are talking about *habitus* (modes of being), which are the middle term between *who we are now* and *who we are called to be.* In this sense they constitute, as it were, the subject's second nature, because the human person's own nature is modified and qualified by them, in such wise that all his dynamisms are integrated and directed toward the goal to which he is called.[32] The virtues do not concern only an external facility of achieving the Good and executive efficacy in attaining it: they are intrinsic constituents of excellent action. In reality, for an action to be good it is not enough that it be in external conformity to the moral rule *(secundum rectam rationem);* it is also necessary that it be done virtuously *(modus virtutis),* that is, with awareness, with a choice (election) motivated by

---

31. See G. Abbà, *Lex et virtus,* 171–73.

32. See P. J. Wadell, *The Primacy of Love: An Introduction to the Ethics of Thomas Aquinas* (New York and Mahwah: Paulist Press, 1991), 106–24.

love for the Good and in a stable and constant way.[33] In other words, only the act that springs from virtue is truly good, because only in it is the subject interiorly engaged in an actuation that anticipates the fullness of the end and participates in it from the very beginning.

Virtue concerns not only the subjective aspect of interiority, not only the objective aspect of execution: it renders good at one and the same time both the one who acts and his deeds.[34] It is here crucially important to understand the spiritual character of virtue. It is a "good quality of mind whereby one lives rightly and which no one can use badly" *(bona qualitas mentis qua recte vivitur et qua nullus male utitur)*. This is an Augustinian definition of virtue, historically codified by Peter of Poitiers, which Saint Thomas Aquinas accepts and defends.[35] Virtue concerns the mind *(mens):* the spiritual dimension of the person, at the same time cognitive and affective: it regards the soul in its bent toward perfection by means of acting. It is impossible to make bad use of virtue because it is not a partial technical ability of a man (for example, being a good musician, who, knowing how to play an instrument can willingly make a mistake), but is rather the goodness of the man as such; insofar as he is related fittingly to the different intelligible human goods a virtuous man cannot want to sin. The good of man insofar as he is man is precisely the spiritual sphere of the virtues.[36]

At the same time the doctrine of the virtues corresponds to an integral anthropology of man, who is the subject of acting in the

33. Saint Thomas Aquinas, *Sententia Libri Ethicorum,* II, 4, 49–76; *Summa theologiae,* I–II, q. 100, a. 9.

34. *Summa theologiae,* I–II, q. 55, a. 3: *"Virtus est quae bonum facit habentem et opus eius bonum reddit."* It is this intrinsic connection between subjective interiority and action, between intention and choice, which is lost in the theories that separate and counterpose "goodness" and "rightness." See B. Schüller, "Zu den Schwierigkeiten, die Tugend zu rehabilitieren," *Theologie und Philosophie* 58 (1983): 535–55, which reduces virtue to a good subjective will *(Grundhaltung),* while on the other hand J. F. Keenan, in *Goodness and Rightness in Thomas Aquinas's "Summa Theologiae"* (Washington, D.C.: Georgetown University Press, 1992), reduces the virtues to abilities of a technical nature for accomplishing what is "right."

35. See Romanus Cessario, *The Moral Virtues and Theological Ethics* (Notre Dame, Ind.: University of Notre Dame Press, 1992), 52ff.

36. Here it is good to consult E. Schockenhoff, *Bonum hominis: Die anthropologischen und theologischen Grundlagen der Tugendethik des Thomas von Aquin* (Mainz: Mathias Gruenewald Verlag, 1987).

integral reality of his being *"corpore et anima unus"* (one in body and soul).[37] The moral subject is not pure reason or pure autonomous freedom: he is also bodily, with instincts, emotions, sensibilities, passions. All these components cannot be repressed and suffocated, but must be integrated into a harmonious whole, which finds its point of reference in reason, which, in the light of the truth about the Good, orders everything in view of the end. Thus virtue, overcoming the difficulties and fragilities of human action, makes it possible for man to do the good easily, stably, and with joy. The virtues are therefore a principle of integration within the human composite, which does not sacrifice any component but orders everything in a hierarchy established by reason with regard to the end. The moral perspective of the virtues reflects a positive evaluation of the creatureliness of man, of whom an essential part is the body with its emotional and passionate reactions.

The virtues are therefore rooted in practical reason. At their heart is a rational and universal principle: the "seeds of the virtues" are also at the same time the truth about the human goods, which freedom is called upon to love and pursue, that is, they are the principles of the natural law. The virtues make us love what is truly worthy of love, the true Good. Thanks to the virtues, human affectivity can react and incline man not only *"secundum rationem rectam"* (according to right reason) but above all *"cum ratione recta"* (with right reason).[38] This removes talk about the virtues from the danger of the subjectivism of arbitrary tastes and the historical relativism of different cultures and social contexts. The intrinsic constitution of virtues, distinguishing them from spontaneous inclinations, from conventional dispositions, and from cultural habitudes, is prudence, *recta ratio agibilium,* the right reason regarding things to be done; there is, in truth, no moral virtue without prudence, which establishes the reasonable measure of acting, one rooted in the rational principles about the Good. Nonetheless, true moral intelligence of the concrete particular cannot be realized without the moral

37. *Veritatis splendor,* no. 48, citing *Gaudium et spes,* no. 14.
38. Saint Thomas Aquinas, *Summa theologiae,* I–II, q. 58, a. 4, ad 3.

virtues: prudence cannot exist without the moral virtues.[39] The mature Thomistic synthesis articulates a theory of practical reason that begins with the universal principles, the expression of the truth about the Good (the natural law), but that can develop the light of those truths in concrete action only in a synergistic union with the virtues, by reason of a connaturality with the good of the moral subject as a whole. The rationality of the virtues is not rationalism.[40]

At the heart of the virtues freedom is also found. In fact, virtue is not a mechanical predisposition for a standardized and uniform behavior. It is totally different from a habit.[41] Virtue does not diminish freedom but rather potency. It is therefore wrong to draw a parallel between virtue and vice, putting them on the same plane. Virtue does not primarily concern the execution of the external act but rather the execution of the internal act, that is, the choice. It is a *"habitus electivus"* (an elective habitus).[42] And the act of choice is not predetermined by the virtue, which only perfects the motivational orientation, but does not preestablish the concrete object: in the technical terms of Scholaticism it is said that the proper end of virtue is not the object of choice *(id quod eligitur),* but on the contrary that for whose sake the choice is made *(id cuius gratia eligitur).* Thus the act of choice always remains ulterior and decisive for the confirmation of the personal orientation and for self-determination. The Thomistic ethic of virtue does not take away the primacy of acts and the centrality of choices.

There is yet more: the heart of virtues is love. The freedom that talk about virtue presupposes is not the "freedom of indifference," but the "freedom of quality," the freedom, that is, that is ordered to the Good as its end.[43] Virtue allows for the love of the true Good.

---

39. On this, see my book *La conoscenza morale,* 191–202.

40. In contrast to voluntarism, in Saint Thomas the intrinsic and constitutive rationality of virtues and of prudence in particular is emphasized. See D. Westberg, *Right Practical Reason: Aristotle, Action, and Prudence in Aquinas* (Oxford: Clarendon Press, 1994).

41. See Servais Pinckaers, *La renouveau de la morale,* chap. 4, "La vertu est tout autre chose qu'une habitude" (Paris: Tequi, 1964), 144–64.

42. See A. Rodriguez Luño, *La scelta etica: Il rapporto tra liberta e virtu* (Milan: Ares, 1988).

43. See S. Pinckaers, *The Sources of Christian Ethics,* 327–78.

Therefore it is possible to affirm that virtues are the "strategies of love": they let the gift of self live in relationship to the different human goods, the objects of human choices.[44] The Augustinian perspective on virtues as different manifestations of charity[45] does not annul the multiplicity of virtuous ends, of the moral goods and virtuous dispositions to be acquired, but shows their intimate connection and ultimate finalization to love as the gift of self.

In this sense, a morality centered on virtues is totally different from a morality of self-sufficiency. It is necessary here at least to offer a token rebuttal to a theological objection of Protestant inspiration,[46] according to which basing moral theology on the virtues would signify condemning oneself to a naturalism and a Pelagianism, in which one ends up by attributing a stable and autonomous capacity of man to do the good, ultimately making man independent of grace. In the Catholic concept, the perfection of the virtues is realized in charity, which is the mother and form of the virtues. But charity is a particular kind of friendship with God,[47] which fulfills all the other virtues. Without charity the other virtues are still true, but incomplete. But charity, as friendship with God, is possible only if God graciously takes the initiative toward man. It is through supernatural grace that we have charity, the form and mother of the virtues. This heals the wounds of sin, which tends to center desire on one's own self, and elevates nature beyond itself. In the life of charity the virtuous man becomes ever more dependent on God, ever more capable of being docile to the suggestions of the Holy Spirit, mediated through his gifts, which adapt the virtues to the movements of the Holy Spirit. The virtuous person lives charity, and is therefore open to a relationship of radical welcoming of another and gift of self, which goes beyond nature and which is utterly opposed to a self-sufficient naturalism.

---

44. Thus P. J. Wadell, *The Primacy of Love . . .* , 90.

45. Saint Augustine, *De moribus ecclesiae catholicae,* I, XV, 25.

46. On the reasons why Protestants are diffident about the theme of virtue in ethics, avoided as pregnant with naturalism and Pelagianism, see E. Herms, "Virtue: A Neglected Concept in Protestant Ethics," *Scottish Journal of Theology* 35 (1983): 481–95.

47. Saint Thomas Aquinas, *Summa theologiae,* I–II, q. 65, a. 5.

Finally, we should underscore another important element in the perspective of a morality of virtue: the recognition of the historical and dynamic character of the moral life. Man is born incomplete and inadequate for the act for which he is made. Only through education, which can develop the germs of the virtues in him, can he grow and make himself adequate for the task for which he exists. This is a constitutive dynamism, which derives from the unfinished character of the human creature; and this dynamism fulfills itself by means of free choices, which take place in relationships with others, within a community, that is, within history.[48]

6. FIRST CONCLUSIONS REGARDING A MORAL THEOLOGY OF THE VIRTUES

We can now trace some first conclusive findings regarding the question that has guided our research: the possibility and advantages of a moral theology grounded upon virtues.

The perspective of an ethics that assumes norms as its principles of departure (what we have called the ethics of the third person) implies a twofold exteriority of morality:

a. This has already been pointed out at the philosophical level: it implies that the norm (which concerns human acts conceived first of all as external acts) is external to the person. It is a concept that reflects an imposition of the norm as a "morality from the perspective of the third person" (the observer: the impartial judge or confessor) and which takes as its starting point the confrontation of the external act with the norm.

b. To this now must be added something from the theological level: this (a normative ethics from the perspective of the third person) entails making Christ extrinsic to the person: He stands before me as the "lawgiver." A starting point marked by an extrinsicalism of this kind with regard to awareness of theological factors (the Church, the magisterium) inevitably produces a potentially conflicting situation between conscience and the Church, between con-

---

48. Stanley Hauerwas is particularly attentive to this fact; see his *A Community of Character: Toward a Constructive Christian Social Ethics* (Notre Dame, Ind.: University of Notre Dame Press, 1981).

science and the magisterium. The alternative, the route taken by the moral theology condemned by the encyclical *Veritatis splendor*, of a subjectivistic reduction of the revealed and objective element, implies a total loss of the sacramental character of the Christian event and a radical subjectivization of Christian morality.

A more adequate starting point for meeting the requirements of the renewal of moral theology as presented in *Veritatis splendor* can be seen in the perspective of a morality of the first person, of happiness and virtue. In it the concept of the norm is not eliminated, but is "redimensioned" internally within the perspective of an ethic of the first person (or of the acting subject). In the next chapter we will try to show how this integration is possible.

Here I will only note some of the advantages provided by this starting point for a moral theology:

a. In this perspective *the aspiration for the good,* characterized by the originating practical situation, is integrally assumed. It is related to the truth ("the truth of desire" of C. Vigna,[49] or the "truth about the good" of Karol Wojtyla), but it also includes the passions. Contrary to a rationalistic and therefore voluntaristic starting point for morality, which attributes the knowledge of the norm to speculative and deductive reason (a Spinozistic *"ethica more geometrico demonstrata"*) and to an executive will, here the privileged role is given to a conception of practical reason enervated within the totality of the subject (including his intellect, will, reason, and passions), "one in soul and body." The knowledge of the moral good, as the "good of the person" (and not simply as the rectitude of external acts) is achieved through the exercise of freedom within the ambit of its own internal dynamisms, perfected now by the virtues.

b. In this way the *reference to Christ* is more global and less external: he is not a lawgiver who stands before me, but the foundation who sustains me and the end who attracts me, as well as "the friend

49. See C. Vigna, "La verità del desiderio come fondazione della norma morale," in an anthology by various authors, *Problemi di etica: Fondazione, norme, orientamenti,* ed. E. Berti (Padua: Fondazione Lanze / Gregoriana Libreria Editrice 1990), 69–135; I note also my contribution, "Desire for Happiness and the Commandments in the First Chapter of *Veritatis splendor,*" *The Thomist* 60, no. 3 (1996): 341–59; reprinted in *"Veritatis splendor" and the Renewal of Moral Theology,* 143–60.

who counsels me" (Saint Thomas Aquinas, in his treatise on the *lex nova*). Charity, Thomistically understood as friendship with Christ, is "the form of the virtues." More developed is the "Christocentrism of virtues" proposed by Saint Bonaventure:[50] the moral virtues are understood as participations in the virtues of Christ, the *origo, forma, et finis* of the moral life, which is destined to prepare the *deiformitas* (the deification) of man. In the *Breviloquium* Christ not only offers man *the precepts (praecepta)* but also *documents, examples, and benefits (documenta, exempla et beneficia)*. We will dwell more extensively later on this Bonaventurian theological direction.

c. A specific perspective for applying this starting point is found in considering *marriage and the family:* subjects crucial to morality. The norms governing them are not extrinsic and in opposition to passions and desire. Conjugal chastity is not the "repression of instincts" (as it is in the Stoic and Kantian concepts, which John Paul II overcomes in his Wednesday Catechesis), but the true integration of instinct and human affectivity within the dynamic of love: the virtue of true love. From the theological perspective, it is possible in this way to think about marital love as a participation (mediated by the virtue of charity) in the love of Christ for his Church, allowing an authentic moral theology and even a "theologial" morality.

---

50. A. Nguyen Van Si, *Seguire e imitare Cristo secondo San Bonaventura* (Milan: Ed Bibl. Francescana, 1995), with essays by P. Delhaye, J. Chantillon, and A. Pompei.

∞

CHAPTER THREE

An Ethics Founded on the Truth about the Good of the Person

*T*he rediscovery of virtues in moral theory has not taken place without serious gaps and a one-sidedness, so much so that its plausibility, both philosophical and theological, has been compromised.[1] To show how it differs from the rationalism of the modern ethics of the obligatory norm, some have defined virtue simply as a "character trait," a disposition reflecting only the desires and interests of the individual.[2] But if there is no reference to an objectively good end, a firm distinction between virtue and vice becomes impossible; one can easily fall into the irrationalism of subjective tastes. Other authors, seeking a greater objectivity, have recognized the importance of particular communities and their constitutive narratives for the formation of character. They have thus traced talk about virtue back to the particularity of a specific historical social context, where they have found, along with a particular vision of the world, an interpretation codified around the meaning of human action.[3] But in this approach virtue talk is not without the risk of falling into a traditionist conformism and even into relativism. The practical and debatable consequences of these theories are even more evident when they are applied to specific areas of professional

1. See G. Abbà, *Felicità, vita buona e virtù: Saggio di filosofia morale* (Rome: LAS, 1989), 123–30.

2. Philippa Foot, *Virtues and Vices and Other Essays in Moral Philosophy* (Berkeley and Los Angeles: University of California Press, 1978).

3. Stanley Hauerwas, *A Community of Character: Toward a Constructive Christian Social Ethics* (Notre Dame, Ind.: University of Notre Dame Press, 1981), 121: "Any theory of virtues is necessary relative to the history of a particular community."

and social life, for example, to medical ethics.[4] On the basis of a historical relativism, it has been said that the doctor's virtues should be defined only within the context of the social practice of medicine, as set by the dominant cultural conception.

The insufficiency of these views is shown in the radical opposition between *virtues* and *norms* in which the preference given to virtue as outlined above implies the rejection of any normative ethics. At the root of this deficiency, in my opinion, lies the absence of the moment of truth as a constitutive rational reference for an authentic virtue ethics. Only truth allows us to overcome the sterility of subjectivism and relativism. Moreover, on such a foundation, the normative dimension of virtue can also be integrated and can find its meaning and its function. Therefore, we will pursue our study of the renewal of moral theology in the light of *Veritatis splendor,* using the truth about the good of the person as the adequate foundation for an ethics of virtue. We will develop the question in two main sections: first, we will reflect on the nature of moral truth, inquiring into the bond between freedom and truth; second, we will study in depth the content of moral truth as the truth about the good of the person. In this context the issue of the relationship between ethics and anthropology is certainly a primary concern.

I. FREEDOM AND TRUTH

John Paul II's encyclical on morality brings to light the decisive character of the bond between freedom and the truth, and identifies the breaking of this bond as the cause of so many dangerous deviations in ethics: "At the root [of the opposition to the moral tradition] is the more or less obvious influence of currents of thought which end by detaching human freedom from its essential and constitutive relationship to truth" (*Veritatis splendor,* no. 4; see also nos. 34 and 84).

As a matter of fact, the modern and contemporary age, in its theoretical expressions and in the common conscience of people, is characterized by the one-sided emphasis given to freedom, which

---

4. See the contributions of M. W. Wartofsky and E. L. Erde in *Virtue and Medicine: Explorations in the Character of Medicine,* ed. E. E. Shelp (Dordrecht, The Netherlands—Boston, Mass.—Lancaster, U.K.: Reidel, 1985), 175–99, 201–21.

"appears as the highest good, to which all the other goods are subjected."[5] The claim of truth, by contrast, is regarded with suspicion, as if it were pregnant with the danger of oppressing freedom. Freedom, it seems, would be better preserved by skepticism, which refuses absolute and immutable assertions and is constrained to recognize the constitutive impotence of thought regarding ultimate questions. In a radically pluralistic society, democracy should be founded on a rigorous agnosticism and guard against the threat that comes from any claim of truth, which is immediately exorcized with the defamatory epithet of "fundamentalism." Such a position surely reflects an understandable reaction to the legalism of an ethics in which law is conceived as an expression of the will of a lawmaker in opposition to the will of the subject.

But this issue goes beyond such a legitimate reaction. From this position any limitation imposed on freedom by any factor would appear as a violation of its rights of autonomy and a dangerous tendency toward absolutism. To be free, it is necessary to remove not only the exterior presence of laws, but also any normative references to some truth about human nature. In this way an "ethics without truth"[6] is proposed, where independence from truth coincides with the demand of a will related to no one and to no thing, because it recognizes no one and no thing as prior to its decisions. Cardinal Ratzinger has correctly identified the theological nucleus of this radical desire for freedom in the delirious claim of rejecting one's own nature as a creature in order to "become like God" (Gn 3.5), and to be independent from everything, because one lacks a given nature and constitutive relationships with other subjects, which represent sources of responsibility and moral obligations.

Freedom, detached from truth, opens the way to the predominance of technological reason, which dominates everything and arranges everything to be used, placing all things at the service of a power that no longer has any limitations. The extraordinary ability to produce means—or better, to reduce everything to means, for

---

5. Joseph Ratzinger, *La via della fede: Le ragione dell'etica nell'epoca presente* (Milan: Ed. Ares, 1996), chap. 1, "Libertà e Verità,"13–36.

6. U. Scarpelli, *L'etica senza verità* (Bologna: Il Mulino, 1982), 111.

there is no longer any end and every thing is but manipulable matter at the service of the desire and of the will to power—implies therefore the more and more impending danger of the loss of equality, with the consequent domination of the strongest over all others.[7] Freedom detached from truth becomes the arbitrary and unlimited power of the few, which enslaves all the others.

If this possibility looms threateningly on the horizon at the social and world level, other frightening consequences are already at work at the individual level. Even from a strictly existential perspective, the freedom of a man without a nature is disoriented, meaningless, and condemns itself to the absolute void. In the extreme though coherent theorizing of Jean-Paul Sartre, anarchic freedom, lacking metaphysical and moral connections and abandoned to itself, becomes an infernal damnation to absurdity and isolation. In the end "the liberation from truth does not produce pure freedom, but takes it away."[8]

Freedom, in order to be saved, must be reconciled with reality and recognize its condition: it is the freedom of a created being, which can be fulfilled only if it takes the form of responsibility toward the human essence and the orientation to the Good that is naturally inscribed in it. Unless it wants to lead to self-destruction, freedom must accord with truth and correspond to the nature of our being.

The Distinctiveness and Originality of Moral Knowledge

Thus far our problem has only been formulated and remains far from solution. We have stated a need, but we have not yet found the adequate way to meet it. In fact, as soon as the problem of truth is posed in the debate about the foundation of ethics, another issue inevitably arises, namely, the well-known and widely discussed "Hume's law."[9] This law condemns every effort to deduce an

---

7. See Hans Jonas, *Dalla fede antica all'uomo tecnologico* (Bologna: Il Mulino, 1991), 262–63.

8. J. Ratzinger, *La via della fede*, 24, referring to Josef Pieper, "Kreaturlichkeit und menschliche Natur: Annerkungen zum philosophischen Ansatz von J. P. Sartre," in Pieper's *Uber die Schwierigkeit, heute zu glauben* (Munich: 1974), 304–21.

9. See David Hume, *A Treatise on Human Nature*, III, I, sec. 1; in *British Moralists, 1650–1800*, ed. D. D. Raphael (Oxford: Oxford University Press, 1969), vol. 2, 504; and

"ought" from an "is," a moral precept from an ontological affirmation, as "naturalistic paralogism." To be sure, it does not belong to speculative reason to ground moral imperatives. Nevertheless, the error of such a prohibition (the so-called great division between facts and values) lies precisely in excluding the moment of truth from the sphere of ethics, and consequently attributing to moral affirmations only the meaning of subjective preferences founded on emotions. In this way we misunderstand practical reason: reason is thought to be able to express descriptive statements about facts exclusively and not to be able to move itself to action. The fact that practical affirmations (whose distinctiveness with respect to "speculative" knowledge is rightly perceived by "Hume's law") possess a different nature does not necessarily imply that praxis excludes a knowledge that permits us to reach judgments about the truth or falseness of certain actions.[10]

It is therefore necessary to dwell upon the distinctiveness of the practical dimension of rationality and in particular upon the nature of moral truth. Practical reason is not a faculty distinct from speculative reason, which knows only "in order to know"; rather, it is the same reason, now inserted within the dynamics of appetites and operations. Practical reason is reason itself insofar as it guides intentional human actions. As we have said, practical knowledge does not depend on speculative knowledge for its principles; it finds its proper principle or starting point in an aspiration for a good that can be participated in through the mediation of freely chosen acts. In its specifically moral and not purely technical dimension it has its origin in the aspiration for *the good of man as man,* realized practically through a human act. In a strict and rigorous sense, moral knowledge does not arise through the deductive application of metaphysical statements about human nature, but rather as a light of the truth concerning the human good, which radiates toward the reality of action

---

G. E. Moore, *Principia Ethica* (Cambridge: Cambridge University Press, 1903), chap. 10, 24–25.

10. See C. Vigna, "La verità del desiderio come fondazione della norma morale," in *Problemi di etica. Fondazione, norme, orientamenti,* ed. E. Berti (Padua: Fondazione Lanze/Gregoriana Libreria Editrice, 1990), 69–135, esp. 77.

and guides it.[11] The good of man, which constitutes the principle of practical reason, is also the end toward which natural inclinations are ordered. The first act of practical reason is, therefore, according to Saint Thomas, the discovery of the truth about man's ultimate end.[12] The Good does not appear as good to purely speculative reason, but precisely to practical reason, which always implies a participation of will and a determination of freedom in its encounters.

Truth of Desire and Truth about the Good

Let us now return to what we said in the previous chapter about the originating situation and the modality of desire by which man relates himself to the Good. The term "desire" expresses the relationship that establishes itself between the needy and incomplete human subject and the end of fullness to which he is called and of which he has had a foretaste or anticipatory glimpse in the originating experience of love. Its value is not only instinctual, but, according to the great Augustinian tradition, also transcendental, orienting man to the fulfillment of his entire being.

Desire is therefore the foundational locus of the meaning of human action. The demand for fulfillment, which lies at the base of the imperative character proper to the norm, appears in desire. But because desire tends to turn back upon itself, to be satisfied with objects inadequate to its breadth, to fall away from its original tension toward the infinite,[13] reason must keep vigil over its dynamics

---

11. On this, see my *La conoscenza morale: Linee di riflessione sul Commento di San Tommaso all'Etica Nicomachea* (Rome: Città Nuova Editrice, 1987). See also J. de Finance, "Aux sources de la metaphysique et la morale," in *L'ouverture et la norme: Questions sur l'agir humain* (Vatican City: Libreria Editrice Vaticana, 1989), 111–38; G. E. M. Anscombe, *Intention*, 2nd ed. (Oxford: Blackwell, 1985); W. Kluxen, *Philosophische Ethik bei Thomas von Aquin*, 2nd ed. (Hamburg: F. Meiner Verlag, 1980); and M. Rhonheimer, *Praktische Vernunft und Vernünftigkeit der Praxis: Handlungstheorie bei Thomas von Aquin in ihrer Entstehung aus dem Problemkontext der aristotelischen Ethik* (Berlin: Akademie Verlag, 1994).

12. See *Summa theologiae*, I–II, q. 3.

13. In my essay, "'The Desire for Happiness and the Commandments in the First Chapter of *Veritatis splendor*," in *"Veritatis splendor" and the Renewal of Moral Theology*, ed. J. A. DiNoia, O.P., and Romanus Cessario, O.P. (Chicago: Midwest Theological Forum, 1999), 143–60, I pointed out the etymological richness of the term *desiderium*. It refers to stars *(sidera)*, thus manifesting both a wandering retreat and a constitutive nostalgia.

and safeguard its faithfulness both to the originating experience of anticipated fullness and to its *true* end.

Making freedom rely on truth, according to the Gospel directive "The truth shall set you free" (Jn 8.32), therefore necessarily implies a reinterpretation of freedom itself with respect to the modern understanding. Freedom does not mean "indifference,"[14] but love of the true Good. The theme of desire for happiness is integrated into ethics as the original and constitutive inclination of freedom, but it is oriented by a judgment of reason. Thus, the desire for happiness is not an empty psychological formula left to subjective interpretation, but indicates the tension toward the ultimate end of that aspiration, which is guided by reason.[15] It thus belongs to reason to verify the relation to the end according to the truth, to point out which is the true Good that deserves to be pursued, and to set order in the desires so that the particular ends stand in hierarchical harmony with what is worthy of being loved in itself, above all else, as the ultimate end.

Desire, fully reinstated in the dynamics of freedom and morals, is not a naturalistic passion, with only an empirical and psychological value, but a conscious openness to the fullness of the horizon of the Good, which is manifested to reason in the original experience of love. At the root of the mistrust of desire and the natural inclinations there lies, perhaps, a reductive prejudicial interpretation of them, which places them at the level of sensible experience. It is therefore crucial to rediscover their specific spiritual dimension: the desire for happiness is the expression of our *spiritual nature* in its spontaneous aspiration for the True and the Good.[16] Far from leading back to the particularism of sensible experience, such a nature, understood theologically as the manifestation of God's image, opens the person to the universality of the spirit.

Thus the *truth about the Good* mediates between desire and its full satisfaction, between original aspiration and its final fulfillment. Freedom is enlivened by an aspiration that must be rediscovered and

14. On this, see Servais Pinckaers, O.P., *The Sources of Christian Ethics,* trans. Sister Mary Thomas Noble, O.P. (Washington, D.C.: The Catholic University of America Press, 1995), 354–78.

15. See M. Rhonheimer, *La prospettiva della morale: Fondamenti dell'etica filosofica* (Rome: Armando Editore, 1994), 44–49.

16. See Servais Pinckaers, O.P., *La morale catholique* (Paris: Cerf, 1991), 71–88.

maintained in its original openness: this is the purpose of the commandments and the virtues.

In this regard, it is helpful to touch on the thesis of the philosopher Karol Wojtyla concerning the *authentic integration of desire*,[17] which may be considered the philosophical background of and which allows us to grasp the meaning of this theme in the encyclical. Man's freedom is made for the gift of self to the other; desire is also integrated into this gift: submitting itself to truth, desire is willing to recognize the primacy of the other and to fulfill itself ecstatically. It is a gradual process that assumes the instincts, impulses, emotions, and feelings, but it can successfully integrate all these elements only in truth. Indeed, the reference to truth conditions the authentic freedom of self-determination and allows transcendence over any determinism.

At this point, the meaning and the role of the commandments and norms emerge within an ethics of virtue.[18] A commandment is the expression of the normative character of the truth about the Good for human freedom. True Good, in fact, recognized by reason, imposes itself as an interiorly binding rule for freedom. Moral norms do not represent, therefore, what opposes desire, repressing it, but the rule of truth that saves it, keeps it open, and leads it to its fulfillment, in faithfulness to the deepest spiritual dynamic that animates it.

Ethics and Anthropology

The content of the moral norm is therefore not the arbitrary will of a lawmaker, but a truth about the good of the person, to which it

17. Karol Wojtyla, *Love and Responsibility*, trans. H. T. Willetts (New York: Farrar, Straus, Giroux, 1981), 114–18; and *The Acting Person*, trans. Andrzej Potocki (Dordrecht, The Netherlands, and Boston: D. Riedel, 1979), 255–60.

18. Here we are not making rigid distinctions between "laws," "commandments," "precepts," and "norms." The terms "laws" and "commandments" are typical of biblical morality and also classic philosophical ethics; they express the character of obligational rule, by virtue of a transcendent authority, based on the wisdom of the lawgiver; they refer mainly to general and fundamental directives. The term "precepts," on the other hand, indicates a particular aspect of a moral rule, which is instructive about the Good. The concept of "norm," originally referred to the juridical sphere, imposed itself in ethics during the Enlightenment and Kant; it indicates the character of the interior obligation of a particular moral rule.

is right to direct one's aspirations and to adhere with one's choices. If normativity as such cannot be deduced from purely speculative knowledge, and if it is a characteristic proper to the practical-moral dimension of reason, the content of the truth of the norm nevertheless forms an object of evaluation that is also speculative in nature. "Every normative propositional form inevitably implies a speculative (veritative) moment as its content."[19] The modality of the relationship between anthropology and ethics is thus delineated.

Although it cannot be deduced from ontology, ethics nonetheless requires ontological and, in particular, anthropological foundations. On the one hand, starting from the ethical experience, it is possible to elaborate an anthropology and, more radically, a metaphysics that justifies it.[20] The ethical dimension is in fact full of meaning for speculative reason, which ascends to ultimate causes, and which aims to understand them as the ultimate explanation of being and therefore also of moral experience. On the other hand, anthropological truths are necessarily implicated in the practical knowledge of ethics, ordered to action. They are assumed and integrated in the light of fundamental moral principles and converge to create more determinate moral norms.

In light of all this, we must conclude that in the dynamic of practical reason, the normative aspect is secondary and subordinate with respect to the virtues. At the foundation of the practical-moral exercise of reason there are principles that express the truth about the basic goods in which people find their fulfillment and which, when participated in through action, bear the fruit of a good life. In Thomistic language, these principles are the ends of the virtues, which indicate those intelligible human goods desirable for a good life. They are also the principles of the natural law, as an order that human reason, participating in the divine wisdom, establishes in human choices and actions. The reason why it is necessary to live in harmony with these principles is offered by the concept of the "good life," as the ideal and ultimate telos of man. It is an original, self-imposing concept, which also gives rise to the experience of

---

19. C. Vigna, "La verità del desiderio . . . ," 81–84.
20. See W. Kluxen, *Philosophische Ethik bei Thomas von Aquin,* 57–66.

duty. What is noble and excellent deserves to be loved and pursued. Besides, when we need to determine concretely what our duty is, only virtue can come to our aid, helping us in our discernment and inclining us to fulfill it. It is here that we find "virtuous circularity" between prudence and the moral virtues, which makes possible the ultimate exercise of practical reason and the choice to engage in truly good actions in the concrete.

Norms are therefore reflective-linguistic formulations of principles. They express, from the perspective of the third person, the concrete consequences of the principles of practical reason, that is, the exigencies of the rational ordering of choices, of moral virtues.[21] From the epistemological point of view, the comprehension of the authentic meaning of norms always refers to the original dimension of the ends and to the virtuous connaturality with these. In fact, the virtuous is the rule and the living measure of the Good.

To affirm the secondary and derivative character of the norm compared to virtues does not thereby mean that norms are superfluous. The relationship that Saint Thomas established between the interior and principal element of the new law and its exterior and secondary element[22] can be analogically applied here to the virtue / norm pair. From an educational point of view, the end of the commandments and norms is to make men virtuous. Aquinas states it clearly: *"Finis vero cuiuslibet legis est ut homines efficiantur iusti et virtuosi"* (The end of every law is that men become just and virtuous).[23] The man who lives virtuously remains under the obligation of law, even if he no longer perceives it as an exterior constraint but rather as an interior spontaneity: by a virtuous connaturality he fulfills spontaneously through love, guided by the Spirit, what the law commands.[24] And it is precisely from the perspective of the virtues, whose fullness is charity, that the deep meaning of freedom in fact

21. See M. Rhonheimer, *La prospettiva della morale,* 269–97.

22. *Summa theologiae,* I–II, qq. 106–8. About the subordinate, but not accessory, character of the "written" and exterior element of the new law, see E. Kackynski, *La legge nuova: L'elemento esterno della legge nuova secondo San Tommaso* (Rome and Vincenza: 1974).

23. *Summa theologiae,* I–II, q. 107, a. 2.

24. Saint Thomas Aquinas, *Super Ep. ad Galatas,* chap. 5, lect. 5, no. 318 (Turin: Marietti, 1964).

finds fulfillment. In fact, "he who avoids evil not because it is evil but only because God orders it through the law's precepts, is not free. On the contrary, the one who acts pushed by an interior inclination toward the Good is free, and not the one who is compelled by an exterior norm."[25]

2. THE PERSON'S NATURE AND HIS GOOD

Let us now focus on the specific question about the truth content of the norm, which implies the anthropological foundation of Christian ethics. According to the directive given in the pastoral constitution *Gaudium et spes*, "[I]t is not enough to take only the good intention and the evaluation of motives into account; objective criteria must be used, criteria drawn from the nature of the human person and his acts" (no. 51). Similarly, *Veritatis splendor* declares that "the true meaning of natural law" must be understood in reference "to man's proper and primordial nature, the nature of the human person" (no. 50). It later says that the criterion of moral judgment is the conformity of a choice with "the dignity and the integral vocation of the human person" (no. 67). But what is this nature proper to the human person? And how does it become the foundation of moral normativity? And what is the relationship between the reference to nature and the dignity and vocation of the person?

As we said earlier, the moral question is a question of the good of the person as such. The person is called to be fulfilled in Christ through his free acts, following his noble vocation to participate in the divine life. The reference to a Christologically founded personalism is clear in recent magisterial teachings; but what kind of relationship is established, at the moral level, between the reference to the nature of the human person and his acts and the unique and unrepeatable dignity of the person taken individually? This is exactly the problem we are about to face.

Person: Between Common Nature and Existential Singularity

According to Saint Thomas, the concept of person expresses "the most perfect thing in all nature, i.e., a being who subsists in the

25. Saint Thomas Aquinas, *Super Ep. ad Corinthios,* chap. 3, lect. 3, no. 112 (Turin: Marietti, 1964).

rational nature."[26] While the term 'man' refers to human nature universally, to the common species that expresses itself in many exemplars, the term 'person' designates the individual human being in his concrete individual reality. The concept of person is intimately associated with that of a special dignity.[27] The philosophical definition is therefore intimately connected to a specific and original moral conception of the ontological dignity that must be honored. It is in the person that human nature reaches its ultimate perfection, the act of being, the perfection of all perfections: *". . . magna dignitatis est in rationali natura subsistere"* (. . . great is the dignity of subsisting in a rational nature).[28]

Now we must carefully observe that the proper and specific reason for the respect due to each human being is not the common human nature in which he participates but his being a "unique and unrepeatable" person, as John Paul II says.[29] There would not be any decisive moral objection against the destruction of a single human individual, insofar as his perfection can be found also in another human being. Plato, who was able to analyze the greatness of the human spirit open to truth in a wonderful way, did not have any moral difficulty in admitting the murder of defective infants.[30] If a human being is but the replaceable exemplar of a specific nature, if he is simply the realization of a species, then nature and species are more valuable than the individual, and the individual human being can be subordinated and possibly sacrificed to the general well-being of the species.

---

26. *Summa theologiae,* I, q. 29, a. 3: "Persona significat id quod est perfectissimum in tota natura, scilicet subsistens in rationali natura."

27. Ibid., ad 2: "Impositum est hoc nomen *persona* ad significandum aliquos dignitatem habentes. . . . Propter quod quidam definiunt personam, dicentes quod persona est *hypostasis proprietate distincta ad dignitatem pertinente."* (The name "person" is imposed to signify those who have dignity. . . . For this reason some define person by saying that a "person is a hypostasis distinguished by having dignity.")

28. Ibid. On this, see G. Perini, *Il "trattato" di teologia morale fondamentale* (Bologna: Ed. Studio Domenicano, 1996), 113–20.

29. See, e.g., his encyclical *Redemptor hominis,* nos. 17, 3; see, among his philosophical writings, "Subjectivity and the Irreducible Element in Man," in *Investigations at the Intersection of Philosophy and Psychology,* ed. A. T. Tymienicka, *Analecta Husserliana* 7 (1978): 107–16.

30. Plato, *The Republic,* 5, 460.

The reason for the singular and eminent dignity of a human person is not simply his rational nature, but his incommunicable mode of existing.[31] Even if innumerable men exist and have existed in the course of history, each person exists as if he were unique: he is *"sui iuris et alteris incommunicabilis" (sui iuris* and not communicable to another). He is a truly concrete whole in which the nature of the species with all its characteristics is included, but this nature is appropriated to the subject in an altogether and absolutely singular way, so that its existence transcends that nature in an eminent manner. Richard of St. Victor's formula *"intellectualis essentiae incommunicabilis existentia"* (the incommunicable existence of an intellectual nature)[32] surpasses and specifies Boethius's definition of person as *"substantia individua naturae rationalis"* (an individual substance of a rational nature).[33] Saint Bonaventure emphasized three characteristics of the person: *singularity, incommunicability,* and *surpassing dignity*.[34] The value of the concretely existing totality transcends the common nature and the sum of the parts. As Romano Guardini said, "The person itself is the fact that it exists in the form of belonging to itself" *(in der Form der Selbsgehörigkeit)*.[35]

The incommunicability of the person, as the fundamental character of his unique dignity, does not mean a solipsistic closure to communication with other persons. On the contrary, it is precisely this character that grounds the possibility and the richness of dialogue. Only because there exists a personal uniqueness of each human being is it interesting to enter into relationship with him. So the relational value of the person presupposes his irreducible ontological value, and not vice versa.

On the one hand, therefore, the person has a "nature." Against a

31. See John Crosby, *The Selfhood of the Human Person* (Washington, D.C.: The Catholic University of America Press, 1996), 61–81.

32. Richard of St. Victor, *De Trinitate*, 4.23.

33. Boethius, *De persona et duabus naturis: Contra Eutichen et Nestorium,* 3.4–11; cited by Saint Thomas Aquinas in *Summa theologiae,* I, q. 29, a. 3.

34. Saint Bonaventure, *In III Sententiarum,* dist. 5, art. 4, qu. 1, ad 1 (Quaracchi ed.), 133.

35. Romano Guardini, *Welt und Person* (Wurzburg: 1962), 128: "To the question, 'what is your person?' I cannot answer 'my body, my soul, my reason, my will, my freedom.' All this is not yet the person but the whole of which the person is made. The person itself is the fact that it exists in the form of belonging to itself."

vague or dualistic personalism, which would oppose the person to nature and reduce the person to a spiritual freedom detached from any ontological foundation, we must affirm that "the human person cannot be reduced to a freedom which is self-designing, but entails a particular spiritual and bodily structure" (*Veritatis splendor,* no. 48). The pope is talking about "man's proper and primordial nature, the nature of the human person, which is the person himself in unity of body and soul, in the unity of his spiritual and biological inclinations and of all the other specific characteristics necessary for the pursuit of his end" (*Veritatis splendor,* no. 50). On the other hand, the value of the person as such consists in his existential incommunicability, which makes him unique and unrepeatable. The person has a value and must be affirmed for himself, and not for the generic nature of the human species or for some accidental quality he may possess.[36]

3. "GOOD OF THE PERSON" AND "GOODS FOR THE PERSON"

In the encyclical *Veritatis splendor* a personalistic interpretation of the classical doctrine of the natural law has been proposed, based on the distinction between the "good of the person" and "goods for the person" (see *Veritatis splendor,* nos. 13, 48–50).[37]

The "Good of the Person"

It is first of all necessary to understand what "the good of the person" means from the perspective proper to morality, that is, the good of the person *insofar as he is person (ut persona)*. This consists in the perfecting of the nature of the human being, constitutively incomplete, by means of the exercise of self-determining freedom.

36. Wojtyla, *Love and Responsibility,* 40–44, where the author proposes and reflects on the "personalistic norm" as the principle of morality. *Persona est affirmando propter se ipsam.* In that sense J. F. Crosby, in the volume already cited, is justly opposed to the so-called Beethoven argument against abortion: one should evade procuring abortions in order not to risk depriving humanity of the genes of the great musical composer from Bonn.

37. The distinction can be traced to Wojtyla's *Love and Responsibility* and his *Czlowiek w polu odpowiedzilnosci* (Rome and Lublin: 1991), cf. *The personal structure of the self determination,* in AA.VV., Atti del Congresso Internazionale di San Tommaso d'Aquino nel suo settimo centenario, ed. Domenicane, Napoli 1974, 379–90, but it has been developed and elaborated by his disciples T. Styczen and A. Szostek.

It is therefore that good that depends only on the free self-determination of the person and that is conditioned in no way by factors extrinsic to his freedom. As Carlo Caffarra has brilliantly affirmed, "[T]he ultimate perfection of the person is an act of the person: the act by means of which the person—and no one else—actuates and dynamizes himself."[38]

We are concerned with the perfection of the *personal being* of the person as such, quite distinct from the perfection of *having*. The moral good is in fact the good of the person insofar as he is a person, a good actuated by means of freedom, an *operable good,* therefore a *practical good.* It is precisely at this level that the incommensurability of the good of the person *as person (ut persona)* with respect to all the other goods must be understood: "What does it profit a man to gain the entire world and suffer the loss of his own soul?" (Mt 16.26). For this reason one must be disposed to lose everything, even goods intrinsic to personal being, the goods of the person *as a nature (ut natura),* goods such as physical life, for instance, in order not to lose the good of the person as such. This is the meaning of the celebrated saying of Juvenal: *"Summum crede nefas animam praeferre pudori et propter vitam vivendi perdere causas"* (Remember that the greatest shame is to prefer life to honor and, for the sake of an inordinate attachment to life, to lose the very reasons for living).[39]

The good of the person is not a partial, sectoral good, distinct from other goods: it concerns that good of the personal being proper to the person that depends on the exercise of his own freedom, that is, the good of action not as a production of goods external to the agent but as the perfection of the acting subject himself. The originality of this moral perspective, as a practical perspective, is constituted epistemologically by the irreducibility of the good of the person *as person (ut persona)* with respect to the goods of the person *as nature (ut natura).*

---

38. Carlo Caffarra, "'Primum quod cadit in apprehensione practicae rationis': Variazioni su un tema tomista," in *Attualità della Teologia Morale: Punti fermi-problemi aperti,* In Honor of the Rev. P. J. Visser, C.Ss.R., "Studia Urbaniana" 31 (Rome: Urbaniana University Press, 1987), 143–64.

39. D. Iuni Iuvenalis, *Saturarum libri,* 8, 83f.

The Ideal of a Good Life as an Ideal of Love among Persons

But all this is still a bit too formal and requires a more precise delineation of its content. The good of the person in fact expresses an *ideal of the good life* of the person, that is, the free realization of the person within relationships with other persons: with God, first of all, and with his neighbor. In fact, the originating experience of the Good is an experience of fullness in love, in which is contained a promise of perfect communion with God and with others. Human actions correspond to the good of the person to the extent that they promote the communion of persons in love. The ideal of a good life therefore has regard to the human person not as an individual in solipsistic isolation but in the communion of persons. Authentic personalism identifies the good of the person in the just relationship with other persons, who are affirmed for themselves as ends and never as means. Love, as the recognition and practical affirmation of the personal dignity of the other, is a condition of the truly personal truth of the subject. The great personalistic affirmations of Vatican Council II and of John Paul II are illuminated profoundly in this context: "Man, who is the only creature on earth that God has willed for itself, can discover himself fully only in the sincere gift of himself."[40] "Man cannot live without love. He remains a being that is incomprehensible for himself, his life is senseless if love is not revealed to him, if he does not encounter love, if he does not experience it and make it his own, if he does not participate intimately in it."[41] This ideal mystery of the communion of love, as the pastoral constitution *Gaudium et spes* says, reflects "a certain likeness to the union of the divine persons and the union of the children of God in truth and in charity."[42]

The properly moral level of that originary experience in which love consists can be adequately defined with the expression to which

---

40. Vatican Council II, Pastoral Constitution *Gaudium et spes*, no. 24.

41. John Paul II, encyclical *Redemptor hominis*, no. 10. On this see the wonderful reflection on love as the foundation of morality by Professor T. Styczen, *L'amore come comunione con gli altri e il senso della vita* (Rome: 1985), which I possess however only in an Italian translation made from the original Polish text, to which I am not able to refer.

42. See Vatican Council II, Pastoral Constitution *Gaudium et spes*, no. 24.

Saint Thomas attributes an extraordinary importance and which recurs time and again in his works: *"in hoc praecipue consistit amor: quod amans amato bonum velit"* (love principally consists in the fact that the lover wills the good for the beloved).[43] This definition emphasizes the specificity of love with respect to other operations of the human soul: love, as an act of the will, an act that surpasses by means of choice the merely affective level, is directed to two objects and not merely to one.[44] That is, love is simultaneously directed to the other person and to the good of the other person. One cannot will the good for a person without also willing his good. The moral goodness of love therefore consists in the choice to will the good of the other.

Here appears the moment of the truth about the Good, as a condition of the very truth of love: the adequate knowledge of what is good for the other person verifies the authenticity of love. As Karol Wojtyla affirms: "The act [of love] is in fact what it is through means of the moment of truth—that is, of the truth about the Good—and this confers on it the form of an authentic *actus personae.*"[45]

The "Goods for the Person"

The good of the person is given its detailed content at the level of the "goods for the person." As has been said, the objects of human actions are particular goods to be realized. Here we treat of the goods that correspond to the desires of the person. But how should we distinguish between authentic goods and apparent goods, those

43. Saint Thomas Aquinas, *Summa contra gentiles,* book 3, chap. 90 (no. 2657, ed. Marietti). For an analysis of Thomistic texts on the definition of love, see J. J. Perez-Soba Diez del Corral, *¿La Interpersonalidad en el amor? La respuesta de Santo Tomas,* a doctoral thesis that I directed in Rome in 1995 at the Istituto Giovanni Paolo II per studi su Matrimonio e Famiglia, partially published under that title in Rome in 1997.

44. See *Summa contra gentiles,* book 1, chap. 91 (no. 763, ed. Marietti): *"aliae operationes sunt circa unum solum obiectum, solus amor ad duo obiecta ferri videtur"* (other operations are concerned only with one object, but love alone seems to bear on two objects).

45. Karol Wojtyla, *The Acting Person.* For a study of the concept of the "truth about the good" in Wojtyla's thought, see E. Kaczynski, "Il 'momento della verità' nella riflessione di K. Wojtyla," *Angelicum* 56 (1979): 273–96, and "Verità sul bene nei diversi elementi della morale," *Rivista di Teologia Morale* 49 (1981): 419–31.

attractive only because of artificial conditions? And what are the fundamental goods *for* the human person?

The Thomistic tradition has always referred to certain *natural inclinations.*[46] There is first of all the inclination to self-preservation, to conserve life, which expresses the bounty of being as such and which is common to all creatures. Second, there is the inclination to sexual union which, while being common to all animals, has in man a specific spiritual dimension: it is open to communion with a person of the other sex, in a stable and faithful union, oriented toward the generation and education of children. Third, there is the inclination to life in society, which is not limited to the need each one has of help from others and to the material advantage that comes from living in society but is extended to the enrichment and spiritual expansion that derives from a common life together. There is finally a specifically human inclination to know the truth, in which the eminent dignity of the human spirit, of the human spirit called to joy in the light of the truth, is expressed.

Let it be noted that here we are concerned with natural dimensions of the person in his unity of soul and body, dimensions that identify the basic or fundamental goods of the person. These inclinations are not only at the "animal" level but are always assumed into the "personal" level, and it is the personal level that qualifies a determinate good as a "good for the person." The term "good for the person" must not be thought to be concerned with goods of a merely instrumental character confronting a spiritual subject who would know himself as something distinct from them.[47] Here the distinction between "good of the person" and "goods for the per-

46. See *Summa theologiae,* I–II, 94, 2. See the clear and simple exposition of these, which we follow, in S. Pinckaers, *The Sources of Christian Ethics,* chap. 17, 400–456.

47. In this sense, using a different terminology, I find myself in perfect agreement with the substance of a criticism given by William E. May, in "The Sacredness of Life: An Overview of the Beginning," *Linacre Quarterly* 63 (1996): 87–96, to a dualistic concept that sees in physical life merely a "good for the person," a merely instrumental good at the disposal of the person's spiritual freedom. For a critique of this dualism, see also Germain Grisez, "Dualism and the New Morality," *Atti del Congresso Internazionale su San Tommaso d'Aquino nel suo settimo centenario,* Vol. 5: *L'agire morale* (Naples: Edizioni Domenicane, 1977), 323–30.

son" is not taken to signify an ontological dualism between the dimension of autonomous freedom and the bodily dimension, considered at the purely spiritual level, but rather it indicates the primacy of the moral dimension that integrates within itself, in the originality of the practical perspective of love, goods intrinsic to the person respect for which is essential for the truth of love.

The "goods for the person," which objectively qualify the content of the good of the other person, which I am called in love to will, therefore also represent the verification of love. Only if I respect and promote the "goods for the person" in reference to the "good of my own person" and of the other person is love true love. *Human acts* are therefore acts of *operable practical goods,* relevant to the different goods of the person, acts that permit the realization of the communion of persons in the truth.

The goods for the person are not of themselves the foundation of morality. It is only at the level of the "good of the person" that one enters fully into the sphere of ethics. This [the good of the person] in fact is the unifying and qualifying factor. Beyond all the inclinations previously enumerated is nurtured an original and irreducible tendency of the human spirit to the good of the person as such, which is constitutive of practical reason in its moral dimension: "love and do the good and avoid evil." Here we are not dealing with an empty and formal orientation: it expresses an original knowledge of a good that attracts by reason of its own intrinsic preciousness and value (an "honest" or a "noble" good), and not by reason of the pleasure that it provokes (a "pleasing" good), or by reason of the advantages that it promises (a "useful" good). In this sense, this tendency is not located at the level of the other inclinations and provokes a dynamism of the will ecstatic in nature: it expresses the rational comprehension of a value that precedes me and requires the homage of my freedom, independent of disadvantages and sacrifices; to give homage to this good is a condition of the truth of my very own person. Here we must speak of a principle rather than an inclination, of the first principle of practical reason.[48] To it corre-

48. Germain Grisez, "The First Principle of Practical Reason: A Commentary on *Summa theologiae,* I–II, q. 94, a. 2," *Natural Law Forum* 10 (1965): 168–96, interprets it as

sponds the twofold commandment of love of God and of neighbor, on which depend the Law and the Prophets (Mt 22.34–40).

The personalistic interpretation identifies the moral good with the "good of the person" and the fundamental norm of morality with the personalistic norm: "the person is to be affirmed in and for himself,"[49] thereby extricating it from indetermination and formalism. Here is the proper level of morality, which springs from the relationship of the will not with particular external goods but with the good of the person. The person has a singular dignity precisely because he is called to love. The moral vocation is a vocation to love: to be God's image, loving and seeking the Good and the True even more than oneself, as a condition for being oneself.

The Relationship between the "Good of the Person" and the "Goods for the Person"

This is a crucial question for morality: What is the relationship between the "good *of* the person" and the "goods *for* the person"? First of all, it must be noted that the goods for the person do not have moral value save in reference to the good of the person. Morality consists precisely in the intrinsic relationship of the partial good realized by means of action (the "goods for the person") with the total good of the person (the "good of the person"). That action is morally good that pursues the good for the person in such a way that it affirms in this choice the good of the person in his wholeness. Thus is avoided biologism or naturalism, which derives moral value from the biological or natural dimension. The natural inclinations that identify the basic goods for the person have a heuristic value in

---

a "practical" and not a "moral" principle, one of formal character only. See Aurelio Ansaldo, *El primer principio del obrar moral y las normas morales específicas el el pensamiento de G. Grisez y J. Finnis* (Rome: Pontificia Università Lateranense, 1990). I am of the opinion, on the other hand, that, at least in the thought of Saint Thomas, we have here a principle pregnant with moral significance regarding the "good of the person," which surely must then be determined with reference to the "goods for the person." See my *La conoscenza morale,* 78–84.

49. This is the precision of Karol Wojtyla, in which is assumed the second Kantian formula of the categorical imperative—"always act in such a way as to treat the other as an end and never as a means." The character, which is not purely formal, of the principle is documented in the reference to the "good of the person."

the discovery of moral values, but it is reason, in its specifically moral dimension, which in the light of the fundamental principle of morality (the personalistic norm), that represents the decisive hermeneutical instance. In this sense there is a primacy of the person, grasped by reason, in the constitution of the natural law.

Second, one must note that these basic goods (the goods for the person) are integral to the person himself, who is not pure spiritual freedom but a being that has a nature. Endowed with this nature (bodily and spiritually) that comprises him in part, the person is called to assume it in the dimension proper to the moral good. From this one can conclude that it is not possible "to affirm the person" save by means of his basic goods, respecting these goods. The person is not absolute freedom, but a unity of soul and body, with a creaturely nature, which is entrusted to his freedom for its development. Freedom is responsibility confronted by this natural gift, which is part of the person; freedom is not arbitrary creativity. If what is given by nature is not recognized, the principle of respect for the person is empty and purely formal.

One must then conclude that the relationship to the good of the person is established by means of the recognition of the moral values deriving from the goods for the person. Once naturalism is repudiated by affirming the primacy of the person, one must then say no to the creative autonomy of a reason unfettered by a truth about the good that precedes it. The human reason that has moral value is a participation in the eternal reason of God. That is expressed in a moment of spontaneity, which precedes and is the basis for interpretation *(ratio ut natura)*.[50] The nature that is at the foundation of morality is that of the created reason of man, which participates in the divine wisdom by welcoming and recognizing the fundamental orientations inscribed in personal being.

Third, the goods for the person, to the extent to which they are seen within the perspective of a voluntary choice (as "practical

---

50. See M. Rhonheimer, *Natural Law and Practical Reason,* trans. Gerald Malsbary (New York: Fordham University Press, 2000); originally published as *Natur als Grundlage der Moral: Eine Auseinandersetzung mit autonomer und teleologisher Ethik* (Innsbruck: Tyrolia, 1987).

goods"), have moral value; they are the expression of the good of the person that is reflected at the level of the different aspects of human existence, at the level of different dimensions of life (see *Veritatis splendor,* no. 13). Every dimension of the person, therefore, is always measured by moral value: it is not merely a "premoral" good; insofar as it is cultivated by reason in the perspective of the affirmation of the good of the person, every good for the person has an intrinsic moral relevance.

Fourth, the goods for the person are not without their own internal relationships: in the light of the fundamental value of the person, they are found to be *hierarchically organized.* The hierarchy is established according to orders of fundamentality and of importance. These two criteria afford an evaluation of the rank of preeminence among the goods, according to different perspectives, but they are not in conflict on the moral level, if one takes into account the preeminent unitary value of the good of the person.[51] In this sense, a criterion of urgency can make preferable and obligatory in the concrete a value more fundamental (for example, that of life), even if it is less important. Nonetheless, the choice intentionally to negate a true good for the person, intrinsically connected with his nature, can never be in conformity with the good of the person. To put the goods for the person into a hierarchy does not mean that one denies true goods for the person or that preferring a superior good means violating an inferior good.

Fifth, and finally, knowledge of the moral relevance of the goods for the person always occurs in a determinate historical context, within a particular culture. Moral knowledge is therefore marked by this context, which conditions it both positively and negatively. Nonetheless, it is knowledge of a truth that transcends its context and is universally valid. It is thus necessary to distinguish between the conditions of an act of knowing and the truth content attained by that act. That is, there is a transhistorical and transcultural truth that measures the act of knowledge. In particular, there are goods for the person so linked in an indissoluble bond with the good of the

---

51. See Carlo Caffarra, *Living in Christ: Fundamental Principles of Catholic Moral Teaching,* trans. Christopher Ruff (San Francisco: Ignatius Press, 1987), 91–95.

person that human reason naturally is in a position to perceive that their violation constitutes an outrageous attack on the moral good itself of the person.

Goods such as life, sexuality, and the truthfulness of communication are immediately expressive of the person. These are so tightly connected with the good of the person and pertain so greatly to the nature of the person that respect for them cannot be something merely instrumental without violating at the same time the dignity of the person, who must be affirmed always as an end and never solely as a means.[52]

The Goods for the Person and Moral Norms

The goods for the person, seen within the moral perspective as objects of choice that affirm the good of the person, are the basis of particular moral norms. These last, in fact, are judgments that express the truth about the good of the person in relationship to actions that have to do with the goods for the person. They (particular moral norms) declare whether a specific act, insofar as it is a choice of the will focused on the pursuit of a particular good, is or is not in harmony with the total good of the person.

Here, first of all, we must acknowledge a fundamental principle, according to which the person must be affirmed for himself. It is in the light of this principle, with reference to reason and to moral experience, that more definite moral norms are formulated, norms expressing the knowledge, at times partial and limited, of a moral good grasped as a value. Moral value therefore precedes and is the basis for the norm. In its turn the value is not the fruit of a merely subjective experience but has an objective character: it designates a truth about the good of the person, grasped by human reason, that participates in the divine wisdom.

The process leading to the determination of specific norms is clarified by the distinction between *principles* and *norms*. Principles (for example, those of the natural law) affirm an ethical value in gen-

---

52. See R. Spaemann, *"La responsabilità personale e il suo fondamento,"* in *Etica teleologica o etica deontologica: Un dibattito al centro della teologia morale odierna,* Quaderni CRIS, nos. 49–50 (Rome: 1983).

eral, while norms apply a principle to a determinate and specific act. Recall here what has been emphasized already: in the passage from the fundamental norms to specific norms, from general principles to specific precepts, there necessarily enters the contribution of rational knowledge which depends on experience, on culture, on scientific knowledge, and so on. In other words, the mediation is marked by an anthropology that assumes empirical data. There is nonetheless a basic truth about man that can be known and which constitutes the criterion of verifying different anthropologies, which are in fact elaborated in history and in human societies.

In relation to the question of determining norms with respect to principles, this annotation implies that the more a moral good is basic and the norm that refers to it is limited to giving a negative judgment on behaviors that violate it, the easier it will be to know it and to interpret it. On the other hand, the more detailed and particular the normative judgment, and the richer the positive indications for the action, the more will the judgment be characterized by cultural conditions and have need for further interpretation by personal conscience.

At this point it is necessary to refer to the decisive distinction between affirmative (positive) moral norms and negative ones, a topic authoritatively taken up by the encyclical *Veritatis splendor*.[53] Affirmative moral norms (those expressing in an affirmative way what one ought to do) are always valid, but not in every single case. In fact, a particular good for the person must be fulfilled by taking into account the hierarchy of the goods, because only in this way does the choice of that good affirm the good of the person. These norms therefore require of their nature a situated interpretation, which can be given only through the judgment of prudence. One perceives, in other words, that forgoing the realization of a value (because one must take care of the realization of another more important or more fundamental value) does not signify the denial of

---

53. See no. 52. The principal references in the works of Saint Thomas are: *Summa theologiae*, II–II, q. 33, a. 2; *De malo*, q. 7, a. 1, ad 8; and *Super Ep. ad Romanos*, chap. 13, lect. 2. See, on this, William E. May, "*Veritatis splendor* and the Natural Law: From First Principles to Moral Absolutes," *Rivista Teologica di Lugano* 2 (1996): 193–215.

the value left unpursued. But, on the other hand, *negative* moral norms (those that prohibit a certain specific behavior as intrinsically opposed to the good of the person) are valid always and forever *(semper et pro semper, semper et ad semper),* in every instance, without any possible exception, every time the moral species of an act of this kind is known to be at stake. These norms are absolute not by reason of the particular good for the person that they protect (for it is a contingent and limited good), but by reason of the necessary bond that truly exists between the direct violation of this particular good and the good of the person: by choosing to violate this particular moral good one necessarily also violates the fundamental moral good of the person. The freedom that chooses to violate the good of the person is necessarily in contradiction to the good of the person.

What can be said, then, of the phenomenon of *progress* in the knowledge of moral goods, and therefore in the formulation of norms? This must be understood as contained in the growing knowledge of what respect and affirmation of the good of the person requires. We can think of the relatively recent moral condemnation of slavery and torture—to give simply a few examples. There is, therefore, an incontestable growth in the perception of the intrinsic connection between some goods for the person (for example, freedom and equality of civil rights) and the good of the person as such. That growth depends on cultural developments and social situations. As a consequence, even moral norms progress in the formulation of what the affirmation of the value of the person as such requires: the obligatoriness to avoid certain behaviors, whose moral wickedness was not so evident earlier, is better grasped today. Nonetheless, it cannot happen (from the axiological perspective and not from the perspective of phenomenology which recognizes also the possibility of regression in the knowledge of morality) that a behavior once judged wicked by moral reason can become morally good under the same aspect and under the same conditions.

Here the decisive factor is the influence of moral virtues in the perception of the morally relevant goods for the person. Virtues, in fact, do not have a merely executive meaning; not only do they help one to attain with greater facility a good already established, but they also have a primarily epistemological relevance: they help one know what the true good of the person requires.

By taking the virtues as a starting point, a systematization of the goods for the person is possible, in a perspective more linked to the subject and to his dynamisms according to the order of the cardinal virtues. *Justice* concerns the affirmation of the good of the person in relationship to others and the just measure of external acts. *Fortitude* has regard for equilibrium in defending the goods of one's own personal life, while *temperance* has to do with the right measure in the appetite for pleasurable goods. Finally, *prudence* assures the just means of reason within each virtue.

The Moral Good in a Christological Context

We have thus far developed a personalistic interpretation of the traditional doctrine about the natural law. Now we have to see how and at what level the Christological context affects the passage from principles to norms. Christian revelation offers, first of all, a deeper and definitive knowledge of the "good of the person." Not only does it radically justify the perception of the unique and unrepeatable value of every person, who is willed and created immediately by God in his image and likeness, it also opens up the perspective of an unexpected fulfillment in the gratuitous participation in the life of the Trinity. In Christ the person is called to the communion of charity with the Father in the Holy Spirit. In the same Spirit the person receives the call to charity toward his brothers and sisters. Jesus Christ has lived the perfection of charity as divine person in a human existence like ours in every way save sin. He is thus the living and personal law to follow (see *Veritatis splendor,* no. 15). He reveals the person to himself. In each of his choices Jesus shows the ultimate and perfect meaning of the natural law and of the Mosaic law as expressions of the will of the Father and of the supernatural call to charity.

In this new horizon of understanding of the definitive vocation of the person, the "goods for the person" are grasped in their fundamental and permanent value, and they are both confirmed and made relative. Natural inclinations are the first signs of the vocation to charity, to love. They remain valid as the original datum of creation, but they are located in a dynamics of charity that transcends them.

Love for life is revealed in the perspective of the gift of self. *Conjugal love* is grasped as the sacramental sign of God's love for man, of Christ's love for his bride, the Church. At the same time the new way of virginity for the reign of God is opened, confirming the meaning of vocation to the spousal gift but now fulfilling it without the earthly sign of genitality. *Sociality*, with its rule of justice, is transcended in charity, which, without denying the natural and rational needs of equity, puts them in the superior context of communion, of which the Church is an anticipation. Finally, the *search for truth* meets the Truth made flesh. The gift offered in faith does not deny the search and its rational needs, but directs them to a never-ending deepening.

Thus particular moral norms, the fruit of rational hermeneutics, are put into a new context and transcended toward a further fulfillment. To grasp the significance of the Christological context, we must remember here the importance of anthropology in the mediation between general principles and specific moral norms. The Christian perspective does not eliminate or substitute the principles of the natural law, but, in keeping them, integrally gives them a new definitive interpretation, with consequences also on the normative level. This perspective allows a better grasp of the bond between the goods for the person and the good of the person, and enables us to formulate norms in an ever more adequate way. Revelation, once more, does not take reason away but opens the possibility for a search and for progress.

Here we must remember the qualifying character that the Beatitudes have for Christian ethics. The great Catholic tradition, from Saint Augustine to Saint Thomas, has always grasped their decisive importance. They are not normative indications in the strict sense. They express a sort of "self-portrait" of Jesus,[54] describing his fundamental attitudes in relationship to human goods and to the situation of trial in which we find ourselves. They show the Disciples the way to follow Jesus in every action. In their known aspect they are "gen-

54. See J. Ratzinger, *Guardare Cristo: Esercizi di fede, speranza, e carità* (Milan: Jaca Book, 1989), 47–53.

eral moral truths, which mediate between the principles of the natural law and the specific moral norms of the Christian."[55] They teach humility, detachment, mildness, hunger and thirst for justice, mercy, simplicity, love for peace, and availability to the gift of self, even in persecution.

It is a "justice that goes beyond that of the Pharisees," that is, of the pure respect for the Law, but that does not eliminate the Law. Thus, on one side the permanent value of the Decalogue is stressed; it is a confirmation (a purification and clarification) of the datum of the natural law. In fact, the specifically Christian character of normative ethics is not at the level of the negative commandments: what is strictly necessary, a minimal threshold to respect, is sufficiently set by the old law.[56] On the other hand, the way to a further positive interpretation is opened. The commandments are not to be understood only as extreme boundaries to respect, but as ways to follow in order to accomplish moral value (see *Veritatis splendor*, no. 15). In this way, according to Saint Thomas, the new law expresses itself more through counsels than through precepts.[57]

The specific new norm of love of enemies expresses both the imitation of the Son who makes himself servant (Jn 13) and the new knowledge of the Father that believers have in Christ.[58] In fact, he sends rain on the just and unjust. He who knows him in his mercy, the mercy that shines on the face of Christ, acts henceforward by imitating him in forgiveness (Lk 7.27–36). This is a characteristic that distinguishes Christians from pagans, who follow the norms of a strictly commutative justice (see Mt 5.47).

4. THE UNIQUENESS OF PERSONAL VOCATION AND CHRISTIAN PRUDENCE

After affirming the obligatory character, without exception, of norms known as moral absolutes, norms founded on the "nature of

---

55. On this, see Germain Grisez, *The Way of the Lord Jesus*, Vol. 1: *Christian Moral Principles* (Chicago: Franciscan Herald Press, 1983), 627–59.

56. See Saint Thomas Aquinas, *Summa theologiae*, I–II, q. 108, a. 2.

57. Ibid., a. 4.

58. See R. Tremblay, C.Ss.R., *L'"homme" qui divinise: Pour une interprétation christocentrique de l'existence* (Montreal: Ed. Paulines, 1993), 193–209.

the human person and his acts," the encyclical *Veritatis splendor* asks a further and decisive question: "how can obedience to universal and immutable moral norms respect the uniqueness and unrepeatability of the person" (no. 85)? It is the other side of the question about the good of the person.

The human person, who has a nature, is at the same time more than the common nature. Since the person is not simply an example of the species, his moral task is more than to respect the general moral norms. The person does not merely have to fulfill the universal aspect of nature but to correspond to a unique and singular call that comes from the personalizing relationship that each person has with God.

Universal moral norms have a constitutive limitation. Concrete moral action does not have universal and immutable essences as its objects, but choices concerning singular and contingent realities that can change in many ways according to particular circumstances. "Human actions concern singular and contingent things, that change in infinite ways and cannot be collected under the same general species."[59] In this sense, the universal moral norm, the object of ethical science, is always the fruit of an abstractive process that grasps the common species but leaves out particularities.

For this reason Saint Thomas has clearly seen the *insufficiency of moral science as such* for the ultimate direction of human action. According to Aristotelian understanding, the object of scientific knowledge includes only universal and necessary realities, among which permanent links can be established.[60] But the actions targeted by moral knowledge are realities that change in infinite ways, and so are unreachable by science.[61]

---

59. Saint Thomas Aquinas, *Sententia Libri Ethicorum*, 6, 1, 190–214. See S. A. Dinan, "The Particularity of Moral Knowledge," *The Thomist* 50 (1986): 66–84.

60. See Hans G. Gadamer, *Il problema della conoscenza storica* (Naples: Guida, 1974), chap. 4, "Il problema ermeneutico e l'etica di Aristotele," 61–73.

61. See Saint Thomas Aquinas, *Sententia Libri Ethicorum*, 6, 3; and *Summa theologiae*, I–II, q. 94, a. 5. On this, see my book *La conoscenza morale*, 171–72, 225–31; and K. Hedwig, "Circa particularia, Kontingenz, Klugheit und Notwendigkeit im Aufbau des ethischen Aktes bei Thomas von Aquin," in *The Ethics of St. Thomas Aquinas* (Vatican City: Libreria Editrice Vaticana, 1984), 161–87.

As far as concrete actions are concerned, considered in their contingency, a demonstrative universal knowledge is impossible; it is impossible to establish univocal links that derive compelling conclusions from principles. Concrete actions can be the objects of advice, but not of demonstration. Because of this, practical reason is perfected in a form of knowledge that is not 'scientific' in the Aristotelian sense. It is perfected in the knowledge of *prudence,* which alone can know what is contingent precisely in its contingency and particularity. Prudence is the virtue that, perfecting practical reason, allows it to grasp what is right in the concrete, overcoming the shortcomings of science. It is an intellectual virtue because it pertains to practical reason, but it is also a moral virtue because it presupposes the rightness of appetite concerning both the ultimate end and the immediate ends of human life. Precisely because of its mixed nature, prudence predisposes the subject (by connaturality) to know the moral truth about the contingent and particular realities of acting, providing efficacious directions about them. Hence, specific moral knowledge is most adequately oriented to its object whenever it is structured as a reflection on moral virtues.

Prudence, nonetheless, is not an isolated and incommunicable knowledge, separated from and opposed to that of moral science.[62] Indeed, it is possible to have a knowledge of contingent things too; they are never so particular that they do not also have universal and unchangeable aspects. Thus moral science, as a practical science, can express, in the light of the first principle of morality, a normative judgment about these universal factors of moral action: thus, for instance, it is always true that intentionally killing innocent human persons is always gravely immoral.

On the other hand, the claim to the individual uniqueness of moral truth, especially important today, is fully realized in the *sequela Christi* proposed by the encyclical as "the essential foundation and the origin of Christian morality" (no. 19). It is through his

---

62. D. M. Nelson, *The Priority of Prudence, Virtue, and Natural Law in Thomas Aquinas and the Implications for Modern Ethics* (State Park: Pennsylvania State University, 1992), opposes systematically a deformed idea of the natural law to an ethics of the virtues, holding an individualistic notion of prudence, foreign to the thought of Saint Thomas.

encounter with Christ that the rational creature receives a unique name, a singular task and mission, and so really becomes a "person" according to the anthropological vision of Hans Urs von Balthasar.[63] Thus in following Christ the spiritual subject becomes more and more personalized. The contingent nature of the signs implied by vocational circumstances requires that we value in full the virtue of prudence; this latter is prudence "in Christ," real participation in his knowledge, through the gifts of the Holy Spirit, which make us attentive and sensitive to every suggestion made by the Friend, and which enable us to act in a way worthy of the supernatural end that has been gratuitously granted to us.[64]

Christian Prudence

If the perfection of practical reason is realized in the virtue of prudence, it becomes concrete for the Christian in the new dimension of his being "in Christ" through faith, hope, and charity. Saint Thomas explicitly states that there cannot be true prudence without charity.[65] In fact, only through charity is man oriented toward his true ultimate end. This is the condition that enables prudence to be exercised. Indeed, according to Philippians 1.9–11, the capability to discern is the flourishing of charity *(he agape humon perisseue en epignosei kai pase aisthesei)*. Charity, by uniting us to God as the end of our desire, permits us also to better grasp the value of human realities as ways to reach him. For this reason Saint Augustine defined prudence as "a love that discerns"[66] and Saint Thomas noted that charity can be said to exercise discernment because it stimulates reason to discern.[67] Charity animates prudence from within, and, by ordering it to the ultimate end, generates *imperium,* its proper act.

---

63. Hans Urs von Balthasar, *Theodrama,* vol. 2 (San Francisco: Ignatius Press, 1985); see also E. Babini, *L'antropologia teologica di Hans Urs von Balthasar* (Milan: Jaca Book, 1988), 171–83.

64. Thomas Aquinas, *Summa theologiae,* I–II, q. 108, a. 4, sed contra: *"Sed Christus est maxime sapiens et amicus"* (Christ is our best and wisest friend). See Romanus Cessario, *The Moral Virtues and Theological Ethics* (Notre Dame, Ind.: University of Notre Dame Press, 1991), 60, 76–79.

65. *Summa theologiae,* I–II, q. 62, a. 2.

66. Saint Augustine, *De moribus ecclesiae catholicae,* 1, 15, 25.

67. Saint Thomas Aquinas, *Summa theologiae,* II–II, q. 47, a. 1.

We can say that charity, becoming prudence, corresponds to the dynamic proper to Christian love, which demands to express itself in exterior works (see Mt 6.22–23); according to Saint Augustine's comment on the Lord's Sermon on the Mount, the eye is the upright intention of charity, which must enlighten the body, that is, human actions.[68]

A suggestive comment of Origen on Exodus 7.10ff places Christian prudence in relationship to wisdom.[69] Aaron's staff, which turns into a snake and devours the other snakes belonging to the Egyptian magicians, is interpreted as Christ's Cross, true wisdom (see 1 Cor 1.18), which, coming into touch with earthly realities, turns into a snake, that is, true prudence (see Mt 10.16) and destroys false prudences, which have only a human nature. True Christian prudence is not an expression of human caution, but of the light that the divine wisdom, revealed in Christ's Cross, sheds on earthly realities. If in its primary aspect the gift of wisdom is that supernatural knowledge of divine things, due to the infusion of the Holy Spirit, with respect to human realities and to the good of man, it becomes and acts as prudence.[70]

The gift of *counsel* corresponds to the virtue of prudence at its proper level, preparing reason to be directed and moved directly by the Holy Spirit, in discerning the good about single and contingent things.[71] At the same time, this availability to the suggestions of the Spirit is not a denial of the rational and human level of prudence, but an "aid and fulfillment." This availability respects prudence's natural light, and subsumes and orders it to its true objective in the supernatural perspective.

From a practical point of view, the prudence of the one who lives "in Christ" allows a spiritual understanding of the Law as a way to the Father, in imitation of the Son. Christ's voice *(intimior intimo meo)* neither substitutes for nor overlaps with the voice of con-

---

68. Saint Augustine, *De sermone Domini in monte,* 13, 45 (edited by A. G. Hamman; Paris: 1978), 120–21.

69. Origen, *In Exodum Homiliae,* 4 (ed. W. A. Baerhrens; Leipzig: 1920), 177.

70. See Saint Thomas Aquinas, *Summa theologiae,* I, q. 1, a. 6; II–II, q. 47, a. 2, ad primum.

71. Ibid., II–II, q. 52, aa. 1 and 2.

science, but reveals it to itself, showing the depth of charity's requirements, far beyond what is strictly compulsory and in respect of the Law, of which not one jot will fail (see *Veritatis splendor,* no. 53).

In this way charity is really at the center of morality, even in the concrete discernment of the Good, so that an organic link and a continuity between spirituality and morality is established, albeit in the necessary distinction of steps. That dangerous separation between morals, ascesis, mystical life, and spirituality that became dominant in the teaching of the manuals, with deleterious effects on the "Christian" and theological understanding of morality, can be overcome insofar as we understand that even the most elementary level of moral life (obedience to the negative precepts) makes sense only in relationship to virtues, which are an inner movement toward perfection.[72] Only in the full image of charity can the meaning of the preparatory stages be understood.

72. See Servais Pinckaers, O.P., "Qu'est-ce que la spiritualité? 1. Morale: Ascétique, mystique, spiritualité," *Nova et Vetera* 1 (1990): 8–19. On this, also see D. J. Billy, C.Ss.R., ed., *Spirituality and Morality: Integrating Prayer and Action* (New York: Paulist Press, 1996).

CHAPTER FOUR

A Morality of Faith

∞

THE SALVIFIC RELEVANCE
OF MORAL ACTION

*F*aced with opinions that claim for morality an autonomy from any reference to faith, and faced with the situation of an increasing secularization of the praxis of Christians, the encyclical *Veritatis splendor* strongly affirmed that there exists "an intrinsic and unbreakable bond between faith and morality" (no. 4). For that matter, it had already emerged in the debate that developed in the 1970s around the question of what in morality is "specifically Christian" that the linkage between action and faith was one of the crucial problems of moral theology.[1] In this context, Hans Urs von Balthasar had introduced his noted "Nine Propositions on Christian Morality" with this flat statement: "The Christian who lives by faith has a right to motivate his moral behavior in the light of his faith."[2]

But at what level does the faith influence the Christian's moral behavior? In the general and transcendental dimension of attitudes or also in the concrete performance of works? The problem is decisive for understanding what the authority of Sacred Scripture is and consequently what weight is to be given to the magisterium of the Church in moral teaching.

---

1. See the essays in *Readings in Moral Theology*, Vol. 2: *The Distinctiveness of Christian Ethics*, ed. Charles E. Curran and Richard A. McCormick, S.J. (New York: Paulist Press, 1980).

2. Hans Urs von Balthasar, "Nine Propositions on Christian Ethics," in Joseph Ratzinger, Heinz Schurmann, and Hans Urs von Balthasar, *Principles of Christian Morality* (San Francisco: Ignatius Press, 1981), 77–102.

At the root of these questions lies a theologically more decisive problem that concerns the salvific import of the Christian's moral actions: What value has moral behavior with regard to achieving salvation? What is decisive on the level of the response of human freedom in light of the eternal beatitude promised by Jesus? Hence we begin from this last and most fundamental question, situating it, however, in its original historical context, that is, in the perspective of the Lutheran split between justification through faith and justification through human works. We shall take note of the consequences on the level of the concept of Christian morality.

I. THE LUTHERAN SPLIT BETWEEN JUSTIFICATION THROUGH FAITH AND WORKS.
THE DISTINCTION BETWEEN "HEILSETHOS" (THE MORALITY OF SALVATION) AND "WELTETHOS" (EARTHLY MORALITY)

William of Ockham had previously separated the morality of the positive divine commandments, which was demanded for eternal salvation, from the natural morality of reason, which was valid with regard to human welfare in this world. While inheriting this fundamental distinction of the nominalist theology of the *Venerabilis Inceptor,* Luther further transformed it in the the perspective of his doctrine of justification by faith.[3] The construction of moral theology as an autonomous discipline separate from dogmatic theology is confirmed by the Lutheran notion of ethics as a theological doctrine of duties and not as a doctrine of natural and supernatural virtues.[4]

The Lutheran Secularization of Morality

As is well known, the justification of sinful man before God, according to Luther, comes about through the gratuitous attribution of divine justice, which God grants to the sinner through the merits of Christ. It is in virtue of a faith that opens itself in total

3. I am following the interpretation advanced by G. Abbà, in *Quale impostazione per la filosofia morale? Ricerche di filosofia morale* (Rome: LAS, 1996), vol. 1, 141–45.

4. See M. Theiner, *Die Entwicklung der Moraltheologie zur eigenständigne Disziplin* (Regensburg: 1970).

trusting abandonment to acceptance of this gratuitous justification that man is made just and is "saved," while man's moral actions and works make no contribution whatever. As the Father of the Reformation said, "Good works do not make a good man, but a good man does good works."[5] Therefore before God it is faith alone that gives value to man's identity and not his works, with regard to which the Christian now becomes free. Morality thus loses all decisive importance for salvation; it is a concern of this world that is involved with social relations with a view to the earthly welfare of society.

Morality is thus reduced to a secular problem, to the issue of calculating what promotes the exterior and temporal welfare of society. Prudence, previously spurned as egotistical wisdom bent only upon seeking its own advantage, thus simultaneously receives both a reevaluation and a radical transformation. In contrast to unselfish love, it becomes a rational calculation for shaping society with a view to the common civil well-being.[6]

Thus, on the level of this secularized morality, it may be necessary and even obligatory, according to Luther, to perform actions *against* the divine law. Hence these would be only a lesser evil to be entrusted to the divine mercy. In a historical situation marked by sin, the divine law has an *elenchticus* value in that it refutes the claim that one is just through one's own works. In this sense, the law is absolute but impracticable for sinful man. It also has a secondary value, *civilis* or *politicus,* in that it promotes harmonious social intercourse, but then it no longer obligates in an absolute way. The passage from the perspective of personal morality to that of social utility brings with it concurrently a transformation from the prudence of a *genitrix virtutum* (mother of virtues) stamp to that of the *gubernatrix artium* (the principle of government by technical calculation).

The Lutheran concept further involves a transformation of charity. It is no longer a theological virtue: indeed, it is no longer directed to God as love, because at this "theological" level the space is occu-

---

5. Martin Luther, *A Treatise on Christian Liberty,* in *Three Treatises* (Philadelphia: Muhlenburg Press, 1943), 271.

6. With regard to this, see B. Wald, *Genitrix virtutum: Zum Wandel des aristotelischen Begriffs praktischer Vernunft* (Munster: 1986).

pied solely and wholly by faith. Charity becomes primarily love for one's neighbor. And this love, separated from the perspective of salvation, takes on primarily the character of care for the temporal welfare of others and of concern for material needs, opening the door to humanistic philanthropy.

Therefore, in the Lutheran perspective, morality, disjoined from its connection with salvation and from a rootedness in faith, finds two roads open to it: on the one side, it becomes social utilitarianism, on the other, philanthropic altruism. Through careful historical research, on the results of which these brief comments are founded, Giuseppe Abbà has demonstrated how the theological utilitarianism of the Scottish Anglican clergy was the first example of utilitarian morality and constituted the decisive link in the passage to classical philosophical utilitarianism.[7]

The Contemporary Separation between the Order of Salvation and the Order of This-Worldly Morality

The separation of morality from the salvation context therefore represents an important factor in the development of modern ethics. It has also had repercussions with regard to Catholic moral theology. In fact, the acceptance of the concept of the rational autonomy of morality, and consequently of the proportionalist method, was brought about through a theological distinction, in my opinion one strongly inspired by the Lutheran concept described above. This involves a differentiation, of which mention is made in *Veritatis splendor* at no. 37, between a this-worldly ethical order *(Weltethos)* and an "order of salvation" *(Heilsethos)*.[8]

The order of salvation is linked to the moral goodness of the person and his "transcendental" attitude toward the Good as such. It is in this interior and formal sphere of the intention, of his acceptance or not of God and of his brothers, that the eternal destiny and the salvation of man is played out. And this is also the sphere in which

7. Cf. G. Abbà, *Quale impostazione,* 145–63.
8. A good example of this thesis is given by Joseph Fuchs in his essay, "Moral Truths—Truths of Salvation?," chap. 4 of his *Christian Ethics in a Secular Arena,* trans. Bernard Hoose and Brian McNeil (Washington, D.C.: Georgetown University Press, 1984), 48–69.

moral absolutes may be advanced that are valid without exception, but that may be referred precisely only to general attitudes. At this level a fundamental freedom is operative, one that has reference to the free choice of the subject as a whole and is therefore athematic: the level, in a word, that it is usual to call "fundamental option."

The order of this-worldly ethical action, which moves on a horizontal plane, is linked instead to the area of the rightness of concrete actions. It is found in the proportion that actions promote a better state of affairs in this world, and hence it depends on a rational calculation of the advantages and disadvantages deriving from the action. On this level of action, taken in its exteriority, the calculating reason is completely autonomous in establishing particular norms for actions that will have only general and indicative value and which are always to be further evaluated in concrete circumstances. On the level of the "category" of action, it would not therefore present ethical norms that are "specifically Christian." An error in this area would not have consequences in the order of salvation but only negative consequences on the exterior plane.

There derives from this a cascade of ecclesiological consequences of the greatest seriousness: if the moral area that concerns salvation is the transcendental one of the goodness of the person and not that of the rightness of the acts, then Sacred Scripture has nothing "revealed" to tell us about this-worldly activity but only exhortations about general attitudes. These have only a "parenetic," exhortative, and not instructive character. Consequently also, tradition and the magisterium could not claim any specific authority concerning concrete norms for acting, a task that would belong exclusively to the autonomous reason. Salvation would, in fact, be decided in a fundamental transcendental option and not in the concrete choices involved in particular actions.

Before outlining in a positive sense a response adequate to the questions that have just emerged, we must enter a little more deeply into the arguments involved in the distinction between "goodness" and "rightness" and the fundamental option, pointing out and criticizing their philosophical presuppositions.

2. THE DISTINCTION BETWEEN THE "GOODNESS" OF THE PERSON AND THE "RIGHTNESS" OF ACTS

The supporters of proportionalism maintain that a differentiation between two levels of moral judgment is central in dealing with ethics: the level of goodness and that of rightness.[9] The character of rightness is attributed to a normative matter if a certain action is morally correct for efficaciously promoting human welfare in certain circumstances. In contrast, the character of goodness is referred to the interior dispositions of the acting subject, to his motivations, which alone would define his will.

An occasion for working out this radical differentiation is offered by consideration of two extreme cases well known in ethics: the case of an invincibly erroneous conscience and that of pharisaical hypocrisy. One may indeed perform a morally wrong action without compromising one's interior goodness: this is the case with one who acts guided by a judgment not culpably erroneous. At the same time one may perform something that is morally right from the exterior point of view but hold interior dispositions and subjective motivations that are morally bad: this is the situation in the pharisaical hypocrisy that is so many times denounced in the Gospel. But the extreme cases become here a hermeneutical tool for the interpretation of actions.

One begins by observing that what is right is not always by that very fact *good,* and that correspondingly even when it is subjectively *evil,* it may come about in actions that are not necessarily *wrong.* The level of *rightness* is therefore interpreted as a quality of the exterior

9. The most systematic text on this subject is James F. Keenan, S.J., *Goodness and Rightness in Thomas Aquinas's "Summa Theologiae"* (Washington, D.C.: Georgetown University Press, 1992); see also the article by Keenan (a disciple of Fuchs), "Distinguishing Charity as Goodness and Prudence as Rightness: A Key to Thomas's *Secunda Pars,*" *The Thomist* 56 (1992): 407–26. L. Dewan, O.P., has severely criticized Keenan's interpretation of Saint Thomas in his essay, "St. Thomas, James Keenan, and the Will," *Science et Esprit* 47, no. 2 (1995): 153–76. The first to introduce such a distinction at the level of ethical philosophy was W. D. Ross, in his *The Right and the Good* (Oxford: Oxford University Press, 1930), but it was widely adapted by influential authors such as C. D. Broad and W. K. Frankena. In moral theology it was received by B. Schüller and J. Fuchs. For a pertinent philosophical critique, see M. Rhonheimer, "Gut und Böse oder Richtig und Falsch: Was unterscheidet das Sittliche?" in *Ethik der Leistung,* ed. H. Thomas (Herford: 1988), 47–75.

act insofar as it is adequate for promoting a better state of things: this depends on a capability for making an exact rational calculation. *Goodness,* however, which cannot be an attribute just of "intelligent" calculators, concerns only interior intentions and hence what motivates the will. Thus we have a radical separation between the rational side (calculated prudence) and the volitional side (intention of love) of actions.

On the level of theory of action, the result is a dichotomy between intention, purely subjective and unverifiable (goodness of the will), and an exterior and objective moment that considers the act simply as an event that happens and that has consequences that are more or less positive (rightness as a rational calculation of the advantages and disadvantages). In an approach of this kind, it is precisely the ethical substance of human action that gets lost, the heart of praxis, where intention and execution meet, that is, choice. Choice, however, has an intrinsic intentional content that defines it. It is in choices that intentions are realized and that exterior actions acquire their human importance.

Together with the unity of human action, the practical reason's own area also gets dissolved. Prudence gets unlinked from moral virtues, and hence reduced to a technical calculation of what is suitable. On the other hand, the moral virtues, separated from reason, serve only to ensure subjective good intention, but they have no importance with regard to the choice made. In these ethical proposals there are thus juxtaposed and oddly combined two elements rigorously independent the one from the other: a subjectivistic ethic of the intention and a pragmatic ethic of the execution. The formal goodness of the will is made independent of the material rectitude of the acts and is made to depend solely on rational appraisement of its efficacy.

3. FUNDAMENTAL CHOICE AND PARTICULAR ACTS

As has already been mentioned, the question of "fundamental option," which is certainly one of the best known and most diffused theses of postconciliar moral theology, is also inserted within this whole problem area. It presents, however, a whole variegated range of interpretations, diversified and divergent among themselves and sometimes not entirely clear internally, in part because of their being the fruit of combinations that are themselves marked by contradictions. Some interpret it simply as a *planned choice of life;* others as *profound orientation at the intentional level (Grundintention);* others again as an *athematic option* at the level of transcendental freedom; others, finally, as *final option,* placed in the passage from time to eternity as before God.[10] Aware of the considerable pastoral repercussions and of the dangers present in several of these theological proposals, John Paul II, in the encyclical *Veritatis splendor,* subjected the thesis of the fundamental option to critical discernment in the light of "sound teaching" (see 2 Tm 4.3; no. 29). The papal document, recognizing the positive contributions of renewed attention to the dynamism of personal freedom and its different dimensions (no. 65), does not totally reject the thesis of a "fundamental choice which qualifies the moral life and engages freedom on a radical level before God" (no. 66). The beginning point for this discernment is, in my opinion, the dogmatic affirmations of the Council of Trent, quoted at nos. 68 and 70, relative to mortal sin. It is from these that the critical point of verification is put into evidence, which consists of the relationship between fundamental option and acts. No. 65 of the encyclical takes into consideration the proposals of those authors who advance "a much more radical revision of the relationship between person and acts."

Critique of the Thesis of Transcendental Fundamental Option

According to a current inspired by a transcendental anthropology of Rahnerian stamp,[11] two levels of freedom ought to be clearly dis-

10. For an elementary description of these variations on the thesis of the fundamental option and for reference to the authors, I take the liberty of making reference to chap. 3 of my own book: *Morale. Tra crisi e rinnovamento: Gli assoluti morali, l'opzione fomdamentale, la formazione della coscienza* (Milan: Ares, 1993), 63–79.

11. See Karl Rahner, *Foundations of Christian Faith: An Introduction to the Idea of Christianity,* trans. William V. Dyck (New York: Seabury Press, 1978), 93–106; "Theology of Freedom," *Theological Investigations,* vol. 6 of *Concerning Vatican Council II,* trans. Karl-H. and Boniface Kruger (Baltimore: Helicon, 1969), 190–93; and "The Theological Concept of Concupiscence," *Theological Investigations* (Baltimore: Helicon, 1962), vol. 1, 385–420.

tinguished: alongside a freedom of choice, which is placed on the categorical level, there is another more fundamental level of the exercise of freedom, a *transcendental* one. Categorical freedom is one that is expressed in the choice of acts with reference to contingent goods: the choice of doing this, that, or the other thing. It deals with a fully conscious dimension of freedom because it concerns something objective put by the subject outside of himself or herself. Fundamental (or transcendental) freedom, however, is one in which the subject makes a disposition of himself or herself as a whole, not with regard to this or that particular good, but with regard to the Absolute Good. It is always a presupposition of every act of particular choice and never resolvable in it. It is always, so to speak, "at one's side," because the subject can never make a choice of himself or herself as a whole by fully objectifying himself or herself: something inevitably escapes from objectivization and therefore from conscious choice. Hence this level of freedom remains only athematically a conscious one and never thematically reflective. It is a condition for the possibility of choices, their transcendental horizon, but it cannot be resolved into one particular choice among others. Furthermore, the partial character of the goods around which choices are made would prevent freedom from coming into being as intentionally totalizing self-determination with regard to the Absolute Good.

The supporters of this thesis do not deny the existence of a nexus between the two levels of freedom. *Veritatis splendor* carefully recognizes that for them it is only through particular choices that transcendental freedom is exercised (no. 65). Nevertheless, the nexus affirmed is not a necessary one. Although mediated by its objectivizations in choices, the fundamental freedom can never be identified with a particular decision nor with the sum of all decisions. This implies affirmation of a *structural difference* between fundamental freedom and its concrete historical determinations.[12] Although real-

12. See A. Szostek, *Natur, Vernunft, Freiheit: Philosophische Analyse der Konzeption "schöpferisher Vernunft" in der zeitgenössischen Moraltheologie* (Frankfurt am Main: Peter Lange, 1992), 83–109. See also Joseph Boyle, "Freedom, the Human Person, and Human Action," in *Principles of Catholic Moral Life,* ed. William E. May (Chicago: Franciscan Herald Press, 1980), 237–66.

ized together with the particular choices, the decisive level of self-determination with regard to the Absolute Good would be actuated outside of the historical conditions of the exercise of freedom. We can conclude that the salient feature of this position is the affirmation that there exists a different freedom than that of choice, one more fundamental than it, and that precisely this freedom is decisive for the moral identity of the person.

From these anthropological presuppositions derives also the thesis of the *transcendental fundamental option* developed by several moralists. This, putting itself on the level of transcendental freedom, is not an act of thematically conscious choice. Particular acts, the object of categorical freedom, may be at most signs or symptoms of its being actuated, without being able to claim an incontrovertible character. In other words, the nexus between the fundamental transcendental option and deliberate choices is of the "occasional" kind and not consciously thematic.

The Human Person and Acts

So what in reality is the relationship between person and acts? The thesis of the transcendental fundamental option makes it very ephemeral: only occasionally would the person express himself or herself in a particular act in history. The real place of the manifestation of freedom is separated from the temporal, corporal, and interpersonal conditions in which particular choices that are the object of conscious reflection are made.[13] This undergirds an anthropology that tends toward a dualistic character,[14] in which man is conceived primarily as "spirit" that self-determines himself, while the concrete circumstances of his "incarnation" in space and time are held to be

13. The limits of the transcendental concept of fundamental option in regard to historicity and interpersonal conditions have been well delineated by A. Guindon, "La liberté transcendentale à la lumiére d'une explication constructiviste de l'option fondamentale," in *Questions de liberté*, ed. J. C. Petit and J. C. Breton (Montreal: Desclée/Novalis, 1991), 197–230. However, the author, despite a desire for realism, does not succeed in overcoming a subjectivistic interpretation and ends up by bringing the problem of moral development back to the narrational stages of the subject himself.

14. See the critical comments of the encyclical, which are found in nos. 46–50, on a spiritualist dualism that sets freedom and nature in opposition.

secondary with regard to his moral identity since they involve obstacles and resistance on the part of nature. The person is identified with the freedom of a pure spirit, while nature is seen as something subpersonal, secondary, opaque, and limiting; that is, as something ultimately not decisive.

It might be said that this is an interpretation of the person and of human freedom that tends toward the "angelic."[15] The unrepeatable uniqueness of the person is thought of as outside the universal coordinates of nature. Freedom, unlinked from the historical and corporeal dimensions of its exercise, lacks reference to what is universal and is therefore ruled only by the interior dynamism of self-realization, starting from which acts of choice draw moral value. Particular behavior would hence be good not because it corresponds in itself to the truth concerning the good of the person that is inscribed in its nature, but because it is the expression of his self-determination in fundamental freedom.

John Paul II sets in opposition to this concept a realistic vision of the person as a "substantial unity of soul and body": it is only "in the unity of soul and body that it is subject to its own moral acts" (see no. 48). This means that freedom is to be thought of as an existential act of the person in his concreteness. Freedom is real in the corporeal, temporal, and interpersonal conditions of its exercise. It is from this starting point that it is necessary to interpret self-determination and not the contrary.

According to Saint Thomas, acts of intelligence and will are acts of the person in his single concrete totality and are exercised only in connection with sense experience.[16] A decision in principle that does not come about in a choice that is circumstanced and binding in time and with regard to others remains one that is uncertain and vague. It is not in fact in generic intentions but in concrete choices that moral battles are won or lost. In the personalistic vision, freedom is essentially relational, intentionally referred outside oneself to

---

15. See A. Szostek, *Natur . . .* , 86–89.

16. For a critique of fundamental option theory from a Thomistic perspective, see Giuseppe Abbà, *Felicità, vita buona, e virtù: Saggio di filosofia morale* (Rome: LAS, 1989), 161–62, 165–66, 264; and "Una filosofia morale per l'educazione alla vita buona," *Salesianum* 53 (1991): 273–314.

a personal interlocutor: the interpersonal relationship is the path to discovering the intrinsic link between freedom and responsibility. In this sense, human freedom is inseparable from its acts, because man discovers that he is free in his acts and through his acts. The encyclical arrives thus at defining the conditions within which the thesis of the fundamental option may be accepted: it, "to the extent it is distinct from a generic intention and hence one not yet determined in such a way that freedom is obligated, is always brought into play through conscious and free decisions" (no. 67). This, according to *Veritatis splendor,* is also the sense of the biblical teaching that "conceives the fundamental option as a genuine choice of freedom and links that choice profoundly with particular acts."

Thus the terms have been established for responding to the urgent demand that has spurred recent moral theology toward overcoming a reifying and fragmentary view of acts. It is a question of rediscovering the profound intentional dimension of choices. In reality, the most particular act of freedom does not have solely an exterior dimension, that of an event that happens in the world and changes a certain state of affairs. It changes first of all the subject who makes it, qualifies him morally and determines his profound spiritual physiognomy (no. 71). *Veritatis splendor* quotes in this connection a striking expression of Saint Gregory of Nyssa, who says that through our acts "we are, in a certain way our own parents, creating ourselves as we will, by our decisions." Thus he who chooses to steal becomes a thief, he who chooses to kill becomes a murderer, and he who chooses to commit adultery becomes an adulterer.

Self-determination, which works in such a way that every free decision is before all else a decision about oneself, is therefore a constituent dimension of choice on the same level as *intentionality,* and involves the opening of the will to its object.[17] Thus, as we cannot separate the person from the acts, likewise we should not dissociate the intention from the choices. Human freedom, which is not angel-

---

17. See Karol Wojtyla, *The Acting Person,* trans. A. Potecki (Dordrecht, The Netherlands, and Boston, Mass.: D. Reidel, 1979), 149–87; and A. Rodriguez Luño, *Etica* (Firenze: Le Monnier, 1992), 133–37.

ic freedom, determines itself through historical choices: intentions are defined through behavioral choices. Actions that imply for their moral object a disorder relative to its ultimate purpose and that are contrary to the moral welfare of the person are bad in themselves *(intrinsece malum)* and, if they are made the object of a conscious and free choice, qualify freedom negatively. Only this doctrine of the object is capable of ensuring the absolute value of the moral precepts taught by the Church and of upholding the proclamation of the magisterium, which, on the basis of the Council of Trent, affirms that "mortal sin is sin whose object is grave matter and which is also committed with full knowledge and deliberate consent" (no. 70). And as we were saying, this is the point of Catholic doctrine that constitutes the touchstone for all discussion about fundamental option, the distinctive element that in the logic of the encyclical permits critical discernment.

4. THE INTRINSIC RELATIONSHIP BETWEEN "MORAL TRUTH" AND "THE TRUTH OF SALVATION"

Up to this point we have analyzed several philosophical premises concerning the theory of action that are implicit in the theories that introduce a separation between the this-worldly ethical order and the order of salvation; we have also tried to grasp in a positive way what the relationship is that exists between intention and choice, between fundamental choice and concrete acts. We must now address the basic theological question. The affirmation that we wish to demonstrate and which constitutes the doctrinal position of the encyclical *Veritatis splendor* is the following: an intrinsic and unbreakable bond exists between "moral truth" and "truth of salvation"; due to this nexus particular ethical contents and not just transcendental attitudes come to belong to the truth of salvation. We consider this "intrinsic and unbreakable" bond (see no. 4) from two points of view: first, starting from moral truth, and then from the truth of salvation.[18]

18. In this demonstration I am following several arguments developed by Carlo Caffarra, in his "La competenza del magistero nell'insegnamento di norme morali determinate," *Anthropotes* 4, no. 1 (1988): 7–23.

Moral Truth as Truth of Salvation

Moral truth, as has already been said, is truth as to the good of the person, and precisely as to that good of the person that depends on his freedom and that defines him as a person. It is not the partial and particular good that is the object of technical and artistic activity (poiesis), but the global and final good of the person as such, that object of his acting (praxis) on which his very dignity as a person depends. It is to this that the saying of Jesus refers: "For what will it profit a man, if he gains the whole world and loses his own soul?" (Mt 16.2). Technical activity may help us to gain the world, but it is only on moral praxis that the salvation of the soul depends. Moral truth is hence the "serious case" of life: it is not concerned with penultimate goods (those that concern physical or psychological welfare, social harmony, and the like), but with the ultimate good that makes the person good, that is, the subject "related in truth and in justice to God." Accordingly, moral truth coincides with the truth of salvation.

Furthermore, and this is the second item of the argument, the moral truth of the person does not involve just the formal goodness of the intention but concerns particular contents relative to what *Gaudium et spes* has called: "the nature of the person and of his acts" (no. 51). *Veritatis splendor* (at nos. 48–51) speaks of the moral truth about the good of the person with relation to the contents of his nature. As we have already said, the person is not a spiritual freedom that is then related to the world and to the body in an instrumental way.[19] He is a substantial unity of soul and body. Hence, "the moral act cannot be dissociated from the bodily dimensions of its exercise" (no. 48). As moral truth regards the whole person in its reality as composed of soul and body, so salvation regards not just interior intentionality but the whole person. From this follows the conclusion that moral truth that is also the truth of salvation necessarily involves particular contents relative to specific moral goods.

---

19. See Germain Grisez, *The Way of the Lord Jesus,* vol. 1 of *Christian Moral Principles* (Chicago: Franciscan Herald Press, 1983), 137.

The Truth of Salvation Involves Particular Moral Truths

Let us see the problem now from the other perspective, that is, beginning from the nature proper to that *Veritas salutaris* which belongs to Christian revelation. It is not a merely formal truth, which does not bring with it any change in existence. It is rather an existential truth that calls to conversion: it is a truth whose acceptance by the intelligence involves a radical change of life. As Carlo Caffarra says, "*Salutaris* means that the eternal salvation of man depends on the fact that the freedom of man decides or does not decide to actuate its own personal being, fulfilling or not fulfilling that truth."[20] The truth of salvation regards in the first place certainly the revelation of the gratuitous love of God which in Christ redeems from sin and calls man to participate in the divine life. But this gift does not exclude, but rather includes in itself, the response of human freedom. The salvific truth is efficacious for the individual man through its free acceptance. Saint Augustine himself, the Doctor of Grace, has said: "*Qui creavit te sine te, non servavit te sine te*" (The one who created you without you, will not save you without you).

Hence the truth of salvation intrinsically involves a moral truth not only to know but to do. "Not every one who says to me, 'Lord, Lord,' shall enter the kingdom of heaven, but he who does the will of my Father who is in heaven" (Mt 7.21). And this truth to be done ("Christian praxis") is not just formal but involves specific and definite contents. This conclusion follows necessarily from the doctrine according to which Christian salvation is integral salvation, embracing the whole man and not just his spirit or just his intentionality, as instead a certain Lutheran pietism reductively thinks, which constituted the humus from which the Kantian ideas blossomed on the philosophical level.

Veritatis splendor (no. 53) cites relative to this a very important text of Saint Thomas Aquinas from the treatise on the new law in the *Summa Theologiae* (I–II, q. 108, a. 1). Here Aquinas asks himself whether this law, which is an interior law of the Spirit, must neces-

---

20. "La competenza del magistero . . . ," 11.

sarily also contain particular precepts that prohibit specific works or whether it limits itself to spiritual motivations. In the language of the proportionalists the question would be formulated this way: Does the new law concern only the goodness of attitudes or also the rectitude of the exterior acts? The definitely affirmative response of the Angelic Doctor calls as witness the very essence of Christianity, the central nucleus of the Incarnation. His response was of this tenor: "Yes, the new law necessarily brings with it precepts concerning exterior works, because 'the Word was made flesh.'" The Word of God, that is, did not remain transcendental but descended into the categorical in order to save the whole man.

For the rest, in all of Sacred Scripture the observance of particular precepts is taught as the indispensable condition for salvation (see *Veritatis splendor,* no. 76). Faithfulness to the commandments of Sinai is indeed a necessary condition for remaining in the covenant and for entering the promised land. Jesus himself, in the dialogue with the rich young man (Mt 19), reconfirms that in order to enter into eternal life it is necessary to obey the commandments. And Saint Paul teaches the first Christians: "Do not be deceived; neither the immoral, nor idolaters, nor adulterers, nor homosexuals, nor thieves, nor the greedy, nor drunkards, nor revilers, nor robbers will inherit the kingdom of God" (1 Cor 6.9–10).

It is clear therefore that particular moral truths that are necessary for salvation definitely belong to the Revelation transmitted in Sacred Scripture, and that hence it is the responsibility of the Church as the "way" of salvation, and in particular to its magisterium, to teach them authoritatively.

5. ACTION IN THE WORLD AS AN EXPRESSION OF FAITH

Let us ask ourselves now at what level is the nexus, always affirmed by Catholic tradition and the magisterium, between faith and works? In order to investigate this link between faith and morality, let us begin first of all from the faith and its content.

The Fundamental Choice of Faith

The distinction between *fides qua* (*creditur* understood; that is, the faith as a subjective act through which one believes) and the *fides quae* (*creditur* understood; that is, the objective content, what one believes), is classical. In the perspective of transcendental theology, the *fides qua* is interpreted as a transcendental option that is a condition for the possibility of acts, but it cannot be identified with an individual act of choice. There follows from this a change in content in the *fides quae* as well: it is no longer definable as consent to a Revelation event present in history, but as an attitude of fundamental freedom with regard to an athematic presence of God to conscience, as a transcendental boundary of it. Thus a certain philosophical interpretation of freedom comes to have primacy and to determine the theological understanding of the content of the act of faith itself. Or rather, it provokes a reductive interpretation of the content of the faith itself. The methodological change that is imposed consists instead of beginning from the *fides quae,* from the objective content of the faith, so as to then understand the *fides qua,* the act of fundamental choice of our freedom.

Vatican Council I and Vatican Council II define the faith as a free and total response to God who reveals himself. The more objective and intellectualist description of faith in Vatican I is assumed and integrated into the personalist perspective of Vatican II.[21] "The obedience of faith must be given to God by which man freely commits his entire self to God, making the full submission of his intellect and will to God and willingly assenting to the Revelation made by him" (*Dei Verbum,* no. 5). The coming of God in history absolutely precedes man's response: hence the nature of the act of faith must be deduced from the nature of the content presented to freedom and not vice versa.

Now the Revelation in the historical event consists of the initiative by which God spoke to us through the Son in Jesus Christ (Heb 1.1–2). He, Jesus Christ, the Word made flesh, sent as a man to men, speaks the words of God (Heb 1.1–2). Hence the act of faith cannot be understood otherwise than as a human act of adherence to the

---

21. In, respectively, *Dei Filius,* chap. III: DS 3008, and *Dei Verbum,* no. 5.

person of Jesus, the event in whom God communicates himself. In the Christian Revelation God enters into history and calls man to a historical covenant through a response that is a choice made in history.

The act of faith is produced in us by grace, but it is also, at the same time (*simul,* according to Saint Thomas),[22] a free act of man, a decision of his freedom. *Veritatis splendor* has pointed out the fundamental nature of this decision for Christian moral life, the character of commitment it has relative to action as well. At no. 88 it is said that "faith is a decision involving one's whole existence," for it is "a new interpretative and operative criterion for existence."

We understand this better in meditating upon our personal relationship with Christ. He is a person; our relationship with him cannot be exhausted in a merely intellectual assent to conceptual truths regarding him. That would mean emptying the faith of its existential content. He asks of us a response of our whole person, which is expressed through the fidelity of our will to his commandments. "The way we can be sure of our knowledge of him is to keep his commandments" (1 Jn 2.3). Faith is thus a global and concrete response to the person of Christ and to the historical and concrete demands of being his follower.

The witness of faith demands that it be expressed in the "flesh," that is, in existence according to its concrete historical connotations. To follow Christ is to accept living with him the fulfillment of the will of the Father through the offering of one's own "body." The new sacrifice through which we accomplish the will of the Father is the offering of our own body, participating in the sacrifice and the offering of his body made once and for all by Christ (see Heb 10.5–10: "Wherefore, on coming into the world, Jesus said, 'Sacrifice and offering you did not desire, but a body you have prepared for me; holocausts and sin offerings you took no delight in. Then I said: behold I come to do your will, O God.'"). The offering of the body refers to the institution of the Eucharist and to the sacrifice of the Cross. The gift of the body is the offering of the concrete totality of the person. The fulfillment of the will of the Father is hence inti-

---

22. *Summa theologiae,* I–II, q. 113, a. 3.

mately linked to the offering of the body. Salvation is not realized in the transcendental interiority of intentions but in the "categorical" concreteness of free choices that involve concrete existence. It is there that faith expresses itself in action.

With Christ's act is associated the response of Christians: "And now, brothers, I beg you through the mercy of God to offer your bodies as a living sacrifice holy and acceptable to God, your spiritual worship. Do not conform yourselves to this age but be transformed by the renewal of your mind, so that you may judge what is God's will, what is good, pleasing, and perfect" (Rom 12.1–2). Once more in this passage of the Letter to the Romans, and this time with explicit reference to Christian action, the offering of the body is found linked to the subject of the will of the Father. Saint Paul emphasizes the realistic and concrete nature of behavior according to the will of the Father. As it is for Christ, the body of the Christian is a place for the expression and the realization of the will of the Father. It is not therefore simply a matter of adhering transcendentally to an aspiration for the good but of doing the will of the Father. What is essential in Christian life is a "bodily matter." The "body" in the biblical meaning in fact designates the person in the concrete conditions of existence—not, accordingly, opposed to the soul but only to an abstract and purely sentimental way of conceiving human interiority and love.

It is thus that we rediscover the supreme and exemplary sense of the offering of the body in martyrdom.[23] In following Christ, the Christian must not offer just the sacrifice of a good fundamental option but that of his concrete body, that is, of all the historical dimensions of his life. In the tradition of the Church, repeated in *Veritatis splendor* (nos. 90–94), concrete fidelity to the moral law, up to the offering of one's own life, has been recognized as authentic witness *(martyria)* to the faith. In this sense von Balthasar has criticized modern transcendental Christianity, because by eliminating the need for martyrdom it has "unfleshed" the faith.[24]

---

23. T. Nadeau-Lacour, "Le martyre comme 'celebration al plus solennelle de l'Evangile de la Vie,'" *Anthropotes* 13 (1997): 297–316.

24. See *Cordula ovverosia il caso serio* (Brescia: Queriniana, 1968).

We can conclude this point with this statement. Because of the intimate nature of the faith, the nexus with morality cannot be established only at the motivational level, independent of the content of decisions, but must be expressed in concrete "categorical action." There are concrete choices that involve faith and demand witness, and which may reach as far as martyrdom. We shall see now, in the final stage of our meditation, what the dynamic of Christian freedom is, that is, how faith turns into works.

6. THE DYNAMIC OF CHRISTIAN FREEDOM

We are concerned here with meditating on the statement of Saint Paul in Galatians 5.6: "faith expresses itself through charity." Faith, which comes from man's center, from his heart, becomes a creator of new life, "a new interpretative and operative criterion," through charity (see Gal 5.6). The intimate link between faith and charity, which constitutes the perfected form of the Christian life, can thus be grasped. If man is gratuitously justified by faith and not by his works (Rom 5.1; Gal 2.16), nevertheless he will be judged "by his works" (Rom 2.6). Understanding this paradox of Pauline theology means grasping the dynamic of Christian freedom.

On one side, as Saint Thomas says, "the movement of the faith is not perfect unless it is informed by charity."[25] Living faith generates hope, and hope charity. On the other hand, charity is the efficient cause of faith with respect to the movement of the will. In this sense without charity "faith itself is dead" (Jas 2.26): it remains in the sinner like a corpse, without the soul that vivifies and permits it to express itself in the performance of acts and hence to conduct toward salvation.[26] The act of faith involves an intentionality that remains oriented toward God and tends to express itself in works. It is again Aquinas who speaks of a *"virtus primae intentionis,"* which perdures and of itself informs every desire of the believer and every decision of his.[27]

---

25. *Summa theologiae,* I–II, q. 113, a. 4: "motus fidei non est perfectus nisi sit caritate informatus."

26. See Council of Trent, Decr. *De iustificatione,* chap. 15: DS 1544.

27. *Summa theologiae,* I–II, q. 1, a. 6, ad IIIum.

Living faith, animated by charity, elicits a dynamic oriented toward works and decisions in conformity with them. This is what Saint Paul expresses in the fifth chapter of the Letter to the Galatians when he speaks of "faith which works through charity" and of the "fruits of the Spirit," which derive from letting oneself be guided by it. In his commentary on the Pauline text, Saint Thomas says that the Christian life consists of charity, whose cause is the Holy Spirit, accepted by faith, which moves hearts to work what is good. Good works are in reality an assent to the Spirit: Christian freedom is adherence to the actual grace that moves it to choose the good. In *lectio VI*,[28] he explains that good works are more properly called "fruits," because they represent the ultimate result of that seed of the Spirit which is the faith placed in us in Baptism. They are the final perfection to which the faith tends and which brings us to merit heaven. Hence works could also be called "flowers," because they anticipate in hope, with their fragrance and their beauty, the very great fruit that is the beatitude of eternal life.

In this dynamic of Christian freedom which from faith through charity arrives at works, the moral virtues are a necessary mediator. They are in fact the necessary instrument of charity, or, as P. Wadell says, "the strategies of love."[29] In order for love to have the capability of expressing itself adequately on the level of acts, it needs the presence of virtuous dispositions relative to the particular contents of human good.[30] The ultimate goal does not indeed do away with the proximate goals and the necessity that human acts be rightly ordered with respect to moral goods. Charity brings to completion (perfects) the moral virtues, of which nevertheless it has need in order to express itself in the dynamism of works. Charity introduces a norm that goes beyond, but never against, the rational rule of the virtues. Hence whatever opposes moral virtue also opposes charity.[31] The God of the Redemption, who gratuitously calls us to the

---

28. *Super Ep. ad Galatas*, chap. V, lect. VI (ed. Marietti, no. 328).

29. See P. Wadell, *The Primacy of Love: An Introduction to the Ethics of Thomas Aquinas* (New York and Mahwah: Paulist Press, 1992), 90.

30. *Summa theologiae*, I–II, q. 65, a. 3.

31. *Summa theologiae*, II–II, q. 24, a. 12.

life of charity, is also the God of Creation, who has disposed the moral order of the virtues.

The link between charity and the commandments also emerges at this point. Observance of the commandments without charity is empty, as is a legalistic fidelity to the precepts that does not involve a fundamental decision of love of God and one's neighbor. Against all pharisaism and in full accord with its Master, the Church reminds us of the centrality of the intention, the primacy of the heart. An authentically Christian moral approach must therefore emphasize the radical importance of charity, of the fundamental response of love for God, the ultimate end of our life, and of our neighbor who bears his image. Only this perspective is capable of giving moral life its unitary character and its soul, its impulse toward a perfection that will never end. We must therefore thank all those moralists who in the recent history of this theological discipline have made us redis-cover the "primacy of love" in the moral life and in that way have again reconnected it with spirituality. So: never again a morality without reference to God as origin and last end, never again a law without a live relationship with the Legislator who has made a Covenant with us, never again precepts that do not refer to a definite Face, that of Christ who invites us to follow him.

But at the same time neither is it possible to make charity vain by detaching it from the commandments (see *Veritatis splendor,* nos. 12, 14, and 24). Our journey toward the end is in fact always determined by the truth of concrete decisions about the means. The relationship with the God of the Covenant is mediated and *verified by observance of the commandments.* Love and following of Jesus is manifested by the putting into practice of his precepts. "If you love me, you will obey my commandments" (Jn 14.15). The commandments express, on the level of decisions about human goods, the demands of love: they are not only the minimal demands of respecting them, as is the case with the "negative" commandments (those that prohibit us from certain actions as intrinsically bad), but also ways to be taken to promote those values, as is the case with the "positive" command-ments (see *Veritatis splendor,* no. 52).

CONCLUSION

The theological proposals that affirm a neat distinction between *goodness* and *rightness* and that support the fundamental transcendental option tend to separate the ethical order from the order of salvation (*Veritatis splendor,* no. 37) and ultimately to establish a dichotomy between faith and morality (*Veritatis splendor,* no. 88). This reflects a widespread temptation in contemporary Catholicism, that of making morality ever more autonomous from reference to God and to God incarnate in Jesus Christ.

Hence, at the center of the subject matter we are dealing with, there stands the reality of the Incarnation and the truth of the Redemption. It is the redemptive Incarnation of the Son ultimately that is at stake, on the level of moral concept as well. It is not by chance that one of the biblical phrases that is repeated by *Veritatis splendor* and that it may be said constitutes an inspirational source from which its thought flows is that of 1 Corinthians 1.17: *"Ut non evacuetur crux Christi,"* that the Cross of Christ may not be made vain. The Redemption took place through the offering by the Son of his body: in this offering of the body he accomplished the will of the Father (Heb 10.10). And the human response too, that response through which our freedom collaborates with grace, comes about through the offering of our body.

As we have seen, Saint Thomas Aquinas, in affirming the necessary presence of particular precepts even within the new law of the Spirit, justifies it by citing the prologue to the Gospel of John, and that is the very heart of the Christian mystery: "The Word became flesh" (Jn 1.17).[32] The Spirit endows the flesh and renews it. The Redemption would not have been true if it had not reached and touched and been expressed in the flesh. It achieves freedom and transforms it in the concreteness of choices, moral actions in the proper sense, which therefore have salvific meaning.

32. See *Summa theologiae,* I–II, q. 108, a. 1.

∽

CHAPTER FIVE

A Christocentric Ethics
of the Virtues

As I have said, the intention of this work is to offer positive suggestions for a renewal of fundamental moral theology in the
light of *Veritatis splendor*. This involves developing a systematic study
of the moral action of the Christian that would be both *theological*
and *scientific*. As we have seen in Chapter One, the challenge presented by the sociocultural and ecclesial context, and also by the
recent history and present discussions of Catholic moral theology, is
that of reconnecting the links between freedom and truth and
between faith and morality. In Chapter Two we went into the characteristics of an ethics centered on the category of virtue, principally from the philosophical point of view. In Chapter Three our consideration of the truth concerning the good of the person
demonstrated the possibility of integrating in a subordinate form
the normative element as well. Chapter Four examined, from the
theological point of view, the relevance of moral action in the order
of salvation, and hence the nexus between faith and morality. Here I
would like to gather together the Christocentric foundation for
moral theology in the perspective of the virtues. This is a synthetic
working hypothesis that I think can adequately meet both the
appropriate theological and the appropriate scientific requirements
of moral theology in the perspective indicated by the encyclical.

In the traditional form in which theological ethics has been structured, at least in the modern era, it has been an ethics of commandments and norms. The reference to fundamental theology has remained rather extrinsic and obscure: *extrinsic,* in that the moral precepts were referred to the will of the Divine Legislator that was imposed on the conscience of the believer, placing limits upon him; *obscure,* because the rational foundation of the precepts, when it was eventually actuated, was realized through a deduction beginning with the nature of man.

Saint Thomas Aquinas in the *Summa theologiae,* with brilliant originality but still in his character as "Common Doctor," proposed a very different form of ethics consistent with the classical tradition and centered on the virtues. It was a profoundly theological ethics, beginning with the fact that the formal perspective is always that of Christian Revelation: the last end is grasped as supernatural beatitude, the human acts that prepare it are placed in the perspective of merit, and the virtues become integrated in the dynamic of love, which is their mother and form. However, the explicitly Christological reference, while present, is very slight. We must frankly admit that the centrality of Christ for morality is not very evident in the moral theology of Aquinas. It is in this direction, however, that Vatican Council II and recent magisterium of the Church invites us to proceed.

I. TOWARD A CHRISTOCENTRIC FOUNDATION: PERSPECTIVES AND PROBLEMS

Vatican Council II, accepting the fundamental intuitions of several German, French, and Belgian theologians (Tillmann, Gilleman, Mersch, Thil, Charpentier, Häring, Delhaye, among others), proposed the Christological reference as essential for moral theology. In the decree on priestly formation the Council affirms that the teaching of moral theology has the task of illustrating the height of the vocation of the faithful *in Christ* (see *Optatam totius,* no. 16). This does not, however, regard only the condition of Christians; in fact, according to *Gaudium et spes,* "it is only in the mystery of the Word made flesh that the mystery of man truly becomes clear . . . Christ, the new Adam, in the very revelation of the mystery of the Father and of his love, fully reveals man to himself and brings to light his most high calling" (no. 22).

For this reason, Pope John Paul II, who considers himself and proclaims that he is "a child and disciple of Vatican Council II," has never stopped saying from the very beginning of his pontificate that "the man who wishes to fully understand himself . . . must, with his disquiet and his uncertainty, and also with his weakness and sinfulness, with his life and with his death, come close to Christ."[1] Reference to Christ is critical for an understanding of man as such and not just as a Christian—that is for any man who wishes to understand his being, his vocation, and hence the ultimate meaning of his acting.

Thus the moral theology proposed by the encyclical *Veritatis splendor* has a character not only Christological but clearly Christocentric.[2] Indeed, we read in it not only that "following Christ is thus the essential and primordial foundation of Christian morality" (no. 19), but also that "he is the 'beginning,' who, having taken on human nature, definitively illumines it in its constitutive elements and in its dynamism of charity toward God and neighbor" (no. 53). I think that this phrase represents the most radical and precise affirmation of the Christocentric character of moral theology. Christ is the ultimate and perfect point of reference not just of the old law revealed to Israel but also of the natural law. He fulfills, as the end toward which man is predestined, all the dynamism of created nature, and accordingly constitutes of this nature the definitive hermeneutical criterion. Christ is the end, in his character as the New Adam, precisely because he was already at the origin of the first Adam, who was created in the light of him, the perfect Image of the Father.

If with Cardinal Giacomo Biffi we define as Christocentric that "vision of reality which makes of the humanity of the incarnate Son of God the subordinate ontological beginning of the entire creation,

---

1. John Paul II, encyclical *Redemptor hominis*, no. 10.
2. For a careful and theologically penetrating study of moral theology in the most recent magisterium of the Church, see R. Tremblay, *Cristo e la morale in alcuni documenti del Magistero: Catechismo della Chiesa Cattolica, Veritatis splendor, Evangelium vitae* (Rome: Ed. Dehoniane, 1996).

in all its levels and dimensions,"[3] then there is no doubt that the moral theology perspective suggested by John Paul II in *Veritatis splendor* is clearly Christocentric. Jesus Christ, in his archetypical humanity, reaches man in his being as his absolute source, as radical ontological beginning, starting from which the moral dynamism of imitation and following develops.[4] If we posit as really original the creative predestination of every man in Christ, then the "natural" dimension too will no longer be juxtaposed as an autonomous premise to Christian moral teaching, but it will have to be comprised and included as creatural "ingredient" in the integral figure of ethics that is manifested in Christ.[5]

Two inescapable tasks are imposed on a Christocentric foundation of moral theology, which are also answers owed to problems and to possible objections in its regard. First of all, there is the question of justifying its claim to universal human validity. In what way does the not simply exemplary but ontological and foundational reference to the historical and unique Christ-event permit the safeguarding of the rational and universal character of the ethical imperative? This is the classical objection of the Enlightenment rationalism that sets the abstract necessity of reason against historical contingency.[6] Without an adequate dogmatic understanding of the uniqueness of Christ, who as "concrete universal" is present in every age as absolute and unique foundation of history, reference to his teaching is in danger of being configured as the particular history of a community without any claim to being universal. The danger of developing a moral theology exposed to criticisms of conventionalism, of relativism, and even of fundamentalist sectarianism can be avoided only by theologically justifying the connection between

3. Giacomo Biffi, *Approccio al cristocentrismo: Note storiche per un tema eterno* (Milan: Jaca Book, 1994), 11.

4. R. Tremblay, in *L' "homme" qui divinise. Pour une interprétation christocentrique de l'existence* (Montreal: Ed. Paulines, 1993), 137–38, offers penetrating theological intuitions on the Christocentric foundations of Christian morality.

5. See I. Biffi, "Integralità cristiana e fondazione morale," *La Scuola Cattolica* 115 (1987): 570–90.

6. With regard to this, see the study of Angelo Scola, "Cristologia e morale," now included in the volume *Questioni di antropologia teologica* (Milan: Ares, 1996), 77–101.

Creation and Redemption and by showing the pertinence of the claim to the universality of the historical uniqueness of the Christian event.[7]

The second question, of a nature more distinctly ethical, regards the modalities of the passage from the Christocentric foundation to the particular determinations of the moral judgment. There has justly been talk of an "inconclusive Christocentrism," diffused at the foundation level of moral theology.[8] The enthusiasm for the new theological basis for moral theology, which is particularly applicable to several approaches to the problem on the part of "dogmatists," is causing neglect of the requirement for philosophical categories of mediation that would permit an adequate interpretation of the ethical experience and the necessary concrete drawing out of principles at the level of directives of action. Thus we have fluctuation between an extrinsic juxtaposing of the new and fascinating Christological foundation together with a normative presentation wholly conforming to the traditional schemes, in which, that is, the foundation had no influence on the norms; and on the opposing side a combination of theological anthropology "in Christ," in the absence of objective moral references, by reason of which the whole applicative aspect is abandoned to the subjectivism of the individual conscience or to an intuitionism without verification of the conformity or lack thereof of the action with the basic Christian condition.

The hypothesis that we are outlining to respond to the demands and challenges of an authentic renewal of fundamental moral theology is that of a "moral Christocentrism of the virtues" in which the Christocentric foundation would find its fundamental ethical mediation in the perspective of the virtues.[9] The normative perspective

7. Wolfhart Pannenberg, in *Grundlagen der Ethik. Philosophisch—theologische Perspektiven* (Göttingen: Vandenhoeck und Ruprecht, 1996), 95–107, sees the problem well but proposes a solution that is, in my opinion, still insufficient, because it is centered prevalently on the eschatological aspect of the Kingdom of God and not on the effective presence of Christ in every age. See the discussion of this book in *Anthropotes* 13, no. 1 (1997): 201–47, and *Anthropotes* 13, no. 2 (1997): 481–92.

8. Cf. G. Perini, *Il "trattato" di teologia morale fondamentale* (Bologna: Studio Domenicano, 1996), 137.

9. I recently found not the formula but expressions analogous to the ones here

would not of course be excluded, but it would be integrated as a subordinate element.

Servais Pinckaers, O.P., whose position is on the wavelength of a moral theology of the virtues, although not in a direction decisively Christocentric, correctly notes that the encyclical *Veritatis splendor* did not make a pronouncement on this subject, leaving the field free for the work of theologians and for their "architectonic" choices, to us the comparisons of Saint Paul.[10] Indeed, in itself the magisterial text on moral theology does not mention the virtues except in passing (no. 82 and no. 100). In order to offer elements for the development of such a prospect and to verify at the same time its plausibility, I would like to propose a course of action in three stages. First I will discuss the essential features of the moral Christocentrism of *Veritatis splendor.* Then I will compare two clearly Christocentric theological proposals that are very distant in time and very different from each other: the Balthasarian proposal of Christ as "concrete categorical norm" and that of Saint Bonaventure of Bagnoregio, which I think can be described as "Christocentrism of the virtues." Finally, I will draw some conclusions.

2. THE MORAL CHRISTOCENTRISM OF "VERITATIS SPLENDOR"

The doctrinal problem that the encyclical intends to deal with is that of "the universality and immutability of the moral commandments and in particular of those which prohibit always and without exception intrinsically evil acts" (no. 115). This concerns a typical question of normative ethics. And it is within this perspective that the discussion in the pontifical document is placed—even though in order to resolve it and to identify the object of the human act, a

---

proposed in the writings of J. G. Ziegler and in particular in the article "Christozentrische Sittlichkeit—christusförmige Tugenden," in *Trierische Theologesche Zeithschrift* 96 (1987): 290–312, where, however, the methodological importance of the prospect for a moral theology of the virtues is not brought into the discussion and the concern is rather to present a form of the moral virtues modeled on Christ.

10. See Servais Pinckaers, O.P., "Linee per un rinnovamento evangelico della morale," in *Annales Teologici* 10 (1996): 3–68, quotation from 60; and "Rediscovering Virtue," in *The Thomist* 60, no. 3 (1996): 261–78.

need was felt to state that it is necessary to place oneself "in the perspective of the acting person" (no. 78). It is not the task of the magisterium to develop theology and to propose architectonic principles of new theological systems. It must be noted, however, that the subject of the commandments is not set against the desire for happiness but integrated with it, and that it is precisely here that a significant possible opening to the subject matter of the virtues is rooted that was not dealt with in the pontifical document.

Encounter with Christ and Desire for Happiness

In the first chapter of the encyclical the connection between the desire for happiness and the commandments is shown in the concrete dynamic of the encounter and dialogue between the rich young man and Christ (Mt 19). The moral journey has its genesis in the meeting with Jesus (no. 7): in this meeting the desire of the young interlocutor, and in him the desire of man in every age, is awakened in all its solemnity as an aspiration for eternal life, for "the fulfillment of his own destiny" (no. 8). It is by the "attractiveness of his [Jesus's] person," by an intuited promise of fulfillment, that the question is reawakened in all its amplitude. In the encounter with Jesus the desire is saved from the possible danger of withdrawal into self and elevated toward an unheard-of goal of fulfillment. Christian revelation proposes a surprising and superabundant fulfillment of the desire for happiness, which resolves the paradoxical tension between the need to find an answer, in order to live and act sensibly, and the impossibility of achieving full satisfaction on this earth.

At the same time this meeting, so full of promise, which happens as an unexpected and unimaginable grace, forces a reformulation of the original question of the rich young man. From the sphere of "doing" that is possible for man, Jesus invites him to turn his attention to the original source of the Good, to him who, being the Absolute Good, constitutes the ultimate end of acting. In the encounter with Jesus the young man discovers on the one side the depth of his own desire that has God as its object, while on the other he is invited to let himself be remade in a historical education through the commandments and by following Jesus. The dynamic of the dialogue, which is emphasized by the encyclical, starting from this impulse of love toward the Absolute and Final Good, continues with reference to the commandments as the "ways" to fulfillment of the desire for eternal life and then to the following of Jesus after abandoning everything else.

The Human Dimension and the Divine Dimension of Christian Moral Theology

The Christocentrism of the encyclical is not, however, a Christomonism: Jesus is the Son of God made man, who points always to the will of the Father. Thus the Christian moral theology that is rooted in him and that takes him as a model is open to the Father: it is a filial moral theology.[11] The Father is the God of Creation who is the author of the natural law and of the intrinsic meanings of human action aimed at the good of the person; the Father is also the author of the revealed law in history as the path of the alliance with a chosen people. To live now no longer as servants but as sons within the new and eternal Covenant means living the irreducible otherness of the relationship with the Creator within the gratuitous newness of the love of "sons in the Son."

It is in Jesus, true man and true God, that the *humanum* and the *divinum* of Christian moral theology meet "without separation and without confusion": neither does the Christology annul the human, nor does anthropology devour and make superfluous the divine.[12] The God of the Redemption who calls us to the perfection of gratuitous love is also the God of Creation who offers the natural law as the first guide for living this same love. The New Adam is also the original archetype of the Adam created in the beginning. Christ, "the way, the truth, and the life" who leads us to the Father, is also Wisdom incarnate, in whom the original truth of the creation is revealed, guarded, interpreted, and elevated to its definitive fulfillment (see no. 19). If the ultimate end of human action is interpreted biblically as a contribution to the building up of God's kingdom in the perfect communion of love of God and love of one's brothers

---

11. Cf. R. Tremblay, *L'"homme" qui divinise,* 151–74.
12. R. Tremblay, *Cristo e la morale,* 37.

and sisters, then all human goods truly constitutive of the good of the person are included in it, transfigured, and definitively guaranteed by this eschatological goal, which will come as a gratuitous gift to fulfill every human effort to love.[13]

The Christological Dimension of the Commandments

Thus the Christological dimension of the commandments is revealed. "From the very lips of Jesus, the new Moses, man is once again given the commandments of the Decalogue" (no. 12). Jesus confirms them and the conditions necessary for salvation that have been established by the creative wisdom of God. In this way the nexus between commandment and promise is established within the relationship of Covenant. In fact, right from the ancient pact, the context in which the commandments were offered by God to his people was that of the Covenant:[14] they have the form of a gift, accepted in trust as the way to the fulfillment of the original promise. Through the commandment the people of Israel entrusts themselves to the Lord, who will bring to fulfillment their desire for happiness (see Dt 6.3). Hence the commandment is the expression of the education of desire through faith. It is the means through which the desire is entrusted by oneself to another for fulfillment. The exterior factor of obedience is lived in the relationship of trust. At bottom, even the commandments of the old Covenant are a way of imitating God.

But the fulfilled form of the commandment is personal. *Veritatis splendor* repeats the affirmation of Saint Ambrose, according to whom *"plenitudo legis in Christo est"* (the fullness of the law is in Christ). He himself becomes a "living and personal law" (no. 15). With regard to man's desire there is no longer the abstract and impersonal expression of precept but the concrete and personal way of life of Jesus. In its definitive Christological dimension the commandment reveals itself to be functional for the imitation of Christ,

13. See Vatican Council II, Dogmatic Constitution *Lumen gentium,* no. 36; see also Germain Grisez, *The Way of the Lord Jesus,* vol. 1 of *Christian Moral Principles* (Chicago: Franciscan Herald Press, 1983), 134–35.

14. See J. L'Hour, *La morale de l'Alliance* (Paris: 1985).

for perfect and free conformation in love to that archetypical image in whom and for whom man was created. The new law, which has its *magna charta* in the Sermon on the Mount and which is actuated in us through the gift of the Spirit, specifies the final and definitive condition of the commandment: it is interiorized as a new instinct, which makes it possible to adhere to every suggestion of the Spirit and to every counsel of Christ, who speaks to us as a friend.[15]

The Commandments as the Way to Perfection of Personal Vocation

In the encyclical *Veritatis splendor* the commandments are seen not only as the way to the end (no. 12), but also as stages toward the maturation of freedom (no. 13), or rather toward perfection (no. 17). The perfection of freedom is realized in the gift of oneself and in charity (see nos. 18 and 87). It is the supreme imitation of God and has its measure in God himself (Mt 5.48 and Lk 6.36 read together by no. 18). Charity is the fullness of the law and, in its Christological reference (see Jn 13.34), the "new commandment." In it the presumed conflict between the egotistical search for one's own happiness (eros) and the gratuitous dedication for the glory of God (agape) (no. 10) is overcome. The desire for happiness, safeguarded in its objective validity and entrusted to the commandment, thus reveals its ecstatic character. It becomes charity that affirms an Other.

At the same time the perfection of freedom is fulfillment of the person in his unique and unrepeatable vocation (nos. 17 and 85). In the appeal of the Good there resounds in fact the echo of a very personal vocation (no. 7), which involves the full accomplishment of one's own destiny (no. 8) in a path of freedom in which the good of the person is affirmed (no. 13). The personalistic side of the moral life is shown ever more distinctly in the encounter with Jesus with passage from the commandments to following him.

---

15. See the brief and superb culmination of Thomist moral theology in the *lex nova*, in *Summa theologiae*, I–II, qq. 106–8, which was given particular recognition by S. Pinckaers in "Linee per un rinnovamento," 17–22.

The Actuality of Jesus Today in the Church, the Dwelling Place of Morality

"Christ's relevance for people of all times is shown forth in his body, which is the Church" (no. 25). It is the dwelling place of the moral life.[16] The profound humanity and the extraordinary simplicity of the moral life are given by the fact that it "consists . . . in following Jesus Christ, in abandoning oneself to Him, in letting oneself be transformed by his grace and renewed by his mercy, gifts which come to us in the living communion of his church" (no. 119). And here the pope quotes a very beautiful passage from the Commentary on the Gospel of John by Saint Augustine: "He who would live has a place to live and has everything needed to live. Let him draw near, let him believe, let him become part of the body that he may have life. Let him not shrink from the unity of the members."[17]

Ecclesiological concern with moral theology is not therefore limited to the institutional elements of the magisterium, which addresses itself to Christians in teaching moral precepts to be observed, but it extends to the sacraments and reaches even to the concrete life of communion in which the Christian moral subject is formed through the moral virtues.

At the end of this rapid presentation let us gather in synthetic form the characteristics that define the moral Christocentrism of *Veritatis splendor:* (1) it is in the encounter with Christ that man's desire for happiness is reawakened and interpreted; (2) the commandments are a form of education of desire so that it may not withdraw into itself; (3) the commandments, within the Covenant, are aimed at the imitation of God and of the person of Jesus in particular; (4) the commandments tend toward an increasing interiorization in the virtues and find their culmination and their sphere in

16. See below, Chapter Six. With regard to the relationship between ecclesiology and moral theology in *Veritatis splendor,* see the contributions of Jose L. Illanes and Jean Laffitte in *Gesù Cristo: Legge vivente e personale della santa Chiesa.* Atti del IX Colloquio Internazional di Teologia di Lugano sul Primo Capitolo dell'Enciclica *Veritatis splendor,* ed. (Lugano, 15–17 giugno, 1995), Facoltà di Teologia di Lugano, ed. G. Borgonovo (Casale M.: Piemme, 1996), 177–209, 211–33.

17. Saint Augustine, *In Joannis Evangelium Tractatus,* 26, 13: CCL 36.266.

charity; and (5) the life of the Church, in which the contemporane-
ousness of Christ to the man of every age is found, is the dwelling
place of morality.

3. THE BALTHASARIAN PROPOSAL: CHRIST THE "CONCRETE CATEGORICAL NORM"

In 1974, Hans Urs von Balthasar, at the direction of the International Theological Commission, prepared a text entitled "Nine
Propositions on Christian Ethics," a work of great theological
importance and density which was approved in general form by the
Commission but which conserved the personal responsibility of the
Swiss theologian.[18] This is a text clearly marked by a Christocentric
perspective and by a "specifically Christian" ethics. As has already
been mentioned, it begins in this way: "The Christian who lives by
faith has the right to motivate his ethical actions by the light of his
faith." And when the content of this faith is Christ, "the Christian
will make the decisive choices of his life from the perspective of
Christ, that is, from the perspective of the faith."

Christ is presented in the first thesis as "concrete norm," as "concrete categorical imperative." The accent is on the fact that this does
not concern a formal universal norm but one that is "personal and
concrete." He in fact lived his eternal obedience to the will of the
Father in a human existence wholly like ours, and thus his concrete
human existence is, in its uniqueness, an unsurpassable normative
form of our moral life.

The perspective of interpretation and of application of the nexus
between Christ and our moral life is that of a "norm," in accordance
with the perspective that dominates the figures of modern ethics, in
particular according to the Kantian figure. However, with this proposal Balthasar intends to set himself precisely against Kantian
morality. He is well aware of the dangers of abstract universality and
of formalism, characteristic of the Kantian ethics of the Law, which
then gets turned upside down in a claim of absolute autonomy for
the practical reason (thesis no. 6). According to the great Swiss the-

18. Hans Urs von Balthasar, "Nine Propositions on Christian Ethics," in Joseph
Ratzinger, Heinz Schurmann, and Hans Urs von Balthasar, *Principles of Christian
Morality* (San Francisco: Ignatius Press, 1986), 77–102.

ologian, this happens precisely when the Law becomes an abstract absolute disconnected from its relationship with the living God. Kantianism is the extreme consequence of the pharisaical temptation of an autonomous justification of man before the Law.

The ambiguity of the Law is resolved only in the personal figure of Christ, a "concrete categorical imperative" and not just a formal one. In him the dialectical opposition between autonomy and heteronomy in which post-Kantian ethics has been involved is overcome. "In Christ" the Law is felt as the expression of the will of the Father filially embraced. In the Garden of Olives the will of the Father is experienced as "other" than his own, but it is made his own in love: "Father, if it be possible let this cup pass from me; nevertheless, not as I will, but as you will!" (Mt 26.39). We too are gratuitously taken up in the Spirit, while as creatures still remaining "something else" *(heteron)* with respect to God, in that relationship of sonship that makes us also "someone else" *(heteros)*. Hence, in the Spirit of Jesus the Christological commandment is interiorized and becomes a "new law" of love, without being able however to eliminate totally, in the terrestrial phase of existence, the aspect of exteriority, which, however, becomes subordinated and polarized in function of the interior element of love.

We have here a powerful theological synthesis of moral theology anchored to the following elements: (1) the main axis is a Christocentric theological anthropology of a filial nature: in Christ we are predestined to be "sons in the Son"; (2) the moral bond is placed within the personal relationship of sons in the Son with regard to the Father; (3) the Law of the Old Testament is summed up in the link of obedience of the Son to the Father, and thus the natural law too becomes a fragment of the Christological whole; (4) the exterior aspect is retained, but it becomes polarized in the Spirit with interiority.

Mention is also made of virtue (proposition no. 7), taken however only as a task of a complete "ethicization" of the corporeal-spiritual nature of the person. Virtue is, in a word, the personalized end of a successful ethical commitment. It must be noted, however, that the key term in the Balthasarian proposal is not "virtue" but rather "norm." In contrast to Kant, it assumes a concrete, personal, and relational character and tends toward interiority in the Spirit.

Regarding the Balthasarian proposal for moral theology, there is also to be noted a reserve relative to the anthropology of the desire for happiness, which is rejected as selfish, while the anthropology of praise, of a biblical character (for example, the Psalms) or of an Ignatian stamp *("ad maiorem Dei gloriam"),* is preferred; only this would ensure the disinterested purity of love.[19]

The critical reserve that one may advance relative to this way of considering the question is that it is perhaps too "theological" and too little "moral," in the sense of its implicitly supposing that once the theological foundation is established, specifically moral conceptual mediation is not after all that relevant. And indeed this is repeated by contemporary normative ethics without critical consideration at this level, taking it for granted that the way moral theology should be presented is the one offered by the modern morality of the norm.

4. THE "CHRISTOCENTRISM OF THE VIRTUES" IN SAINT BONAVENTURE

Already in von Balthasar the personal Christological reference bursts the limitations of the normative presentation. Christ is a special "norm," a new "law," living, personal, and interior. *Veritatis splendor* goes so far as to make a clear and important statement that I would like to take as the starting point for our final stage: "Love and life according to the Gospel cannot be thought of first and foremost as a kind of precept" (no. 23).[20] The preceptive figure of moral theology is, like an old wineskin, constitutionally unable to contain the new wine of Christian moral life, which makes it burst. Of course, this does not mean that we give up norms, but that we must find a more satisfactory context. Accordingly, the proposal that I think may be advanced is that of the virtues.

19. Hans Urs von Balthasar, *Homo creatus est,* vol. 5 of *Saggi Teologici* (Brescia: Morcelliana, 1991), 9–26.

20. See Angelo Scola, "Gesù Cristo legge vivente e personale," in *"Veritatis splendor": Testo e commenti,* Quaderni de "L'Osservatore Romano" (Vatican City: Libreria Editrice Vaticana, 1994), 153–57.

I would like to look into this possibility by alluding to the ethical synthesis that comes down from the great medieval tradition of the Franciscan school, that of Saint Bonaventure, which I think may possibly be described as a "Christocentrism of the virtues."[21] The medieval Franciscan school, following the Augustinian tradition and keeping its distance from the Aristotelian philosophical novelties, was always oriented toward concentrating morality on law. This was also to be the prevalent direction in Duns Scotus and Ockham, with great influence on modern ethics. The so-called *Summa Halensis,* attributed to Alexander of Hales and his Franciscan collaborators, developed the great theological distinctions around the system of laws.

In Saint Bonaventure, however, we find a perspective that is new and original, so much the more significant in that it is distinct from the "school" he belonged to. His moral theology is clearly Christocentric; on this no doubt at all is possible; there is to the contrary explicit polemical reference in it to philosophical ethics of Aristotelian inspiration. But it is also a moral theology centered on the virtues. Oddly enough, an expert on Bonaventure's moral theology, A. Pompei, sets the two elements against each other: "Although favoring a Christocentric morality, [he, Bonaventure] speaks of a Stoic and Aristotelian doctrine of the virtues."[22] He seems to imply that recourse to the concept of virtue may constitute a spurious element of a philosophical character and in tendency contradictory to the theological foundation of Bonaventurian moral theology. In reality, however, there is no opposition but rather integration, and for this reason we can speak of a "Christocentrism of the virtues."

21. The studies of Bonaventuran moral theology on which I rely are those of N. Nguyen Van Si, *Seguire e imitare Cristo secondo San Bonaventura* (Milan: Biblioteca Francescana, 1995); and A. Poppi, *Studi sull'etica della prima scuola francescana* (Padua: Centro Studi Antoniani, 1996). In addition, see A. Pompei, "Influssi di Francesco sul pensiero bonaventurano circa il rapporto tra cristologia e morale," *Miscellanea Francescana* 82 (1982): 534–68; P. Delhaye, "Les conditions generales de l'agir chrétien selon Saint Bonaventure," in *San Bonaventura, maestro di vita francescana e di sapienza cristiana* (Rome: 1976), vol. 3, 184–215; and J. Chantillon, "Le primat de la vertú de charité dans la théologie de Saint Bonaventure," *San Bonaventura,* vol. 3, 217–38.

22. A. Pompei, "Influssi di Francesco," 535.

First and foremost, the unitary and vital concept of theology characteristic of the saintly Franciscan theologian must be shown: the theology is both speculative and practical science; it is at the same time wisdom and love. It is oriented toward the practical and the mystical, but there is no authentic theology without a moral life and a life of prayer. Practical reason is inserted in the spiritual dynamic. The knowledge of divine realities is implanted in the spiritual dynamic. The knowledge of divine realities can never be separated from the practice of the virtues.[23] Thus, morality takes on the character of true theological discourse that shares in the true knowledge of Christ.

Christocentric Moral Theology

In a very deliberate and powerful theological statement Bonaventure proposed a Christological concentration of theology and ethics. Christ is for him the *medium* of all knowledge.[24] Faith in him is the foundation of all virtue, and so Christ is also the ethical "medium," the center of knowledge and of the moral life.

This whole discourse is based on the exemplarist doctrine of Platonic Augustinian origin. In the ethical perspective, Christ is the exemplar of the virtues: *"exemplar excitativum virtutum."*[25] In order to understand this statement, it is necessary to refer back to the metaphysical premises of theological exemplarism. Christ, Word of God, is the original exemplar of the Father. The relationship of the Word with creatures and of creatures themselves with their Creator has its foundation in the relationship of the Son with the Father. Rational creatures receive an impression of the image and are called to express it in a likeness that depends on their free response. The moral life is located between the *"impressio"* of the image and its *"expressio"* in life. It has as its ultimate end the showing forth of the glory of God.[26]

23. See *Breviloquium*, prol. 4, V, 206a; L. Mauro, ed., Italian ed. (Milan: 1985), iii.
24. *Collationes in Hexaëmeron*, Coll. I, II, 10–38 (Italian edition, ed. V. C. Bigi; Milan: 1985), 46–56.
25. *In III Sent.*, d. 35, a. 1, q. 2, concl.
26. On the Bonaventurian doctrine of *impressio/expressio*, see E. Gilson, *La philosophie de Saint Bonaventure*, 3rd ed. (Paris:Vrin, 1953), 210–21.

Through the moral life man is called to *deiformitas,* to take on the very form of God. This, however, is perfectly manifested in the Son, who has revealed divine exemplarity in the charity of the Cross. Hence the moral ideal of man is to model himself on the cruciform figure of Divine Charity *(cruciformitas).* Now this revelation of the image in Christ is personal presence that demands and induces a free response of following, brings one to be enamored of him. Man, in order to act well morally, needs examples more than precepts, and Christ is the perfect example who arouses emulation by his virtues. Christ is the ascending center of morality who leads us to the Father, "from virtue to virtue."[27] This accordingly means to rise behind Christ toward the Father by imitating him in virtue. In this ascent the figure of Francis of Assisi, first and foremost in the experience of conforming himself to the charity of the cross of the Verna, has a decisive role. In Francis there is realized the eschatological manifestation of what it means to imitate Christ.[28] He in fact imitated Christ "in every perfection of virtue."

Exemplarity and Participation in the Virtues of Christ

Christ is not just a legislator for us, but also the origin, the exemplar, and the goal of moral life. He supports us not just with precepts, but also with documents, examples, and gifts of grace.[29] The exemplarist perspective makes a rich abundance of approaches to the Christocentric foundation possible, and this makes its proficient influence effective in many ways. At this point a double path for the imitation of Christ opens up, one centered on the Word incarnate and developed above all in the *Breviloquium,* the other linked to the inspired Word and discussed primarily in the Commentary on the Hexaëmeron.

In the *Breviloquium* there is a triple illumination of the incarnate Word: through symbols, through doctrine, and through examples.

---

27. *In III Sent.,* d. 24, dub. 4 (III, 531b).

28. The nature of the eschatological uniqueness of Saint Francis is involved in the theology of history of Bonaventure. In this regard, see J. Ratzinger, *San Bonaventura: La teologia della storia* (Firenze: Nardini, 1991), 76–80.

29. *In III Sent.,* d. 24, dub. 4 (III, 531b).

Christ is the "master and principal doctor" in the moral field, but the example is much more powerful than the simple word. Through his example Christ conducts us "from virtue to virtue" up to the culmination of the virtues which is the charity of the Cross. Hence the life of Christ is example and unique model of the virtues and of the perfections. For Bonaventure, in fact, it is not so much a question of imitating the concrete actions of Jesus but of imitating his virtues. Virtue is therefore the middle term in the exemplary relationship of Christ for us. His influence as incarnate Word remains, however, in a certain sense predominantly exterior, in that it is a model.

In the Commentary on the Hexaëmeron, on the other hand, contemplation of the inspired Word is prevalent and its influence is made correspondingly more interior. Here in fact it is a question of the interior presence of Christ in man through the Spirit. At the center, here as in the *Itinerarium mentis in Deum,* is a meditation on the Christification of the Verna, in which Francis received the stigmata: "the lover is transformed into the beloved." The inspired Word consents to an intimate participation in the very virtues of Christ. The imitation of Christ thus becomes participation in the virtues themselves, both in acting and in suffering.[30] The moral action expresses the Word incarnate in the world: it is the revelation of salvation by Christ. From the meeting with Christ there comes to life that "fire of love" *(incendium amoris)* that causes one to be virtuous. In the intimate contact of the world with the inspired Word we find the origin of an inflammation by charity *(origo inflammationis caritatis):* the true conversion that makes one cruciform.[31]

Exemplarism of the Virtues and Rectitude of Choice

Attentiveness to the primacy of the virtues in the following of Christ does not lead Bonaventure into neglect of the importance of acts. He places his understanding of action in the supernatural theological perspective of "merit." Merit is the quality of the human act in its being made through grace proportionate to the final end of

---

30. *Collationes in Hexaëmeron,* Coll. VI, 10 (Italian edition: ed. V. C. Bigi; Milan: 1985), 112–21. Cf. also on the same subject: *In III Sent.,* d. 34, q. 1. a. (III, 737a), 1.

31. See J. Chantillon, "Le primat de la vertú de charité," 218, 238.

supernatural beatitude. Christian action has a divine dimension. That does not take away the human dimension but rather presupposes it. To be meritorious, a human act must also be righteous. On the subject of rectitude in acting, the Seraphic Doctor depends strictly on Saint Anselm.[32] To be meritorious, the act must reflect the ecstatic character of a love that, overcoming all withdrawal into itself, turns to the Good, loving it for itself.

Now, and this is the specific contribution of Bonaventure, the rectitude of the act depends on the preceding rectitude of the soul, which is realized only through virtue. The lower part of the soul is rectified by the four cardinal virtues, while the superior part is rectified by the three theological virtues.[33] The three requisites for a meritorious act are ensured respectively by the corresponding virtues: the *vigor virtutis* (the strength of the virtue) by the cardinal virtues, the *splendor veritatis* (the splendor of the truth) by faith, and the *fervor caritatis* (the fervor of love) by charity.[34]

And here we have revealed the probable origin of the title of the encyclical *Veritatis splendor*: "the splendor of the truth" is a necessary condition for the human act in that this act is under the operative influence of the virtue of faith, which is in us a participation in the virtues of Christ and an expression of our being configured in the original Image. Thus, while not changing the classical configuration of the cardinal virtues, the theological study of the great Franciscan saint modified from within the very idea of virtue: from a habit due to personal effort, he has made of it a quality that God himself operates in us, through which, by making us like him, our acts are made proportionate to the goal of our supernatural vocation.

Charity, the Mother and Form of the Virtues

For Bonaventure, the apex of Christian moral virtue is the apex of the imitation of Christ and what makes us "godlike" is the virtue of charity. In it man participates in the superhuman generosity of

---

32. See R. Pouchet, *La rectitudo chez Saint Anselme: Un itinéraire augustinien de l'âme à Dieu* (Paris: Ed. Augustiniennes, 1964).

33. See *Breviloquium*, V, 4, 4. On this subject, see P. Delhaye, "Les conditions générales," 204–5.

34. See *Breviloquium*, V, 1, 6.

the Creator. For him, charity is the root, the form, and the goal of all the other virtues.[35] While following the Augustinian line of the primacy of charity and the acknowledgment of its character as source, Bonaventure does not subsume the other virtues under it: human morality has an autonomy of its own that is to be respected.[36] Charity is not to be confused with the other virtues and, while remaining specifically distinct from them, it does not dispense from practicing them. It has, however, a primacy: in it is actuated the most essential and profound aspect of the imitation of Christ.

It is in the *incendium amoris* (in the fire of love) that is characteristic of charity that the virtues grow. Hence, for Bonaventure, charity is the mother and form of the other virtues. It is "mother," not that it generates them, but that it warms and nourishes them, elevating them supernaturally. And it is their "form" in that it corrects their intention toward God, loved for his own sake above all else; and it is precisely intention that gives form to acts. In becoming the ultimate form of the moral virtues, charity thus also informs acts, turning them toward the gratuitous love of God.

CONCLUDING THOUGHTS

In the light of what has emerged from the study of *Veritatis splendor* and from the theological proposals of Hans Urs von Balthasar and Saint Bonaventure, we can now conclude with several final considerations our thoughts on the direction of a possible renewal of moral theology.

a. First and foremost, with regard to the prospects for a *Christocentrism* of moral theology, in the Bonaventurian theological proposal, which is centered on the virtues, we have met a wealth of forms and of interpretative models of morality and of the corresponding influence of Christ on the life and the actions of the believer. Christ is not just legislator, but also origin, end, and exemplary form of the

---

35. See *Breviloquium,* V, 8, 3–5. On this subject, see J. Chantillon, "Le primat de la vertú de charité."

36. See *In II Sent.,* d. 27, a, 1, q. 1 (III, 589–93). The patristic text, which was the authority for Peter Lombard and for those who traced all the virtues back to charity, is in Saint Augustine, *De moribus ecclesiae catholicae,* I, 14: PL 32, 1322.

Christian life. The theological perspective of a morality of beatitude and of charity makes it possible to go beyond the minimalism of an ethics of the norm, and at the same time to go beyond the age-old extrinsic character of the relationship between morality and spirituality. In Christ man is called to the perfection of the gift of himself in charity. The nexus between the Christian and Christ, mediated by the virtues, becomes intimate and at the same time malleable; it is not a question of imitating the exterior actions but of immersing oneself through the Spirit in the fundamental attitudes of his life.

b. One could further comment that the Christological reference also demands a reformulation of the significance and the hierarchy of the virtues. They are no longer the simple result of human practices but are a gift infused by God. The fundamental primacy of charity and the theological virtues changes the overall significance of the virtuous state, crowned by the gifts of the Spirit. In the reference to Christ, new virtues, unknown to classical philosophy, come into play: humility, obedience, service (see Phil 2 and Jn 13).[37] The specifically Christian character of morality is thus decisively affirmed and the virtues become the expression of a Christlike form of existence in which the glory of God shines forth in the life of man, son in the Son.

c. In the second place, with regard to the category of *virtue*, it offers the human and rational premise for a Christocentric morality of charity that makes it possible to go beyond a morality of pure obligation and to unite the natural dimension and the supernatural dimension.[38] The first-person perspective, which is proper for a morality of the virtues, is the only one that allows us to satisfactorily grasp the moral point of view as praxis through which the subject is called to actuate himself precisely as a person.

d. The organic unity of the Christian moral life, centered on the virtue of charity and on the dynamic toward the sole supernatural

---

37. For the "Christ-forming" virtues of obedience and humility, see J. G. Ziegler, *Christozentrische Sittlichkeit—christusförmige Tugenden;* for the virtue of service, see R. Tremblay, *L'"homme" qui divinise,* 193–209.

38. See M. Rhonheimer, "Morale cristiana e ragionevolezza morale. Di che cosa è il compimento la legge del Vangelo?" in *Gesù Cristo legge vivente e personale della santa Chiesa,* 147–68.

end of beatitude, does not abrogate the difference between the natural human order of the virtues and the supernatural order of charity. The rational dimension of the virtues, subsumed in the superior logic of charity, is respected with regard to its own demands. In the Christocentric perspective, the human and the divine in morality are united "without confusion and without separation."

e. However, to avoid reference to the virtues becoming something too vague and susceptible to subjective or relativistic interpretations, it is necessary to base the virtues on a universal practical rationality, on universal principles of the Good that are those proper to the natural law. In Saint Bonaventure there is a certain reluctance to deal with the content of virtue in terms of philosophical conceptualism. In him a mystical tension and concern prevails. It seems to me to be necessary here to have recourse to the rigorous Thomistic foundation of moral virtue, which has rationality at its heart and is safeguarded by prudence. In the context of these reflections, this matter can only be noted here as a matter that needs to be developed further and verified.

f. Accordingly, the primacy of the virtues is not set against the commandments and can ensure a place for normative concern, one that becomes integrated in a subordinate form in the perspective of the virtues. Indeed, from the point of view of the subject, the commandments are a pedagogical stage relative to the formation of the moral virtues; only the context of the practical reason and the virtues makes it possible to understand the genuine significance of moral norms and to justify their claim to absolute validity without exception. Finally, in this way we understand that in relation to the requirement for concrete action and the particular call of the person to perfection, the commandments, while necessary, are insufficient and must find their fulfillment in charity, which is "the fulfilling of the Law" (Rom 13.10).

∞

PART TWO

Ecclesial Sense and Moral Life

PERSPECTIVES AND DEVELOPMENTS

∝

CHAPTER SIX

Ecclesial Dimensions of Moral Theology

POINTS FOR A THEOLOGICAL "REDIMENSIONING" OF MORALITY

I. PREMISE

*M*oral theology is the area of theological knowledge in which the conflicting tension between the magisterium and theology has been expressed in perhaps its most acute form. The assertion of the autonomy of moral reason in relation to every external authority has been considered a necessary condition of ethical action. Such autonomy has been considered to be an irreplaceable guarantee of interiority and universality in the many circumstances in which ethical action takes place. Consequently, clashes have developed in moral theology, for example, the clash between the need for autonomy and theological aspects of the so-called Christian specificity; between the universality of practical reason and an alleged sectarianism of Christian ethics; between the reflection of theologians and the doctrinal competence of the magisterium; between personal conscience and the teaching of the Church. These clashes seem to presuppose, as a common denominator, that faith is *external* to morality. This common denominator, in turn, flows from an obscuring of the theological foundations of morality, from forgetting that Christian morality is rooted in the "new man" spoken of by Saint Paul. Therefore, it is necessary to reweave the "theological" bonds between moral theology and Christology, theological anthropology, and ecclesiology.[1]

The subtitle of this chapter is meant to suggest the need for a theological "redimensioning" of morality. Such a "redimensioning" involves rediscovering the authentically theological dimensions into which Christian moral behavior and its corresponding theological reflection fit—as in a dwelling. Without this theological *ubi consistam,* Christian behavior loses its proper obligations and is disfigured, becoming at times an extrinsic and extraneous appendage to the faith, or even a substitute for faith. Praxis is then given such exaggerated priority that it absorbs the faith completely. Moral theology is thus in danger of being transformed either into a "theological ethics," in which practical reason alone is ultimately decisive, or into a presumptuous theology of historical liberation, in which the theological contents of Revelation have only symbolic value for all behavior and the criterion of effectiveness takes the place of moral truth.

It should be made clear that "redimensioning" is not at all equivalent to "relativizing" morality,[2] but rather indicates a need for a strong sense of theological "refoundation." In fact, I am convinced that such a refounding alone allows us to avoid the opposite extremes of relativization and absolutization present in the sterile approaches of a mere ethic of theologically inspired reason.

Considering the magnitude of this task of "redimensioning," my essay is intentionally limited, both in its object and in its purpose. I intend only to suggest certain starting points for reflection on the

1. Cf. Hans Urs von Balthasar, "Nine Propositions on Christian Ethics," in Joseph Ratzinger, Heinz Schürmann, and Hans Urs von Balthasar, *Principles of Christian Morality* (San Francisco: Ignatius Press, 1986), 77–102; I. Biffi, "Integralità cristiana e fondazione morale," *La Scuola Cattolica* 115 (1987): 570–90; G. Chantraine and A. Scola, "L'évenement Christ et la vie morale," *Anthropotes* 1 (1987): 5–23; and A. Scola, "Christologie et morale," *Nouvelle Revue Théologique* 109 (1987): 382–410.

2. Certainly not in the sense understood, for example, by J. Blank, "Evangelium und Gesetz: Zur theologischen Relativierung und Begrundung ethischer Normen," *Diakonia* 5 (1974): 363–75. Applying the theory of Adorno's "model" to the New Testament ethos, Blank concludes that the moral directives of Jesus could only be suggestive *(ethische Wetsungen)* but not binding. For an accurate summary of New Testament ethics, see G. Segalla, "L'etica di Gesù da Dodd a Dillman (1951–1984)," *Teologia* 1 (1986): 24–67.

ecclesial dimension of Christian moral behavior, and then to discuss the relevance of the ecclesial dimension for theological and moral reflection. The essay indicates a fruitful course for overcoming the stalemate in which the modern discussion is held, and to which it refers. This direction also develops one of the most characteristic intuitions of Don Luigi Giussani, the founder of the Communion and Liberation Movement, who sees "the Church as the place of morality."[3] We do not deal with the problem here from the perspective of a dialogue between "ecclesiology" and "moral theology"; rather we seek to discuss the relevance of the ecclesial dimension of Christian moral behavior.

2. HISTORICAL ROOTS OF THE CRISIS

It seems appropriate to take a direct historical look at the question. Although brief, this historical overview considers both the roots of the problem in moral theology and the main proposals for solutions. We refer principally to two authoritative studies on the topic: the extensive and excellent study of Herbert Schlögel, which is, however, limited to German scholarship; and the more synthetic study of Giuseppe Ruggieri.[4]

One can understand the essential terms of the present ethical problem only by reviewing the historical process that determined their form. Nietzsche is the most eloquent witness, and yet his roots are sunk in the separation of ethics from religion and metaphysics that occurred in the sixteenth century. The Protestant theologian W. Pannenberg describes this epochal shift:

The position that the authority of ethics for all mankind distinguishes it from the religious question, which is to be left to the private sphere, was characteristic of the early modern period. At that time, in the face of the insurmountable divisions among Christian groups, people were seeking for

3. L. Giussani, "La Chiesa come luogo di moralità," *Communio* (Italian ed.) 34 (1977): 13–18; reprinted in *Moralità. Memoria e desiderio* (Milan: 1980). For an English translation, see L. Giussani, *In Search of the Human*.

4. H. Schlögel, *Kirche und sittliches Handeln. Zur Ekklesiologie in der Grundlagenddiscussion der deutschsprachigen katholischen Moraltheologie seit der Jahrhundertwende* (Mainz: 1981); G. Ruggieri, "Ecclesiologia ed etica," *Cristianesimo nella Storia* 9 (1988): 1–22.

a new basis for human life in community and believed they had discovered it in basic ethical insights.[5]

Since religious wars (the ultimate outcome of the dissolution of medieval Christianity) had shown the faith to be a source of particularism and division, the intellectuals of Europe turned confidently to reason as the means to establish a truly universal ethics for human society.[6]

The pietistic movement emerged from the heart of Christianity during the late seventeenth and early eighteenth centuries. It developed especially in Protestantism, but also had remarkable influence within the Catholic milieu. Pietism emphasized the immediacy of religious experience and the mysticism of practical piety. These were contrasted to a theoretical and rationalistic conception of God and to a rationalized and distant dogma. The ideal of Christianity thus came to be more and more an ideal of moral perfection, practiced in an individualistic way independent of dogmatic truth, which was no longer perceived as relevant for life. The result of this tendency was once again the separation of morality from dogma, and affirmation, at the very heart of religion, of a primitive misunderstanding of morality. Morality was now seen simply as blameless individual conduct.

It is possible to speak of this view—and not without reason—as "the progressive corruption of the Church because of morality" and also as "ecclesiological heresy." For salvation was reduced to an individual "ethos" that was socially useful, while dogma and liturgy were valued only as means to such a goal.[7] The door was thus thrown open to consider Christianity as simply "logical humanism," in which the Christian substance is reduced to what is "truly human." Once love is reduced to an abstract principle, the Gospel

---

5. W. Pannenberg, *Ethics,* trans. Keith Crim (Philadelphia: Westminster Press, 1981), 77.

6. Cf. H. Grotius, *De jure belli ac pacis,* Prologue II (1646): *"etiamsi daremus non esse Deum."* The position becomes radically destructive to the entire Christian tradition in P. Bayle, *Pensieri sulla cometa* (1682), where the identification of atheism with immorality is refuted and, for the first time, a civil society governed by atheists is admitted as possible.

7. See C. Yannaras, *La libertà dell'ethos: Alle radici della crisi morale in occidente* (Bologna: 1984), chap. 8: "Il pietismo, un'eresia ecclesiologica," 119–38.

becomes a "gnosis that would be enough to free itself from its historical shell in order to extract the permanent moral kernel."[8]

The tradition of Catholic apologetics in relation to modernity developed within this horizon of a progressive emancipation of Western social ethics from religious tutelage. This antimodern apologetics argues that only in Catholicism is an authentic morality possible, because only the Church can guarantee freedom from error through the authority of its magisterium. Without this reference to authority, the crisis of a human ethics abandoned to itself and incapable of assuring civil society would be inevitable.

The classical manuals of moral theology, at least up to 1930, do not discuss the relevance of the Church for moral behavior except in a rather extrinsic way: the ecclesiological theme is identified with the authoritative role of the magisterium in the life of the individual. The manuals present the commonly accepted juridical framework of a treatise on functional law and a "morality for confessors."

An important new factor was introduced by the those who worked for a new, more "theological" thrust in manuals (F. Tillman, E. Mersch, G. Gilleman) from the beginning of the 1930s until Vatican Council II. This tendency seeks to reestablish an organic connection between the Revelation of God in Jesus Christ and morality. It singles out a key idea (for example, discipleship, charity, the Mystical Body of Christ), capable of synthetically organizing Christian moral life, and draws out that idea from the fragmentation of an overly juridical casuistry. Even if ecclesiology is not specifically presented as a subject (not in the work of Mersch), the preference for the idea of the Church as the "Mystical Body of Christ" makes significant inroads into the preceding tendency that identified the Church with the authoritative function of the magisterium. Particularly significant are the proposals of the Church as "quasi-sacrament" (B. Häring) and the full appreciation of the moral "common sense" of the faithful as theologically relevant for the formation of moral judgment (R. Hoffman, R. Egenter).

---

8. See Hans Urs von Balthasar, *Punti fermi* (Milan: 1972), 93 (author's translation here). [Translator's note: For an English translation, see *Elucidations* (London: Society for Promoting Christian Knowledge, 1975).]

Rather than initiating a new phase, Vatican Council II codified the most important achievements of the preceding reflection. There are clear signs in the Council documents of a basic biblical and Christological rooting of morality with a more positive presentation centered on the "duty to bear the fruit of charity for the life of the world" (*Optatam Totius, 16*). However, in the period after the Council this Christian rooting has been neglected and somewhat marginalized due to the themes on which the postconciliar debate in moral theology was focused. The central question becomes that of the *proprium* of Christian ethics, while the research concerning universal communicability on a level of interhuman norms gives an even greater importance to the autonomy of reason, however this autonomy was ultimately interpreted. One can say that the ecclesiological elements have become relevant: there were important, but also one-sided, ecclesiological elements of a "people of God" on pilgrimage in history, *sacramentum mundi.* Aspects of a substantial openness to dialogue were stressed in the common search for that *humanum,* to which the Church has a word to speak, even if she does not have ready solutions for every question.

This framework sets the stage for the serious crisis following the publication of the encyclical *Humanae vitae,* which renewed the debate on the question of natural law. Once again, reflection on the relationship between ecclesiology and moral theology was concentrated in the narrow terms of the competence of the magisterium to determine the concrete norms of the natural law. Here we can only point out the two proposals of Joseph Fuchs and Franz Böckle. Joseph Fuchs starts from the clear distinction between the "transcendental" aspect and the "categorical" aspect of morality: if in inspiration and motivation the Christian is "transcendentally" determined by a faith lived in ecclesial membership, at the level of the individuation of the "categorical" contents he can have recourse only to common human reason.[9] For Franz Böckle, it is clear that the new life in

---

9. Cf., for example, J. Fuchs, "Moraltheologie und Dogmatik," *Gregorianum* 50 (1969): 689–718; *Essere del Signore: Un corso di teologia morale fondamentale* (Rome: PUG, 1981), esp. 32–37. In this regard, see G. Grisez, "Moral Absolutes: A Critique of the View of Joseph Fuchs, SJ," *Anthropos* 2 (1985): 155–201.

Christ is the root of the primitive Church's ethics. Nevertheless, the words of Jesus and Church tradition would not offer any immediately practical indication for action. Practical reason illuminated by faith is called to decide what must be done here and now as "the law of Christ."[10]

3. A "DWELLING" FOR ETHICS

The decisive point in correctly defining a theological reflection on Christian moral behavior is to remember that the person's freedom and behavior are absolutely preceded by a gratuitous gift of God. At the source of every initiative, human freedom is preceded by a love that constitutes it, creates it, and redeems it (that is, restores it to itself in forgiveness).[11] Human activity cannot be thought of except as a response of love to Love, rooting itself in the prior love of God.

Without this "abiding," once faith had perceived the gift of God, our action would be inclined to rush around trying to make an appropriate response to God's initiative through compulsive, overhasty undertakings and attempts to change the world. That would be "works" in the sense in which Jesus and Paul reject them.[12]

In other words, the Christian must, before all else, "abide" in the love of God (see Jn 15) precisely because, in Christianity, "to receive" is the absolutely original event. This forgiveness once again shows the complete supremacy of "logos" over "ethos." It is only by start-

10. Cf. F. Böckle, *Morale fondamentale* (Brescia: 1979), 222–59 [Translator's note: For an English translation, see *Fundamental Moral Theology,* trans. N. D. Smith (New York: Pueblo, 1980)]. I also recommend R. Garcia de Haro, "I concetti fondamentale della morale," *Anthropos* 1 (1985): 95–108.

11. For philosophical analyses of this precedence of forgiveness over freedom inspired by the parable of the prodigal son, see A. Chapelle, *Les fondements de l'éthique: La symbolique de l'action* (Brussels: 1988), 19–58.

12. Hans Urs von Balthasar, *The Truth Is Symphonic: Aspects of Christian Pluralism,* trans. Graham Harrison (San Francisco: Ignatius Press, 1987), 116–17. See also *Solo l'amore è credibile* (Rome: 1982), 109–36 [Translator's note: For an English translation, see *Love Alone* (New York: Herder & Herder, 1969)]. For some of the open perspectives on moral theology in the work of Balthasar, I am indebted to the license thesis of A. M. Jerumanis, *Le Christ, fondement ultime de l'agir moral: Etude du rapport christologie—morale dans l'oeuvre de Hans Urs von Balthasar* (Rome: Alfonsiana, 1988).

ing from the fullness of love manifested on the Cross of Christ that the Christian receives the power to act in love.

The fundamental and decisive factors for the moral conduct of the Christian, therefore, precede what is proper to moral theology (just as does human freedom, above all, freedom of choice): predestination, Creation, justification, Eucharist, the call to holiness by participation in the divine life. These factors deal with events that are not primarily and essentially moral but that rather establish morality. Now, this love that precedes and establishes freedom as its dwelling has a constituent ecclesial dimension. The Church is, in fact, the

place where the process of conforming humanity to the person and event of Christ is begun, the place where men dedicate themselves, in a faith that listens and obeys, to this event that is a person, are formed by him (sacramentally), and seek through their lives to make him effective in the world.[13]

With respect to the term "ethics," Aristotle had already indicated an original ambiguity in the Greek vocabulary. At the beginning of the second book of *The Nicomachean Ethics,* he draws attention to the similarity between *"ethos"* with an epsilon (ethics) and *"ethos"* with an eta (habitation).[14] Ethics, therefore, is linked to "habit, custom," but even more profoundly to "inhabit, dwell." In his *Letter on Humanism,* Martin Heidegger probes this term in its philological origins within Homer's epic and the philosophy of Heraclitus. He attaches to *"ethea"* the meaning of "dwelling," sojourn, place of habitation.[15] The famous, and yet obscure, maxim of Heraclitus, *"ethos anthropo daimon"* could, therefore, be translated according to Heidegger, to mean that "man, inasmuch as he is man, has his

13. Hans Urs von Balthasar, *The Glory of the Lord: A Theological Aesthestics,* vol. 7 of *Theology: The New Covenant* (San Francisco: Ignatius Press, 1989), 445.

14. Aristotle, *The Nicomachean Ethics,* trans. H. Rackham (Cambridge, Mass.: Harvard University Press, 1958), II, i, p. 71. 'Ethos' with the epsilon (e[]qo"); 'ethos' with the eta (hjqo").

15. M. Heidegger, *Lettera sull'umanesimo* (Turin: 1975), 123–25. See also the reflections of C. Yannaras who take points from these Heideggerian suggestions, "La morale della libertà: Presupposti per una visione ortodossa della morale," in C. Yannaras, R. Mehl, and J. Aubert, *La legge della libertà: Evangelo e morale* (Milan: 1973), 17–19, and L. Ceccarini, *La morale come Chiesa: Ricerca di una fondazione ontologica* (Naples: 1980), 47–67.

dwelling in God." The ontological interpretation of ethics, in which the indicative of the gift of being precedes and establishes the imperative of having to be free, appears to be more profound and more radical than the axiological interpretation of ethics (which has been imposed almost exclusively in the contemporary West, giving preference to the concepts of "law" and "duty").

Research on the ancient roots of the concept of *"eleutheria"* (freedom) offers interesting results in this regard.[16] It shows how the term is not connected primarily with the horizontal freedom of choice, but rather finds its significance in opposition to the condition of slavery. To be free means, first of all, "to be and feel at home." Freedom, therefore, has to do with the concepts of house and homeland, of a place where the person is among his own and sees his rights recognized. After analyzing the Letter to the Galatians (chaps 4–6), Cardinal Joseph Ratzinger concludes his research on the biblical significance of freedom in this way:

> Freedom, we can now say, is above all participation in a social reality, the people of God. It is a reality beyond the limits of every social entity, the participation in the people of God, the Body of Christ. It is a participation in the divine being, the source of life and happiness.[17]

Morality, as a dimension of human and Christian behavior, is thus found to be absolutely, constituently relational in the semantic memory of language that refers to a "dwelling," a place in which freedom can flourish. Freedom is always preceded by the *gift* of being, which is its dwelling, the place of truth. Even more, freedom is originally guaranteed by that superabundant gift that is the *forgiveness* of the Redemption through the Cross of Christ. As in the parable of the prodigal son (Lk 15.11–32), human freedom, after many vicissitudes far from home in a land of slavery, discovers that man is preceded from within the fiber of his being by the Father's forgiveness. Freedom lives by a *for-give-ness* that constitutes and establishes the moral obligation in a manner even more true and radical than

16. Cf. J. Ratzinger, *Church, Ecumenism, and Politics: New Essays in Ecclesiology* (New York: Crossroad, 1988), 195–201, where the biblical concept of freedom is analyzed, also from the point of view of the original Greek meaning of the term.

17. Ibid., 197–98. [Translator's note: Translated here from the Italian text.]

does the gift of creation itself.[18] Ethics is remaining in this dwelling where one can live the freedom of children, where forgiveness is continuously offered and faithfully develops the dynamic that conforms us more and more to itself.

4. WHAT PRECEDES ACTION:
OUR PREDESTINATION IN CHRIST

The *Cross* is the original place where Love was manifested as "always greater" than any betrayal, and so the for-give-ness by which our freedom exists was granted by way of anticipation. This uncomfortable dwelling cannot be inhabited by us except *in* Christ who "died for us, while we were still sinners," thus revealing God's love for us (Rom 5.8). In the act on the Cross, Christ provided beforehand *for us* (2 Cor 5.14) so that we find ourselves, our place of existence, "transferred" "in Christ" *(en Christo)*. The Pauline formula (see Rom 6.11) above all expresses the objective inclusion of man in Christ, deferring to second place even the sacramental inclusion by which he ratified this filial vocation henceforth bestowed upon all creation. Finally, this formula implies "the sphere of action and life created by the radiation of the universal mission of Christ."[19] On the other hand, if we are "in Christ" it is because Christ is first "in us" (Rom 8.10–11). Thus, in Galatians 2.19–20 the true significance of this *being-in-Christ* according to Saint Paul comes to light: "crucified with Christ, it is no longer I who live, but Christ lives in me."

This is not alienation. We are, in fact, transplanted from the darkness of our sinful and alienated being into the truth and freedom of divine sonship (Col 1.13) for which we were created (Eph 1.4ff.).[20] Man is originally destined to be "son in the eternal Son" of God. Christ was forever predestined for this (Rom 1.4): to be the firstborn of many brothers (Rom 8.29). Thus, our transferal before the world into the place proper to the Son eternally signifies for us not only a

---

18. For all of this, see the suggestive analyses of A. Chapelle, *Les fondements*, 21–58.

19. Hans Urs von Balthasar, *Teodrammatica*, Vol. 3: *Le persone del dramma. L'uomo in Cristo* (Milan: 1983), 229–30. Cf. E. Babini, *L'antropologia teologica di Hans Urs von Balthasar* (Milan: 1988), 157–229.

20. Cf. H. Balthasar, "Nine Propositions," proposition 2.

return to God, considered as our original dwelling, but at the same time also a return to ourselves in the perfect human being: Jesus Christ.

The original and identifying *predestination* in Christ constitutes the foundation of our moral conduct. Even the "natural law" cannot be understood theologically except as an "ingredient" of this complete truth of our being that shines in Christ.[21] The content of predestination is our participation in the image of the Son, the Word incarnate, so that Christ can also be defined as the "concrete norm of moral behavior," which is at the same time "personal" and "universal."

Christ's concrete existence—his life, suffering, death, and ultimate bodily resurrection—surpasses all other systems of ethical norms. . . . The synthesis of the Father's entire will that is achieved in the Person of Christ is eschatological and unsurpassable. Hence, a priori, it is universally normative.[22]

The universalization of Christ as the personal concrete norm of acting is the work of the Holy Spirit. In the Spirit, the person and work of Christ are made present in all times and are actualized in us, in the same manner in which we are also constantly made present in Christ. Through the Spirit, the Law no longer remains abstract and general with the risk of also being vague and therefore minimal. Instead, it becomes a concrete personal imitation empowering each person with a particular personalized mission.

And yet the Spirit is not only subjective. The Spirit's work is also displayed in the building up and enlivening of the Church in the Scriptures, in the sacraments, in tradition, and in ministries. It is what Balthasar calls the "objective dimension of the Spirit" *(Geiste-*

21. On this topic, see I. Biffi, *Integralità.* For the theological foundation of the natural law on the "imago Dei," see A. Scola, *La fondazione teologica della legge naturale nello "Scriptum super Sententiis" di San Tommaso d'Aquino* (Freiburg: Freiburg University Press, 1982). For a general approach to the Christological teaching of predestination, see G. Biffi, *Alla destra del Padre: Nuova sintesi di teologia sistematica* (Milan: Ares, 1970), 86–129, and *Tu solo il Signore Saggi teologici d'altri tempi* (Casale Monferrato: Piemme, 1987).

22. H. Balthasar, "Nine Propositions," proposition 2, 82–83.

sobjektiv).[23] Objective and subjective unity is realized in the Holy Spirit.

Thus, the constituent ecclesial configuration of Christian morality becomes evident. It is in the sacrament of Baptism that our justification is realized through our solidarity with Christ. The baptized person is now "in Christ," in-corporated in him and, at the same time, "con-corporated" with one's new existence. One is incorporated in Christ always and only through the sign of, and in the measure of, a "con-corporation" into the mystery of the Church.

The new commandment imparted by Jesus, which finds its purpose in mutual love, is already infused into the hearts of the faithful as a reality that is a priori more profound than anything of our doing. Through the overflowing of the Holy Spirit with the presence of the Father and the Son, it is the divine "We" of the Most Holy Trinity that comes to dwell in the depths of believers (Rom 5.5). Belonging to Christ as members of one body bestows, at the level of the Church, the gift of the *"we" consciousness,* without diminishing the personal responsibility of each, according to the model of the Most Holy Trinity.[24]

5. EUCHARIST: SOURCE OF THE CHURCH AND THE NEW COMMANDMENT

The moment in which the bond between the ecclesial sense and morality is established and documented with the maximum theological conciseness is in the sacrament of the Eucharist. This is the place from which the Church springs and, at the same time, the place in which we are given the new commandment of Christian morality. The Eucharist is the true "dwelling" of the new man from which derives all his ethics. This dwelling is at the same time an ecclesial dwelling. Let us listen to two witnesses on this subject.

Carlo Caffarra writes:

Through and in the Eucharistic celebration, understood in its totality (sacrificial gift of Christ—consent of the believer to this gift), Jesus the Christ

23. Hans Urs von Balthasar, *Theologik,* vol. 3 of *Der Geist der Wahrheit* (Einsiedeln: Johannes Verlag, 1987), 292–339.
24. H. Balthasar, "Nine Propositions," proposition 2.

snatches the believer from egotistical self-possession and enables him to participate in his own charity. By reason of this event of grace, the believer no longer belongs to himself, but to Christ who died for him and he receives as a gift the commandment to love as Jesus the Christ has loved. At the origin and foundation of all that the Christian *must* do, hence, of Christian morality, one finds his being embraced within the event of the cross through Baptism and Eucharist.[25]

Also, in the same sense, Hans Urs von Balthasar writes:

While Christians break the one bread which is the body of Christ, together they all become one body, that is, precisely the body of Christ (1 Cor 10.16ff.). This is true to such an extent that the entire ethics at the heart of the Church derives from the fact that we are members of one another in the same body, branches of the same vine. The *ontology* of this mystery prescribes the *morality* which follows. Hence, the ontology of a mystery, in which the believer has no introspection, but can only accept in faith, decides the acts which he, with his own great responsibility, must carry out or lay aside.[26]

Here the great Swiss theologian grasps with his original intuition the point of the supreme transcendence of Christian morality in respect to every humanistic morality founded solely on reason. At the root of conduct stands the urgency to respond to the revelation of a love without measure that infinitely surpasses any rational measure, or rather any comprehension by human reason ("as I have loved you"). For what ultimately establishes Christian morality is not the search for perfection, but the folly of love that shines on the Cross of Christ "a scandal to the Jews, absurdity to pagans" (1 Cor 1.23).[27]

25. Carlo Caffarra, *Viventi in Cristo* (Milan: Jaca Books, 1981), 23 [Translator's note: For an English translation, see *Living in Christ: Fundamental Principles of Catholic Moral Teaching*, trans. Christopher Ruff (San Francisco: Ignatius Press, 1987).] See also G. Grisez, *The Way of the Lord Jesus*, vol. 1 of *Christian Moral Principles* (Chicago: Franciscan Herald Press, 1983), chap. 33: "Eucharistic Life as Fulfillment in the Lord Jesus," 789–806.

26. Hans Urs von Balthasar, *La semplicità del cristiano* (Milan: 1987), 66–67.

27. For a discussion of the question of the *"proprium"* of Christian morality according to Saint Paul, I refer to S. Pinckaers, *The Sources of Christian Ethics*, trans. Sister Mary Noble, O. P. (Washington, D.C.: The Catholic University of America Press, 1996), originally published as *Les sources de la morale chrétienne: Sa méthode, son contenu, son histoire* (Fribourg and Paris: 1985), 114–43.

It seems possible to describe the bond between Eucharist, Church, and morality by means of three affirmations that we will present in the following manner:

A. *Christian morality is born from the Eucharist.* The affirmation of Jesus, "I give you a new commandment" (Jn 13.34), is read as the fulfillment of the prophecy of Jeremiah 31 and Ezekiel 36 concerning the New Covenant that God promised to make with his people. God will place his law within the hearts of his people. He will write in these hearts and no longer on tablets of stone (Jer 31); even more, he will give his people new hearts (Ez 36). The commandment is *new* not only in the context that it proposes (the example of Jesus as the model of love: "love one another *as* I have loved you"), but also and above all because it is no longer simply a law promulgated from the exterior, but a new possibility of gift bestowed upon the person in communion with Jesus. The new commandment *(lex nova)* is more than anything a "gift" placed in the heart of man, a real participation in the new man, Jesus, in his sacrificial eucharistic self-giving. The New Covenant written in the heart is established in him. He is the person of the new heart whose most intimate inclinations correspond to the will of the Father ("My food is to do the will of the Father," "Behold, Father, I come to do your will"). He makes his brothers and sisters participants in his activity: "I *give* you a new commandment" (as gift). The gesture by which Jesus gives the new commandment is precisely the eucharistic gesture in which he glorifies the Father by loving his own unto the end. The new commandment, therefore, is given as eucharistic grace (a gift that bears the requirement of a gift). The gift of the new commandment is revealed in the communitarian, or rather ecclesial, context: "I give *you . . .*" (plural). This is the context of the Covenant with the new people of God who receive the law for their life.[28]

Here one could point out a possible development of a eucharistic morality flowing from the idea of *"mysterium sacramentale"* elaborat-

---

28. Although John does not report the historical account of the institution of the Eucharist in his Gospel, it is already suggested in chap. 6, and he describes the essential content in the narration of the washing of the feet (chap. 13) in which the precedence of the service of Jesus is evident as the source of all service by the Disciples.

ed by Scheeben: "that which is hidden in the sacrament, precisely because it is united to the sacrament."[29] The eucharistic occasion bears within itself sacramentally the hidden mystery and the ineffable love of God in Christ Jesus. In this way it becomes the foundational and paradigmatic occasion for all the others. Every moral act is called to shape itself by dependence upon the eucharistic act, so that morality consists in facing every life situation eucharistically and recognizing the mystery hidden within it.

B. *The Church is born from the Eucharist.* Following this line of thought, a few remarks are sufficient to recall a widely discussed topic in theology. Saint Hilary of Poitiers says that the indwelling of Christ within us occurs in a double manner: in Christian love for neighbor and in our being "one" in the sacrament of the Eucharist.[30] Being the body, on the part of the faithful, is given through their unity in the sacrament of the body of Christ.[31] Saint John Chrysostom affirms that union with Christ in his body is effected through Christian love and the eucharistic sacrament.[32] Henri de Lubac can thus synthesize what emerges from his long excursus on the tradition of the Church:

The Church is then truly *"Corpus Christi effecta."* Christ comes among His own, makes Himself their Food; each one of them, thus united to Him, is by the same token united to all those who, like Christ Himself, receive Christ. The Head makes the unity of the Body.[33]

C. *Morality, then, has a constituent ecclesial form.* The new commandment of charity, like the Eucharist, is given first of all to the Church and in the Church. Ecclesial communion is the proper form of the new life that is born from the Eucharist. In Saint Augustine, our union with Christ is realized on three levels, each of which is,

29. M. J. Scheeben, *The Mysteries of Christianity,* trans. Cyril Vollert, S.J. (St. Louis: Herder, 1946), 558–66.

30. St. Hilary of Poitiers, *Comm. in Mt.,* 19, 5: PL 9, 1025; *De Trin.,* VIII, 15: PL 10, 247f.

31. On the bond between eucharistic doctrine and sacramental ethics in some of the Fathers, see J. Ratzinger, *Popolo e casa di Dio in S. Agostino* (Milan: 1971), 207–10.

32. Saint John Chrysostom, *In II Cor. Hom.,* 20, 3: PG 62, 540; *In I Cor. Hom.* XXIV: PG 61, 200.

33. H. de Lubac, *The Splendor of the Church,* trans. Michael Mason (Glenlock, N.J.: Deus Books of Paulist Press, 1963), 88.

however, inserted most intimately into the other in such a way that all three together form an indissoluble whole: *"sacramentum corporis Christi"* (Eucharist)—*"Corpus Christi"* (Church)—*"caritas."*[34] Partaking in the Church is realized by partaking of the visible eucharistic sign: the reality of the sacrament is in ecclesial *caritas*. Thus, as he says: "anyone who wants to live has a place to live, has that with which to live." The new sacrifice of Christians, their spiritual cult, is the *caritas* that comes from the sacrifice of Christ with whom we communicate in the Eucharist. The connection between eucharistic sacrifice and ethics allows the Cross to be the unsurpassable form of the Christian's ethical life.

In the same way, there is also the most intimate union of cult and morality. If the new center of ethics is given in the Eucharist, that means that life becomes liturgy through mutual love in the community of the body of Christ. The *"dilige et quod vis fac"*[35] has its place of authentic understanding in the eucharistic unity of the Church, where sacrifice and mercy are identified. The action of the Cross of Christ becomes the fundamental action of Christian liturgy and of ethics. The Lord's open hands on the Cross are simultaneously raised to the Father and extended toward neighbor, and the two directions make but one.[36]

6. THE PRECEDENCE OF THE CHURCH AS MOTHER IN THE MORAL LIFE OF CHRISTIANS

If the Eucharist is at the foundation of Christian morality as the "gift" of the new law of love, it is not sufficient to highlight the Church's role simply as the result of the Eucharist. It is also true that the Church "makes the Eucharist" and enters with her poor but irre-

---

34. Saint Augustine, *De Civitate Dei* XXI, 25, 3; *In Jo. ev. tr.,* 26, 13: "Oh, great mystery of love! Great symbol of unity! Great bond of charity! Anyone who wants to live, has a place to live and has that with which to live. Let him draw near, let him believe, let him be embodied, that he may live. Let him not flee union with the other members . . ." See J. Ratzinger, *Popolo,* 201–16.

35. Saint Augustine, *In Jo. ep.* VII, 8, PL 35, 2033. See J. Ratzinger, *Il nuovo popolo di Dio: Questioni ecclesiologiche,* 3rd ed. (Brescia: Queriniana, 1984), 47–49.

36. Saint Augustine, *Enarr. In Ps.,* 62, 13: CCL 39, 801.

placeable contribution into the redemptive offering. She, as the Spouse of the Head and the Mother of the Body, is gratuitously associated with Christ's work of salvation and thus precedes believers, generating them into the faith and the Christian life. In effect, the maturity of the Redemption is already achieved and assured once and for all in the two constituent and enduring elements of ecclesial life: in Mary, who perfectly expresses realized personal holiness (subjective sanctity) and in the apostolic college presided over by Peter, who receives the ministerial gift of authentic teaching and forgiveness of sins in view of the sanctification of the entire Body (objective sanctity of ministry). A *mother* like Mary, the Church continues to generate and enable her children to grow in the Christian way of life. The basis of the Church's maternal duty in the moral life of the baptized (generation and education) rests in her priority and preeminence in Christ with regard to each individual Christian. This "gift of the Holy Spirit" is already bestowed upon all the members in its essential subjective and objective aspects in view of their complete sanctification in the same Spirit. If the mission conferred upon the Apostles (Mt 24) remains at the basis of the Church's mission even with regard to morals, then it is necessary to broaden the perspective even to the moment of her birth from the Cross (Jn 19) and by the Spirit (Acts 2). If the universalization of Christ as the concrete moral norm is the work of the Spirit, then one finds the justification of the Church's role in the moral formation of Christians in the bond between the Spirit and the Church as "its temple." This occurs in a double direction: through the authentic interpretation of the *divine law* and its application to the circumstances of history, and through the *forgiveness of sins,* consolation, and pastoral exhortation—*Magistra et mater.*

Thus, one finds that the Christian's moral conduct is inserted into and profoundly nourished by the life of the Church as "Mother" through the gift of the Spirit that works in her living tradition. Such presence and action are realized on a triple level: sanctity, sacrament, teaching (Scripture, doctrinal tradition, and magisterium).

Heinz Schürmann has shown how, in Saint Paul, the ecclesial community is the place of moral conscience, its immediate source.

The other "mediated" sources of moral conscience (Scripture, tradition, and reason) converge in the ecclesial community and find in her their authentic interpretation.[37] The Law of the New Covenant "written in hearts" was promised by the Prophets and given to a community. It involves not only a teaching, but a "being immersed in Christ through the Spirit." The community is the "letter of Christ" (2 Cor 3.3), the spiritual place in which the *Kyrios* through his *Pneuma* makes his will known. Thus, the Church, in the Pauline letters, is presented as the source of moral conscience through a double teaching: the teaching *interior* to each person that is accomplished by the Spirit, and the *exterior* teaching through the work of the Apostles, Prophets, and teachers guided by the same Spirit (1 Cor 12.28; Eph 4.11). An exterior teaching remains necessary because only in Jesus is the law written fully in the heart, since for believers this is only beginning to develop. Thus, the "interior word" and the "exterior word" confront one another as expressions of the same Spirit given by the Church, the Spouse of Christ.

A small sampling of the Latin patristic tradition confirms the scriptural data even if with different and sometimes limited emphasis. For Tertullian, the Church is the "community of discipline" that is called to radiate the image of Christ in believers who are the first to be shielded from sin. The image of Christ is a person who exhibits the conduct of Christ; such conduct is acquired by the Christian through following the discipline of the Church which comprises the two complementary factors of the sacraments (cult) and true, proper moral discipline. The grace of the Lord is not communicated only as an idea *(gnosis),* but rather by concrete insertion into a community of salvation conceived as an ordered common life, both juridical and pneumatic, in which the intimate content is formed by the sacraments and by their life-giving power as the work of the Holy

---

37. H. Schürmann, "Die Gemeinde des Neuen Bundes als der Quellort des sittlichen Erkennens nach Paulus," *Catholica* 26 (1972): 15–37. See also, by the same author, "Du caractère obligatoire des normes et directives morales du Nouveau Testament," in J. Ratzinger and P. Delhaye, *Principes d'éthique chrétienne* (Paris and Namur: 1979), 37–71. For a biblical approach, see E. Hamel, "La scelta morale tra coscienza e legge," *Rassegna di Teologia* 17 (1976): 121–36, and "La legge nuova per una comunità nuova," *La Civiltà Cattolica* 3 (1973): 351–60.

Spirit. Salvation consists, for Tertullian, of the journey of following the image of Christ in the unique historical form of his Church.[38]

For Saint Augustine, too, *"mores"* are constituently ecclesial. His principal tract on morality is entitled *De moribus ecclesiae catholicae*. In this work, the saintly Doctor of Hippo first speaks of the goal of life (happiness in God) and of the way to achieve it (the moral life characterized by the virtues, which are ultimately different expressions of charity). He then presents the Church as the place and society for the Christian's moral activity. The Church is the "mother" of the moral life of the faithful in a double manner: *praedicans ("exercens et docens")* and, above all, *ostendens exempla* of a holy life at her heart, fruit of the Spirit. The divine precepts are everywhere preserved *("late et diffuse")* close to the Church, and morality is preached not as exterior obedience to a law, but as an assent of the heart to the Good. The Church, then, is presented as a hermeneutic of authentic morality and as a community that offers examples of the holy life according to the various states and conditions of life. The Christian community, therefore, is truly for Saint Augustine *"Ecclesia morum regula."*[39]

7. SPIRIT AND LAW IN THE CHURCH

A decisive point to face is the bond between the Spirit and the Law at the heart of the Church. It involves a question that has its determining pivotal point in the interpretation of the novelty of the Gospel at the heart of salvation history: between the reign of the Old Testament in which the Law prevailed (in the sense of "written": *littera*) and the fullness of the eschatological Covenant in which the only law will be the "Spirit" without any need for external instruction.[40] In the present phase of salvation history, the form of

38. Tertullian, *De resurrectione carnis* and *De Baptismate*. The bond between ecclesiology and morality in Tertullian is studied in Ratzinger, *Popolo*, 67–72.

39. Saint Augustine, *De moribus ecclesiae catholicae*, XXX, 62.

40. Even if we do not follow the terminology of Saint Thomas, nevertheless at the basis of all that is said is a meditation on his tract on the *lex nova: Summa theologiae* I–II, qq. 106–08. For an authoritative comment, refer to the French edition of "Somme des jeunes": *La loi nouvelle (Ia–IIae, Questiones 106–108)*, translation, notes, and appendices by S. Tonneau (Paris: Deschée, 1981). The key categories used by Thomas are *lex indita* and *lex scripta*: as seen in the solution he gives to the problem,

the "law" (understood in the sense of an element that gives external instruction about the good to do and the evil to avoid) is at the same time both secondary and unsurpassable.

The *secondary* aspect of the element of "law" is revealed at different levels. Already in the *"lex naturae,"* the order of reason in accord with the eternal law that constitutes its proper content, there is an expression of an original harmony. It is discoverable precisely through the *"inclinationes naturales"* that orient the human person to the Good. Even in the Old Testament the same written law (Decalogue) is given in the larger context of the Covenant, that is, in the context of the free gift of God. He offers the people his faithful companionship, and the Decalogue expresses the intrinsic requirements of fidelity to this divine companionship.[41] In the kingdom of the New Covenant, then, what is specific and dominant *("id quod est potissimum")* is the grace of the Holy Spirit which is given to us through faith in Jesus Christ. The written and external elements of the law are secondary and are concerned with the preparation to receive such grace *(dispositiva)* or its effective exercise *(ordinativa ad usum).*[42] Morality is, therefore, a "covenant with the redemptive and creative Wisdom" of God; a proposal of the truth of the Good, with which the intimacy of the human heart cannot fail to be in original harmony.

At the same time the form of the law, also declared exteriorly by an authority, remains *unsurpassable.* After the disobedience of sin, this aspect of the otherness of the Father's will in respect to "my" will, which dutifully assumes a crucified form, cannot be eliminated. Jesus himself experienced in his agony the burden of the exteriority: "not my will, but your will be done."[43] In the Spirit one is able to fulfill another's will like a child, without being alienated. But that does

---

the *lex nova,* insofar as it is specific *(potissimum),* is the grace of the Holy Spirit, it is the *lex indita (interius data),* while it is written only for the secondary *(secundaria)* elements; *Summa theologiae,* I–II, q. 106, a. 1. Instead, I understand the term "law" only in its accepted meaning of an exterior norm in respect to freedom.

41. Cf. E. Hamel, *Les dix paroles: Perspectives bibliques* (Montreal: 1969); *Loi naturelle et Loi du Christ* (Bruges and Paris: 1964).

42. Saint Thomas, *Summa theologiae,* I–II, q. 106, a. 1c.

43. H. Balthasar, "Nine Propositions," proposition 1.

not mean that this crucified form of obedience, which the Father asked of his own Son, is eliminated.

Nevertheless, it should be made clear that the hierarchy thus described between the Law and the Spirit in the present order of salvation is not at all static. It is rather a dynamic polarization of complementary elements in which the Spirit is called to have more and more control of the Christian's life, making the conformation of freedom to the good interior and almost spontaneous. As was seen, the promise made through the Prophets to the people of the New Covenant (Jer 31; Ez 36) is about a new law written in the human heart. Hence, it is a law in the form of a spontaneous interiority, an *instinct:* "a new heart." The new law can also be called the "law of freedom" precisely insofar as *"ex interiori instinctu gratiae ea implemus."*[44]

The completed form toward which Thomistic ethics tends is not that of an "ethics of the law" or of duty, but rather an *"ethics of virtue."*[45] It is meant to form interiorly in the subject those dispositions that place him in spontaneous harmony with the Good. It fosters within one an increasingly attentive listening to the Spirit as a new instinct of the heart. This "instinct" indicates the penetration of grace into the heart of the faithful together with the theological virtues, the infused moral virtues, and the gifts of the Holy Spirit. On the other hand, the gift of the Spirit is still only partially bestowed upon the Christian and cannot in any way be justified as a type of spiritualistic antinomianism in the sense understood by

44. Saint Thomas, *Summa theologiae,* I–II, q. 108, a. 1, and ad 2. See also Saint Augustine, *De Spiritu et littera.* The relationship between the Augustinian tract and the tract on *lex nova* in Saint Thomas's *Summa* is studied by I. Biffi, in "L'auctoritas' di sant'Agostino nelle questioni sulla legge nuova della *Summa Theologiae* di San Tommaso d'Aquino," *La Scuola Cattolica* 115 (1987): 220–48.

45. An abundant literature is developed on this subject, among which I can point out S. Pinckaers, "La vertú est toute autre chose qu'une habitude," *Nouvelle Revue Théologique* 82 (1960): 387–403; G. Abbá, *Lex et virtus: Studi sull'evoluzione della dottrina morale da San Tommaso d'Aquino* (Rome:LAS, 1983); W. Kluxen, *Philophische Ethik bei Thomas von Aquin,* 2nd ed. (Hamburg: 1980), 218–30; and J. Porter, *The Recovery of Virtue: The Relevance of Aquinas for Christian Ethics* (Louisville, Ky.: Westminster Press, 1990). I have also addressed this topic in the commentary on *The Nicomachean Ethics* in L. Melina, *La conoscenza morale: Linee di riflessione sul Commento di San Tommaso all'Etica Nicomachea* (Rome:Città Nuova Editrice, 1987), 159–63.

Joachim of Fiore. The "letter" remains an indispensable reference point, and the human person cannot refer to interior inspiration alone for the rule of conduct. Thus, for Saint Thomas, the *lex nova* not only contains tendencies of interior attitudes, but also prescriptions for exterior acts. In fact, the grace of the Holy Spirit is given to us through the humanity of the incarnate Son. By this interior grace through which the flesh is subordinated to the Spirit, sensible exterior works are also produced. Some actions are commanded or prohibited, insofar as they are respectively necessary or contradictory to the newness of life in Christ, while others (the greater part) are left to freedom, which is called to discern their suitability in an increasingly perfect dynamic of love.[46]

The eschatological relevance of Saint Thomas's response is noteworthy: "with the Incarnation a kind of interdependence is established between the Spirit and the body, in the Church and in each believer."[47] There is no action of the Spirit expressed that does not involve the body, understood in the physical and communitarian sense. It is by means of the body (visible actions, institutions) that the action of the Spirit becomes real in us. If primacy clearly belongs to the interiority of inspiration and the spiritual character of the ecclesial dimension, these cannot be contrasted to, but rather are harmoniously integrated with, the exteriority of the teaching and institutional visibility of the Church. One and the same Spirit given to us in Christ is the author of both elements.

8. ILLUSTRATIVE APPLICATION TO SOME CATEGORIES OF MORAL THEOLOGY

We only have space here to present a few illustrations meant to give a glimpse or a suggestion, rather than a demonstration, of the necessity and fecundity of the dimensions of the ecclesial sense for moral theology.

A. Regarding *moral knowledge,* it should be pointed out that besides the proper universal moment of moral science, there is the

---

46. Saint Thomas, *Summa theologiae,* I–II, q. 108, a. 1.

47. S. Pinckaers, "L'Eglise dans la loi nouvelle: Esprit et institution," *Nova et Vetera* 4 (1987): 246–62; quotation from 254.

decisive personal practical moment of prudence which grasps the moral good in its concrete singularity. At this level, the virtuous dispositions of the person become determinative by the acknowledgment of moral value. The virtuous person is the measure of the very goodness of an action.[48] Here we recall the classical theme of knowledge "by connaturality" which offers an excellent standpoint from which to evaluate the moral experience lived by the Church. This lived moral experience is a concrete and immanent condition for the formation of an adequate prudential judgment.[49]

Only if one adequately acknowledges at a theological level the precedence of the Church as mother in relation to the individual Christian on the basis of her essential hierarchic element, and only if the teaching of *sentire cum Ecclesia* is consequently emphasized, can one avoid the serious mistakes that lend, even for moral theology, a falsely democratic appeal to the *koinonia* of the Christian community. In such mistaken ecclesiological models, which often claim to refer to the conciliar theme of the "people of God" but incorrectly interpret it, the Spirit, who is given to all without distinction, would normally work through a dialectic between a misunderstood *"sensus fidelium"* and the magisterium. Such a model would, therefore, render legitimate, and even obligatory, public dissent against the latter's teachings.[50] Forgetting the magisterium's charism and specific ministry of authentic interpretation of revealed and natural divine law

48. Saint Thomas, *Sententia Libri Ethicorum* III, 10, 76–79: *"Virtuosus singula quae pertinent ad operationes humanas recte diiudicat et in singulis videtur ei esse bonum id quod vere est bonum";* see also X, 9, 150–58. For the entire question of moral knowledge in the Commentary, refer to my research, cited above: Melina, *La conoscenza,* esp. 191–202, regarding prudential knowledge.

49. On the topic of knowledge by connaturality, see J. Maritain, "De la connaissance par connaturalité," *Nova et Vetera* 55 (1980): 181–87; I. Biffi, "Il giudizio 'per quandan connaturalitatem' o 'per modum inclinationes' secondo S. Tommaso. Analisi e prospettive," *Rivista di Filosofia Neoscolastica* 61 (1974): 356–93; R. T. Caldera, *Le jugement par inclination chez Saint Thomas d'Aquin* (Paris: 1980); and J. M. Pero-Sanz Elorz, *El conocimiento por connaturalidad: La afectividad en la gnoseologia tomista* (Pamplona: Eunsa, 1964).

50. An example of this mistake is the paragraph, "The Morality of *koinonia,*" in J. Mahoney, *The Making of Moral Theology: A Study of the Roman Catholic Tradition* (Oxford: Oxford University Press, 1987), 341–47. A previous study by the same author is valuable for the attention given to the ecclesiological element for moral theology, especially for the study of Saint Thomas's thought, but it is disputable in many of its

leads to the loss of any ultimate guarantee in the discernment of spirits. This would result in being at the mercy of the logic of statistics or the presumed authority of whoever claims to be an authorized interpreter of the "the critical man of today." In this way the "spirit of the world" would be identified with the Spirit given to the Church, and the "people of God" as a way of acting and thinking would be dissolved into the prevailing mentality of the society in which it lives.

B. In addition to the theme of knowledge by connaturality, it is also possible to point out the influence the Church exercises upon the will, when she is lived as a *companionship* in the journey of the moral life. The category of "personal causality" and the influence of interpersonal relationships can be elaborated not only in the sociological field, but also at the properly theological level, by virtue of a different basis and method.[51] The "personal causality" of Jesus through the Spirit continues in the Church as an effect of a person-to-person encounter with him. The effects by which this personal causality are actualized are, according to Mühlen, the impression in the other person, the increase in the other person of the ability for the gift of self, and the actual agreement made between two persons. The encounter with Christ is a person-to-person relationship that occurs through the mediation of the ecclesial community and sacrament. The personal salvific action of Christ for us is realized in the Church. The Church, in her turn, being composed of living and historical persons, constitutes in her humanity immediate access to Christ (certainly within the faith, but always in full fidelity to the

---

conclusions; see *Seeking the Spirit: Essays in Moral and Pastoral Theology* (London: Sheed & Ward, 1981), esp. part 2: "The Holy Spirit and the Moral Life," 61–134. For a correct ecclesiological placement of the *"sensus fidelium,"* see L. Scheffczyk, *"Sensus Fidelium*—Witness on the Part of the Community," *Communio* 15, no. 2 (1988): 182–98.

51. See H. Mühlen, *Una Mystica Persona: La Chiesa come il mistero dello Spirito Santo in Cristo e nei cristiani una persona in molte persone* (Rome: 1968), 352–438. F. Santoro, in *La comunità condizione della fede* (Milan: 1976), 99–127, consistently develops the thesis of Mühlen showing the "way of the Church," by which the personal causality of Christ is exercised today. It is explained in the sense of the causality of the concrete ecclesial community and her members as a possible concrete vehicle for the salvation of all people.

structure of human experience). Through the personal causality of her members in Christ, the Church can be a concrete vehicle for the salvation of every human being.

C. The existence of a tradition, which is not only taught but also "lived," should be valued much more, not only for spirituality, but also for moral theology. The *existence of the saints* should be conceived and accepted as an authentic "theological place": a lived experience in which a personal and paradigmatic modality of the universalization of the Christic norm is demonstrated. Sanctity, a work of the Spirit, clarifies an aspect of the Mystery of Christ in history in the key area of personal discipleship as a possible catalyst for other personal experiences of discipleship. Does this not give a new thrust to the term "to canonize"?[52]

D. The inclusion of the person by predestination in Christ confers upon one's very acts a new dimension, which has a profound ecclesial relevance: *merit*. The Christian's freedom in acting is always shaped to Christ and, in him, to a supernatural destiny. The *"mihi fecistis"* of Matthew 25 shows how every act of charity is always an act measured to Christ, even if unconsciously. No act exists that is only "naturally good." The Tridentine doctrine that the sinner who is not yet justified is prepared for justice by morally good acts indicates that a conscious and free act without value for ultimate human destiny is unthinkable. This ultimate destiny, in turn, cannot be exhaustively understood except in reference to Christ.[53] One must therefore even more radically establish the morality of an act upon its meritorious dimension, which ontologically is primary, even if, in the order of knowledge, we can only take the knowledge of its morality as a point of departure to infer its meritoriousness. Now, the inclusion by predestination in Christ is, at the same time, an ecclesial "concorporation." The *"communio sanctorum"* enters into the most intimate dimension of moral activity so that the good and

---

52. See D. L. Orsuto, "The Saints as Moral Paradigm," in *Spirituality and Morality: Integrating Prayer and Action*, ed. D. J. Billy and D. L. Orsuto (New York: Paulist Press, 1996), 127–40; and L. Gerosa, "Santità e diritto canonico," *La Scuola Cattolica* 125 (1997): 661–74.

53. Cf. G. Biffi, *Alla destra del Padre*, 111–14.

evil freely done find their repercussions in the ecclesial communion.[54]

E. Regarding the topic of *conscience,* here too the same etymology refers back to an intrinsic interpersonality: *"con-scientia."* It is in communion that the innermost subjectivity encounters moral truth. The reference back to the ecclesial "we" becomes the condition of truth for opening to the Spirit given by Christ to his Spouse the Church. Starting from a theological rediscovery of the conscience-Church-Holy Spirit relationship, an earlier moral theology using an autonomous and individualistic conception of conscience must be critically examined.[55] Thus, it seems possible to conceive correctly the conscience-magisterium relationship with a view toward overcoming the initial conflict, provoked on the one hand by an individualistic concept of conscience, and on the other by an extrinsic emphasis on magisterial authority. Conscience and magisterium are not opposed but complementary functions, working at distinct but not separate levels; they originate from the same Spirit, in the Church, for the sake of our conformation to Christ.[56] Since conscience is the ultimate norm in moral activity and the formal condition of its truth, it is undeniably accepted by the Christian. However, one should also remember with Saint Paul that the supreme height where the truth of conscience is fulfilled and transcended is ecclesial charity, which knows how to be responsible for the salvation of the others while respecting their weaknesses (see 1 Cor 8.7–13; 10.23–30). Therefore, the Christian conscience has an intrinsic ecclesial configuration in which reference to the authority of the magisterium is a requirement interiorly counseled by truth, and concern for the edification of the communion is the supreme rule verifying the judgment.

54. Cf. H. de Lubac, "Credo Sanctorum communionem," *Communio* (Italian ed.) 1 (1972): 22–31, which shows that the communion of saintly gifts (*"communio sanctorum"* in the sense of the genitive neuter plural) produces the communion of saints (*"communio sanctorum"* in the sense of the genitive personal plural). For the topic of the "reversibility of merits" in the ecclesial communion, see esp. 26–27.

55. Cf. L. Ceccarini, *La morale come Chiesa,* 132–46.

56. Cf. C. Caffarra, *Viventi in Cristo,* 102–9.

∞

CHAPTER SEVEN

The Call to Holiness in the "Catechism of the Catholic Church"

THE MORALITY AND SPIRITUALITY OF "LIFE IN CHRIST"

*T*he *Catechism of the Catholic Church* (hereafter cited as *CCC*) did not intend, as Cardinal Ratzinger has explained, to lay out a systematic interpretation of faith and morals with individual truths derived from a single basic idea. Leaving this task to theology, "we [the Commission] had to do something simpler: we had to set out the essential elements that were to be considered as conditions for admission to baptism and communal life of Christians."[1]

Nevertheless, even a very superficial glance at the structure of the third part ("Life in Christ") suffices to point out the novelty in the treatment of morality with respect to previous catechetical exposi-tions, for example, the *Roman Catechism (Catechismus romanus)* of Saint Pius V and the *Chief Catechism (Catechismo maggiore)* of Saint Pius X. The part on morals, in fact, is not limited to an explanation of the commandments, but is preceded by an ample section dedicat-ed to "Man's Vocation: Life in the Spirit." The present chapter intends to highlight this novelty and to help in explaining its mean-ing with reference to the problematics of postconciliar moral theol-ogy.

---

1. Cardinal J. Ratzinger, *"The Catechism of the Catholic Church* and the 'Optimism of the Redeemed,'" *Communio* 20 (1993): 469–84; quotation at 479.

I. THE NOVELTY OF THE APPROACH

The novelty of the *prima tertiae* of the *Catechism* essentially consists in two aspects: above all, in the very fact of its existence, and then in interpreting Christian morality within the perspective of a "vocation to holiness."

The encyclical *Veritatis splendor* clearly indicates the motivations that have led the magisterium of the Church in its most recent documents to intervene no longer solely on the level of specific normative matters that are proper to the different spheres of human life, but also on the level of the foundations of morality themselves. "A new situation has come about *within the Christian community itself.* . . . It is no longer a matter of limited and occasional dissent, but of an overall and systematic calling into question of traditional moral doctrine, on the basis of certain anthropological and ethical presuppositions" (*Veritatis splendor,* no. 4). In light of "what is certainly a genuine crisis," and a crisis that as such attacks the very basis of the moral teaching of the Church, the *Catechism* has responded with a "complete and systematic exposition of Christian moral teaching," not only "in its many aspects," but also, and above all, "in its fundamental elements" (*CCC,* no. 5).

But the aspect in which the novelty of the approach adopted by the *Catechism* is largely expressed is described by the perspective of a "vocation to holiness," which constitutes the general framework within which the foundations of morality are explained. If the "Prefaces" to the four parts of the work are important for understanding their spirit, the one that precedes the part on morality (*CCC,* nos. 1691–98) is absolutely indispensable.[2] In it, the *overture* is provided by the exhortation of Saint Leo the Great: "Christian, recognize your dignity" (*CCC,* no. 1691). Before there is moral action, before there is the free response of the Christian, there is the recognition of a gift that constitutes his very dignity. But this dignity is the dignity of a call: "sanctified . . . [and] called to be saints (1 Cor 1.2)" (*CCC,* no. 1695). The redemptive work of God in Christ through the Spirit does

---

2. C. Schönborn, "Breve introduzione alle quattro parti del Catechismo," in J. Ratzinger and C. Schönborn, *Breve introduzione al "Catechismo della Chiesa cattolica"* (Rome: 1994), 93.

not exclude, but brings about and embraces, the free response of man. The gratuitous gift is, at the same time, an appeal to a dynamics of life that supports being "holy as He is holy" (see Lev 19.2). The concluding part of the section is then dedicated to Christian holiness: it is presented as the goal of the moral life (*CCC*, nos. 2012–16). The moral task of the Christian is thus rooted in the gift of an already gratuitously conceded, but yet to be developed, sanctification and is placed in the perspective of a perfection without limits: "Be perfect, as your heavenly Father is perfect (Mt 5.48)" (*CCC*, no. 2013).

The moral life, as a way of perfection in response to a gratuitous call to realize the image of God in us, implies a strict *relationship between morality and dogmatics,* on the one hand, *and with spirituality,* on the other. The *Catechism* thus finds itself in line with that renewal of moral theology sought by Vatican Council II, but in large part not as yet realized. *Optatam totius* has indicated that the principal task of moral theology is to "throw light upon the exalted vocation of the faithful in Christ" (no. 16). Also, the document of the Congregation for Catholic Education on the theological formation of future priests has encouraged the consideration of morality as "a part regarding the process in which man, created in the image of God and redeemed by the grace of Christ, tends toward the fullness of his realization according to the exigencies of a divine vocation."[3] Finally, the encyclical *Veritatis splendor* has also spoken of the commandments as a first stage in a "vocation to perfect love" that regards all struggling "at the service of a single and indivisible charity . . . whose measure is God alone" (*Veritatis splendor,* no. 18).

In reality, the separation of morality from dogmatics and spirituality, which was to become "classical" for modern moral theology, is of relatively recent origin. It prevailed and remained undiscussed with posttridentine manualistic theology.[4] This development has its

3. Congregation for Catholic Education, *La formazione teologica dei futuri sacerdoti* (22 February 1976), no. 97, in *Enchiridion Vaticanum* 5 (Bologna: 1982): 1168–1221; quotation at 1208.

4. See S. Pinckaers, "Qu'est-ce que la spiritualité?," *Nova et Vetera* 1 (1990): 7–19. For a critical judgment on the posttridentine manualistic tradition, one may see the same author's *The Sources of Christian Ethics,* trans. Sister Mary Noble, O.P. (Wash-

roots in a legalistic understanding of moral obligation, viewed as a fact that is justified by itself, which begins with the will of a legislator. Morality thus becomes a doctrine of precepts that are imposed on conscience under the pain of sin. It is detached from its anthropological roots (the ontology of a new creature in Christ) and from the concrete supernatural end of the beatific vision. Separated from dogmatics, it assumes an ever-more voluntaristic character: it becomes a "human" morality organized as a code of precepts of the natural or ecclesiastical law, to be realized by human effort alone. Separated from spirituality and centered on single acts, it is preoccupied only with the minimum for not falling into sin, leaving to ascetics and mysticism the way of perfection—something viewed as optional and only for the few elect.

It has been rightfully noted that this restriction of the horizon of the morality of obligation was due to the prevalence of a third-person perspective, that of a spectator (a judge or confessor) called upon to evaluate acts "from without" relative to their conformity or nonconformity with the law.[5] All appearances notwithstanding, such a perspective has remained intact in contemporary "normative ethics," which, though reacting to legalism, continues to consider human acts simply as "events" that happen and that have consequences. If the norm of action is now to be looked for in the consideration of foreseeable consequences or in the proportion of premoral good and evil, the point of view in which one finds oneself still remains extrinsic to the dynamics of the formation of action. Subjectivism of intention, which is at times juxtaposed to these the-

---

ington, D.C.: The Catholic University of America Press, 1995), originally published as *Les sources de la morale chrétienne: Sa méthode, son contenu, son histoire* (Fribourg: 1985): 258–82; in addition, see L. Vereecke, *Da Guglielmo d'Ockham a Sant'Alfonso de Liguori: Saggi di storia della teologia morale moderna (1300–1787)* (Rome:Alfonsiana, 1990), esp. 643–56.

5. See M. Rhonheimer, *La prospettiva della morale: Fondamenti dell'etica filosofica* (Rome: 1994), 31–34, and "Intrinsically Evil Acts and the Moral Viewpoint: Clarifying a Central Teaching of *Veritatis splendor,*" *The Thomist* 58 (1994): 1–39. Similarly, see G. Abbá, *Felicitá, vita buona, e virtú: Saggio di filosofia morale* (Rome: LAS, 1989), 97–104; and Rodriguez Luño, *Etica* (Florence: 1992), 120–25. The philosophically decisive work for the rediscovery of the perspective of intentionality in theories of action is that of G. E. M. Anscombe, *Intention* (1st ed., 1957; 2nd ed., Oxford: Oxford University Press, 1985).

ories, does not serve to compensate for objectivism in the way of considering moral action.

A way out is possible only in the rediscovery of the classical perspective of the *first person,* that is, the subject of the action who acts precisely insofar as he effects choices, concretizing intentionality in them. Human actions then appear as choices that not only effect an exterior change in the state of things, but above all transform the subject who performs them, either perfecting or perverting him. In this way, the original dimension of "praxis," which qualifies morality as a relative knowledge of action *(agere)* and differentiates it from a purely *"poetic"* (or "technical") consideration of doing *(facere),* comes to the fore.[6] By posing the moral question within the horizon of the "call," and thus by giving preeminence to the end that man is called to realize in Christ through his actions, the *Catechism* invites us decidedly to place ourselves in the perspective of the subject. In the same way, *Veritatis splendor* also reiterates that "in order to be able to grasp the object of an act which specifies that act morally, it is therefore necessary to place oneself *in the perspective of the acting person"* (*Veritatis splendor,* no. 78). All this does not mean that we are yielding to a subjectivism according to which intention alone determines the moral meaning of actions. Rather, it is reason that measures the truth of intention and choice, verifying whether or not they conform to their end, whether or not they are adequate in promoting that true good of the person that is established by divine Wisdom in man's original call.

2. THE PRIMACY OF GRACE

Conceived as a "vocation," morality thus becomes a dialogue between God and man. If man is called, the first actor in the vocation to holiness is God who calls. The original initiative, which creates the space of moral responsibility, is his. It is God who, by creating man in his image and calling him to realize this likeness (*CCC,*

---

6. For the recovery of the classical distinction between *"praxis"* and *"poesis"* (production) in a theory of action, see R. Bubner, *Azione, linguaggio, agire: I concetti fondamentali della filosofia pratica* (Bologna: 1985), 55–109. The German original is *Handlung, Sprache und Vernunft. Grundbegriffe praktischer Philosophie: Neuausgabe mit einem Anhang* (Frankfurt: 1982).

no. 1701), stands at the font of that natural law that is "a very good work of the Creator" (*CCC*, no. 1959). By means of it, every man in the intimacy of his reason is called to realize himself by loving and accomplishing the good and avoiding evil in solidarity with other men according to the design of divine Wisdom. In the revealed law of the Old and New Testaments, the divine call is made more secure and clear, and it even assumes, in the Beatitudes above all, the appearance of Jesus Christ (*CCC*, no. 1717). The moral life for the Christian, the follower of Jesus, thus becomes an appeal to pass through the way of the Cross with the force of the Spirit until perfection of charity is reached. In any case, both in the natural law and in the revealed law, it is always the voice of God that resounds as a call. Underlying the law is a vocation, that is, a Person who makes an invitation of love resound.

This being so, it is also stated that the Christian morality, as presented by the *Catechism,* is inserted in the concrete context of the history of salvation, which is marked by sin and by Redemption. If the structural selection of the *secunda tertiae* is in conformity with the whole preceding Catholic catechetical tradition by following the commandments of the Decalogue, their interpretation is concrete and dynamic and viewed in the Christian context of the Sermon on the Mount, the gifts of the Spirit, and the doctrine of the virtues.[7] The "ten words" find their authentic meaning in light of the grace of Christ, which precedes us and which renews us in the act of forgiveness, thus giving us the capability of realizing them in their fullness. The commandments are by no means simply limits to observe, but are rather open paths "involving a moral and spiritual journey towards perfection, at the heart of which is love" (*Veritatis splendor,* no. 15; compare *CCC,* nos. 2054–55). The primacy of grace definitively expresses itself in the new law of the Spirit, "the perfection here on earth of the divine law, natural and revealed" (*CCC,* no. 1965)—a work of Christ within us that comes to us by means of an interior call of charity.

At the same time, the new law, far from eliminating the moral exigencies of the commandments, confirms their permanent validi-

---

7. Cardinal J. Ratzinger, *"The Catechism of the Catholic Church,"* 482–83.

ty. The Gospel is not to be counterposed to morality, but assumes it in itself, bringing it to fulfillment and elevating the call, originally of a religious nature, conveyed by it. As we have seen already, a tradition of thought, relevant in Protestantism, but also influential in Catholic theology, tends to oppose the Gospel and morality. Avoiding any sort of contraposition, the *Catechism* proposes the authentically Catholic vision for which "God's free initiative demands *man's free response*" (*CCC*, no. 2002).

The primacy of grace and of the Gospel does not annul morality and does not render human effort superfluous, but rather encourages and sustains it. The Ten Commandments are not an Old Testament reality entirely surpassed by the Christian New Testament reality. They cannot be identified with that "Law" from which the grace of Christ has freed us. The "law" to which the Christian is no longer subjected is the economy of the Old Covenant in its *complexus* as it has been fulfilled in Christ and transformed on the Cross.[8] Instead the Decalogue, "revealed in its hidden virtualities" and opened to new exigencies of charity (see *CCC*, no. 1968), is fully confirmed in its validity. It is the first stage in the journey toward perfection. In light of the Sermon on the Mount, the Church pursues an actualized interpretation of the commandments that confirms their permanent validity, applying them to various circumstances (see *Veritatis splendor*, no. 27).

3. A DYNAMIC AND PERSONALIST PERSPECTIVE

As is immediately indicated by the title of the first section of the third part of the *Catechism*, the moral question is radically identified with the question of the vocation of the person: "Man's Vocation, Life in the Spirit." If the gift of grace (life in the Spirit) connotes the integral dimension of the call and makes its ultimate end precise (eternal beatitude in loving vision of God), the creatural datum of being "in the image and likeness of God" (*CCC*, nos. 1701–9) describes its beginning. In any event, as *Veritatis splendor* precisely defines, the moral question "is the echo of a call from God who is the origin and goal of man's life" (*Veritatis splendor*, no. 7). Before

8. Ibid., 482.

being a question of rules, it is, in fact, *"the question . . . about the full meaning of life,"* the aspiration for the absolute Good who attracts the person and who alone can satisfy the desire of the human heart.

The perspective of Christian morality that is placed on view by the *Catechism* is thus that of the dynamic realization of the person in reference to an ultimate end to which he is gratuitously called. Citing *Gaudium et spes* (no. 22), the *Catechism* affirms that "'Christ . . . in the very revelation of the mystery of the Father and of his love, makes man fully manifest to himself and brings to light his exalted vocation'" (*CCC*, no. 1701). In fact, the human person is "'the only creature on earth that God has willed for its own sake'" (*CCC*, no. 1703, citing *Gaudium et spes*, no. 24), and who from conception is destined for eternal beatitude. Such an aim, which begins with the gift of filial adoption in Christ, is not realized without the free consent of human action as a "perfection in charity which is holiness" (*CCC*, no. 1709).

From this, morally speaking, is derived the *primacy of the person* and of his final destination with respect to acts that are therefore seen as ways toward his end. The event of morality cannot be considered as a series of accomplishments isolated from precepts in relation to acts, but as a history of the growth of the person who edifies himself and disposes himself through his concrete choices, which are sustained by grace, toward the beatitude to which he is gratuitously called.

The struggle on the way to this ultimate end, besides strictly linking Christian morality to spirituality, at the same time characterizes it as a limitless journey toward the perfection of charity (*CCC*, no. 2013). On the one hand, rigorism, which does not distinguish between precepts and good counsel and which confers an equal degree of obligation to negative and positive precepts and to good counsel, is avoided; while on the other, commandments are not ends in themselves in their minimal basic demands, but constitute the first indispensable stage and the way for a growth in charity, which has the same divine perfection as an ideal. If negative precepts, by indicating behavior intrinsically contrary to charity, evoke a necessary conversion that is realized in us by grace, positive precepts and good counsel elicit a dynamic of progressive maturation in free response to a continual journey on earth that is sustained by the gift of the Spirit. It is positive precepts, in fact, that realize the increase of charity in the Christian with the collaboration of his freedom and by means of his acts.

4. A UNITARY PERSPECTIVE

It is now time to consider the object of the call directly, or that which gives meaning to Christian moral life, namely, holiness. The human individual, having been made in the image of God, was created in order to know, love, and serve God (*CCC*, nos. 356–58, 1721). He has been gratuitously called to participate in divine life, in the communion of love of the Most Holy Trinity. Holiness, which constitutes the goal of Christian moral life, thus consists of that perfection of charity that is realized in us by the Holy Spirit as a communication of divine, intratrinitarian love. Here the Catechism applies the great conciliar perspective of chapter five of *Lumen gentium* to morality, which is dedicated to the "vocation of the whole Church to holiness," explicitly mentioned in no. 2013. If everyone in the Church, and not just the few elect, are called by force of Baptism to holiness, it is in this perspective that the moral life of each Christian is to be considered.

The citation of Romans 8.28–30, which constitutes no. 2012 of the *Catechism,* underscores the unity of the plan of God who has, at all times, predestined us "to be conformed to the image of his Son, in order that he might be the first-born among many brethren." It is, indeed, "in union with his Savior that the disciple attains the perfection of charity which is holiness" (*CCC*, no. 1709). For all time there has existed in the project of God a unique end for man that is definitively illuminated in Christ, the Son of God incarnate. He is, in his humanity, the final, exemplary, and efficient cause of everything in the universe.[9] Christocentrism in morality means the assumption of

---

9. On this theological theme, one with great relevance for morality, one may consult the recent theological study—noteworthy for its synthetic character and clarity—of G. Biffi, *Approccio al cristocentrismo: Note storiche per un tema eterno* (Milan: 1994), esp. 66–71.

the Christological event, in its singularity, as the exemplary, normative, and insuperable form of Christian moral life.[10] It is in Christ, in his concrete humanity, that the moral journey of man and his call to be a "son in the Son" is placed into relief.

The vocation to holiness, even in its irreducible gratuitousness and superabundance, surprisingly corresponds to the human aspiration for happiness. The Beatitudes, which "express the vocation of the faithful" to reproduce in themselves the features of the face of Christ and of his charity (*CCC*, no. 1717), "respond to the natural desire for happiness" that is also of divine origin: "God has placed it in the human heart in order to draw man to the One who alone can fulfill it" (*CCC*, no. 1718).

Thus, the classical understanding of morality as a question of happiness, that is, of the true good and true ultimate end of man, is proposed in the Christian context of the Beatitudes. This understanding has characterized the great patristic tradition, in particular the Augustinian and Thomistic approaches, but was abandoned in the modern era.[11] In reality, there is no contraposition to an anthropology of the "glorification of God," but rather a fundamental integration that includes beatitude in a Christian manner. After all, the *Catechismus romanus* (also called "of the Council of Trent") had already stated that God, though "being able to force us to serve his glory as slaves without any perspective of reward," in reality "wished instead to found his honor and our happiness in a singular, admirable harmony" (no. 300).[12]

The response to the desire for happiness that man encounters in the Beatitudes is, in fact, at once real, surprising, and paradoxical. While the Beatitudes confirm and sustain the struggle for happiness

---

10. See Hans Urs von Balthasar, "Nine Propositions on Christian Ethics," in H. Schürmann, J. Ratzinger, and Hans Urs von Balthasar, *Principles of Christian Morals* (San Francisco: Ignatius Press, 1986), 77–102. See also A. Scola, "Christologie et morale," *Nouvelle Revue Théologique* 109 (1987): 382–410.

11. In this regard one may cite the already noted works of G. Abbà, *Felicitá*, 12–75, and M. Rhonheimer, *La prospettiva*, 31–85; in addition, see S. Pinckaers, *L'Evangile et la morale* (Fribourg: 1990), 103–16.

12. L. Andrianopoli, *"Il Catechismo romano" commentato: Con note di aggiornamento teologico-pastorale* (Milan: 1983), 315.

that is at the heart of each action and each human undertaking, they widen it beyond every natural expectation and show it to be obscurely anticipated in poverty, affliction, and persecution. They thus show that only through the Cross does the fulfillment of the desire for happiness come to term (*CCC*, no. 2015). It is thus to be expected and received as a gift from the hands of the Father, and not to be earned as a conquest through the merits acquired from one's own works (*CCC*, nos. 2007ff.).

Holiness, which is identified by the *Catechism* as a universal vocation and as a response to the desire for happiness, is thus also presented as the truth of the human person. It is not a question of an arbitrary exceptionality without any relationship with the inherent exigencies of the heart. On the contrary, as it has been incisively affirmed: "[T]he saint is not a superman; the saint is a true man. The saint is a true man because he adheres to God and thus to the ideal for which his heart has been patterned and his destiny constituted."[13] It is a genuine human experience of the unity of the "I" in fondness for Christ and in a never abandoned struggle for the ideal.

5. THE ECCLESIAL DIMENSION OF THE VOCATION TO HOLINESS

"All men are called to the same end: God himself" (*CCC*, no. 1878). They must establish between themselves that fraternity which in some way reflects the union of the divine Persons. The moral appeal is, thus, a call to communality in forming the Mystical Body of Christ in which a vital exchange between the Head and the members, and among the members themselves, is constant. Insofar as it is a call to holiness, the moral dimension is realized in the Church. It is, in fact, the Church that is "holy" insofar as she is the Bride of Christ, who has purified her with his blood and has filled her with the gift of the Spirit for the glory of God (*CCC*, no. 823). Holiness, which is first of all given to the Church, is then communicated by her to individual faithful members through the sacraments, which see to it that they develop in life right up to the perfection of charity. The first

13. L. Giussani, *Moralitá: Memoria e desiderio*, 2nd ed. (Milan: 1991), 41.

sign of holiness is precisely the "communion of the saints," which flows out from the "communion with the holy gifts" (*CCC*, nos. 946–59).

In this perspective, the *Catechism* restores the relevance of the ecclesial dimension for morality that goes well beyond the traditional chapter on obedience to the magisterium to which it has often been reduced.[14] Before treating the teaching of pastors, it speaks, in fact, of the life of the Church who is *Mater et Magistra* for the moral journey of Christians (*CCC*, nos. 2030–31). She is a mother who generates life through the sacraments and an abode that offers shelter and favors growth—an environment in which the witness of brothers, particularly that of the saints, creates a favorable atmosphere for moral maturation. Before being a structure and an institution guaranteed in its essential elements, the Church is, thus, a life. And the growth of everyone in the vocation to holiness happens, as in every concrete human experience of education, above all *through life*, that is, by osmosis. "From the Church," the Christian in fact "learns the *example of holiness* and recognizes its model and source in the all-holy Virgin Mary; he discerns it in the authentic witness of those who live it; he discovers it in the spiritual tradition and long history of the saints who have gone before him and whom the liturgy celebrates in the rhythms of the sanctoral cycle" (*CCC*, no. 2030).

At the same time, the moral life of Christians, as a life of the members of the Body of Christ animated by the Spirit, contributes to the *edification of the Church* (*CCC*, no. 2045). By means of the holiness of her faithful members, the Church grows, develops, and expands. Moral action in which human freedom corresponds to the gift of the Spirit serves to render more evident, by means of charity, the Church's splendor of holiness. It favors evangelization and, at the same time, hastens the coming of the Kingdom of God, the full realization of the goal to which we are summoned.

CONCLUSION

The perspective adopted by the *Catechism* for framing the themes of fundamental morality thus offers an adequate base for the theo-

14. See above, Chapter Six.

logical renewal of this discipline. The dynamics of the "vocation to holiness" permit the rooting of Christian morality in dogmatics, by exalting the primacy of the grace of Christ and the work of the Holy Spirit; it opens up the horizon for an itinerary of perfection to the glory of God the Father, thus intimately linking the ethical dimension to spirituality. At the same time, by overcoming the limitations of legalistic conceptions, it allows for a discussion of the human struggle for happiness in the specific perspective of the moral journey, which is that of the maturation of the human subject in communion with God and the brethren. By means of his choices, the human person, in fact, is called to grow in charity in correspondence with the action of the Spirit, right up to becoming capable of seeing God, loving him perfectly, and enjoying an eternity with him.

∝

CHAPTER EIGHT

Moral Conscience and "Communio"

TOWARD A RESPONSE TO THE CHALLENGE
OF ETHICAL PLURALISM

*W*hat is the relation between Christian moral conscience and ecclesial *communio?* This question itself sounds unusual because we usually pose a more limited question in its stead, namely, that in regard to the rights or obligations of conscience vis-à-vis the ecclesiastical magisterium.[1] As long as we remain in the narrow terms of such a contraposition, however, it is rather difficult for us to find a way out of the extrinsicism in terms of which the concept of conscience is generally articulated. Above all, it would seem that such a framework precludes not only an adequate *prise de conscience* of the ecclesiological dimensions of the crisis in which morality now finds itself, but also the possibility of developing theologically, then implementing, a way out from this crisis. To pose the question of the relation between moral conscience and *communio* is thus to embark on the task of thinking out the ecclesial form of Christian moral conscience.

I. ETHICAL PLURALISM IN THE CHURCH: CONSCIENCE
SUBTRACTS FROM "COMMUNIO"

It would seem to me that, for contemporary moral theology, the truly central question has become that of the ethical *pluralism* that

---

1. See my article, "Coscienza, libertà e Magistero," *La Scuola Cattolica* 120 (1992): 152–71, which has abundant bibliographical references to this theme.

lies at the heart of the Church. This question is not merely one of fact due to the lack of correspondence between profession of faith and concrete behavior. There is really nothing new here. Rather, we find ourselves facing the question of vindicating the legitimacy of following different moral norms, all in the name of personal conscience.

This crisis took on acute proportions as a reaction to *Humanae vitae* and is still in evidence today, more than twenty-five years later, in the defense of the right on the part of conscience not to follow the teaching of the magisterium.[2] From a particular question of sexual morality, a general thesis regarding the status of moral truth has evolved. Since it is a truth that is accessible to reason, at least at the level of "operative" normativeness, this general thesis ought to be autonomously established by the individual rational subject without recourse to divine assistance for any particular application by the magisterium. The teaching of pastors would be binding only in view of the united public witness of the ecclesial community on themes like peace, social justice, and ecology, but not on questions of private morality, as, for instance, in the sphere of sexuality. In sum, the value of salvation for "categorical" moral questions relative to "inframundane" behavior is negated; only "transcendental" attitudes are considered to be relevant.[3]

Moral conscience is thus removed from ecclesial *communio* and claims an autonomy in judgment. Here *communio* exists without a communion of judgment and without the evidence of choices and historical works, and limits itself to communion in the faith and in the proclamation of the *kérygma*. Accordingly, it is not conscious of

2. See F. Böckle, *"Humanae vitae als Prüfstein des wahren Glaubens? Zur kirchen-politischen Dimension moraltheologischer Fragen,"* *Stimmen der Zeit* 115 (1990): 3–16; and Ph. Schmitz, *"Ein Glaube—kontroverse Gewissensentscheidungen,"* in *Gewissen. Aspekte eine vieldiskutierten Sachverhaltes,* ed. J. Horstmann (Lath. Ak. Schwerte: 1983), 60–76.

3. For these theses, see the contributions of B. Fraling, "Hypertropie lehramtlicher Autorität in Dingen der Moral," and P. Hünermann, "Die Kompetenz des Lehramtes in Fragen der Sitte," in *Lehramt und Sexualmoral,* ed. P. Hünermann (Dusseldorf: 1990), 95–129 and 130–56. For the same, see J. Fuchs, "Moral Truth-Truth of Salvation," in his *Christian Ethics in a Secularized Society* (Washington, D.C.: Geargetown University Press, 1992), 59–78.

morality except at the level of common transcendental intentionality or in view of public, outward discipline. What is at work here
is the intrinsic link between *"fides et mores"* that has always been
upheld by Catholic doctrinal tradition in line with the words of
Jesus: "It is not he who says: Lord, Lord, who will enter into the
kingdom of heaven, but he who does the will of my Father who is in
heaven" (Mt 7.21). That the Gospel is not solely a promise without
any tie to the commandments was defined by the Council of Trent
(DS 1570, 1501). Vatican Council II has also repeated this claim, calling
the Gospel "the source of all saving truth and moral teaching" (*Dei
Verbum,* 7). It is the Gospel that has been entrusted to the Apostles
and to their successors in the very act of the Teacher's conferral of
the original missionary mandate: "Go, therefore, and instruct all
nations, baptizing them in the name of the Father and of the Son,
and of the Holy Spirit, *teaching them to observe all that I have commanded"* (Mt 28.19–20; emphasis mine).

To detach the witness of faith from the observance of determinate precepts is to place oneself in contradiction to the dynamics of
the Incarnation, which brings salvation not only to the spirit, but to
the whole man in the concreteness of his own choices. Saint
Ambrose expressed this bond between faith and works in this way:
"And, what is more, you have given witness not only by word, but
also with works. That man is, in fact, a more authoritative and credi-
ble witness; it is he 'who acknowledges Jesus Christ come in the
flesh' [1 Jn 4.2], precisely by observing the norms of the gospel. On
the other hand, he who hears and does not do denies Christ. Even if
he confesses him in words, he denies him in deed. . . . A witness,
therefore, is he who above all attests to the precepts of the Lord
Jesus with the evidence of deeds."[4] In the same way, Saint Thomas
Aquinas resolves the question whether in the new law, which is the
law of the spirit, there have to be precepts regarding outward deeds.
He bases his affirmative answer on the central truth of the Christian
message: "The Word is made flesh" (Jn 1.44).[5] The God of the Law,

4. Saint Ambrose, *Commento al Salmo 118,* Disc. XX, 47–50: CSEL 62, 467–69.
5. See Saint Thomas Aquinas, *Summa Theologiae,* I–II, q. 108, a. 1.

we could say, does not remain in the transcendental and formal dimensions of intentionality, but enters into the categorical in order to save the concrete flesh of human action. To place all this into question by denying the relevance of determinate moral norms for salvation entails an attack at the heart of the Christian message. John Paul II has clearly stated that "the negation of moral truth 'renders vain the Cross of Christ' [see 1 Cor 1.17]. Having become Incarnate, the Word has fully entered into our day-to-day existence and finds expression in concrete human acts; having died for our sins, He has recreated us to our original holiness, which has to express itself in our daily activity in this world."[6]

It has to be frankly admitted that the autonomous way of understanding Christian moral conscience represents a reaction to post-Tridentine manualistic approaches, which have greatly dominated seminary instruction and Catholic moral preaching until Vatican Council II, and which have been diffident toward conscience, denying it any interpretive role in the name of the absoluteness of the law. In a "legalistic" understanding of morality, the moral law is interpreted on the model of positive human law as expressive of the will of a legislator in which minimalist technique is generally applied to a case with a view to defending, as far as possible, the "rights of conscience."[7] In this perspective, conscience has a merely mechanical role applicable to the individual case. In order to guarantee ecclesiastical unity, itself conceived in juridical and outward terms, an ideal of conscience is proposed that tends to sacrifice it to outward obedience. On the other hand, a defense of freedom of conscience leads to an opposition to the excessive meddlesomeness of ecclesiastical law. Here also conscience ultimately remains external to ecclesial *communio*. The relation between the two elements is mediated by a law that is understood as an expression of the will of authority. Given this extrinsicism, which of its nature favors conflicts, one cannot but express oneself in forms of submission, com-

---

6. John Paul II, *Allocuzione ad un Convegno di Teologia Morale* (12 November 1988).

7. See G. Grisez, "Legalism, Moral Truth, and Pastoral Practice," in *The Catholic Priest as Moral Teacher and Guide,* ed. T. J. Herron (San Francisco: Ignatius Press, 1990), 97–113.

promise, and artful exception. One could also say that the autonomous conception of contemporary morality cannot but follow without really overcoming its horizon, namely, the extrinsicist path of post-Tridentine manualistic approaches: it does not put the antinomic character found in principle between conscience and *communio* under discussion, but merely eliminates *communio* from the horizon of conscience.

2. CONSCIENCE AND VOCATION

A confirmation of this interpretation is found in the sixth thesis on Christian ethics of Hans Urs von Balthasar,[8] in which the law is elevated to an abstract absolute that takes the place of the living God and then ends, by dialectical necessity, with establishing "the human subject as his own legislator, as an idealized, autonomous subject who imposes limitations on himself in order to reach perfection."

Moral conscience is understood rather as the scene of a call, of an original vocation of the Good par excellence, God *"qui interius docet, inquantum huiusmodi lumen animae infundit."*[9] One discovers here the great Augustinian tradition concerning moral conscience that interprets it as the "voice of God," "the place in which no other man can enter, where man is alone with himself and where you are alone before God."[10] It is, as Saint Bonaventure says, *"sicut praeco Dei,"* the herald of God who does not speak or command on his own authority, but in the name of God; for this reason, it has the power to oblige.[11] The underscoring of the profound ontological dimension of conscience, itself placed into relief by this tradition, was taken up in particular by Pius XII and Vatican Council II in *Gaudium et spes,* no. 16: "Conscience is the most secret core and sanc-

---

8. Hans Urs von Balthasar, "Nine Propositions on Christian Ethics," in J. Ratzinger, H. Schürmann, and H. U. von Balthasar, *Principles of Christian Morality* (San Francisco: Ignatius Press, 1981), 77–102.

9. Saint Thomas Aquinas, *De Anima,* q. un., a. 5, ad 6; cited by H. Balthasar, in "Nine Propositions on Christian Ethics," 74.

10. Saint Augustine, *Enarr. in Ps. 54:9:* PL, 36, 635; see J. Stelzenberger, *Conscientia bei Augustinus* (Paderborn: 1959).

11. Saint Bonaventure, *Il Sentent.,* d. 39, a. 1, q. 3 (II, 907b).

tuary of a man. There he is alone with God whose voice echoes in his depths."[12]

In regard to the possibility of an erroneous conscience, the Thomist tradition has detailed the intellectual nature of conscience, which is considered rather as a judgment applying knowledge to some particular act.[13] The relation of conscience as a judgment with truth, indeed with a truth that precedes it and from which it derives its obliging force, is thus highlighted.[14] It is a question of the truth of those first principles in the moral order that are naturally grasped by *synderesis* (that is, the *"scintilla conscientiae"*), that reflects the creatural image.[15] At the same time, the noninfallible, human character of the act of judgment of conscience is thus revealed: it is possible that it does not conform to the truth. Accordingly, the need for some *habitus* that might perfect reason such that it can conform to truth is seen. Not only will *synderesis* be necessary, but also moral knowledge and prudence, with links to moral virtue. In this way, the formation of conscience can be understood as a pedagogy that permits a person to acquire these *habitus* in such a way as to be personally able to effect a judgment of true conscience.

From etymological considerations regarding the supposed derivation of *"cumscientia"* using *"cum scire"* (*"cum alio scire,"* *"quasi simul scire"*) as a starting point,[16] Aquinas characterizes the judgment of

12. *Gaudium et spes,* no. 16, recalls the radio message of Pius XII, "De conscientia christiana iuvenibus recte efforrmanda," of 23 March 1952, AAS 44 (1952): 271; for more on this, see K. Golser, "Das Gewissen als 'verborgenste Mitte in Menschen,'" in *Grundlagen und Probleme der heutigen Moraltheologie,* ed. W. Ernst (Leipzig: 1989), 113–37.

13. Saint Thomas Aquinas, *De Veritate,* q. 17, a. 2.

14. See J. Ratzinger, *La Chiesa. Una comunità sempre in cammino* (Alba: Paoline, 1991), chap. 6, "Coscienza e verità", 113–37.

15. For a discussion of the theological foundation of the natural law in Saint Thomas, see A. Scola, *La fondazione teologica della legge naturale dello Scriptum super Sententiis di San Tommaso d'Aquino* (Freiburg: Univ. Freiburg Schweiz, 1982).

16. Saint Thomas Aquinas, *Summa theologiae,* I. q. 79, a. 13; *De Veritate,* q. 17, a. 1. Subsequent to the publication of my "Kirchlichkeit un Moraltheologie: Anregungen zu einer Re-dimensionierung der Moral," in *Internazionale Katholische Zeitschrift Communio* 29 (1991): 62–81, a small, but interesting debate developed in the same review regarding the etymology of the term "conscience" and its communion character (see D. van Nes, 286, and G. Ibscher, 383–84). [Translator's note: A translation of this article (Chapter Six of this book), entitled "Moral Theology and Ecclesial Sense,"

conscience as a *knowing together* with a truth that is of universal character and therefore common. Conscience thus at one and the same time expresses an opening to truth and to others. It is communion in truth with those who seek the Good. The judgment of conscience, which expresses subjectivity at its most intimate and personal level, is therefore always at the same time capable of universalization insofar as it is rooted in all that is objective and common in us. In this sense, R. Spaemann can say that conscience "leads man beyond himself. . . . In order to be sure not to deceive himself, he must live in a continual exchange *with others* regarding the good and the just in the community of moral life."[17] In a similar fashion, the ancient philosopher Heraclitus writes in his second fragment that "one must therefore follow all that is universal." The communion dimension is not an extrinsic or accessory instance with respect to the search for truth that animates moral conscience: it is rather intrinsic and constitutive of it.

Nonetheless, it must be asked how we can explain the relationship between personal conscience and the communion dimension not as a major alienation, but as a safeguarding of the heteronomy of the inner core that constitutes the very dignity of the person. Here we see the question of the relationship between the letter and the spirit in Christian morality.

3. LETTER AND SPIRIT IN CHRISTIAN MORAL LIFE

What form does the ecclesial element assume for Christian conscience? Do we find ourselves univocally on the side of the "letter"

---

appeared in the American *Communio* 20 (1992): 67–93.] Independently of the validity of the etymology of *conscientia* as adopted by Thomas, the philosophical intuition that has given rise to the link between conscience and truth remains valid and, to my mind, also opens up avenues for an immanent communion reference for conscience which can be subject to a phenomenological examination. At any rate, far from wishing to found the theological argumentation on a debatable medieval etymology, it seems to me that the basis for understanding the intrinsic link between conscience and *"communio"* is given—as I shall attempt to demonstrate—in the indwelling of the Holy Spirit, which is at the same time the new law present to the interiority of the believer and the claim that bonds him to ecclesial communion.

17. R. Spaemann, *Moralische Grundbegriffe* (Munich: 1983), 75.

or do we also enter into the moment of the "spirit"? We find ourselves before a theologically dense and extremely delicate point because the physiognomy of Christian morality depends on it. How are we to interpret the "novelty" of the Gospel, the gift of the Spirit in relation to the written law? Here, with the link between conscience and the Church established, we also see the relation between precepts and the new law of love, between institution and charismatic inspiration, between the Old and the New Testaments. An inadequate resolution can make Christian morality fall into a legalism of the Old Testament type, which annuls that newness brought about by the law of the Spirit of life (see Rom 8.2), or project it into an arbitrary anomie without any point of reference and without any recognition that the "full observance of the law is love" (Rom 13.10).

Saint Augustine forcefully rejects the insufficient character of the "letter" of the law: "We are helped to fulfill justice not because God has given us a law rich in good and holy precepts, but because our will itself, without which we cannot accomplish the good, is aided and elevated through the gift of the spirit of grace."[18] The newness of the Gospel is not on the side of the letter. Indeed, even the letter of the Gospel "could kill" if it were not for the interior grace of faith that saves. Now with the gift of grace within us, we are able to love those written precepts outside of us that the law makes us fear.[19] These "are the precepts of justice that we are also obliged to observe."

Saint Thomas Aquinas recalls this doctrine in his splendid treatise on the new law.[20] The primary characteristic element of the new law is not the Gospel as a written text (as the Franciscan School of Alexander of Hales maintained), but the grace of the Holy Spirit that is given to us through faith in Jesus Christ. The primary point of reference of Christian conscience is thus the inner presence of the

18. Saint Augustine, *De spiritu et littera* XII, 20 (Italian edition: ed. S. Iodice, *Lo spirito e la lettera* [Naples: 1979]).

19. Ibid., XIX, 32.

20. Saint Thomas Aquinas, *Summa theologiae,* I–II, qq. 106–8. For a study on the dependence of the Thomist treatise on Augustinian thought, see I. Biffi, *"L'auctoritas* di sant'Agostino nella questioni sulla legge nuova della *Summa Theologiae* di san Tommaso d'Aquino," *La Scuola Cattolica* 115 (1987): 220–48.

Spirit that speaks "from within" as a teacher *(Magister interior)*, as a listening, in the Spirit of Jesus, of he "who is maximally wise and friendly." Nevertheless, contrary to any spiritualism of the Joachim type, which also concerns the earthly regiment of the new law, there remains the necessity of referring oneself to the written Gospel (the visible and ecclesial sacramental economy), which is an external and secondary, but not superfluous, element. In fact, only Jesus has received the Spirit in its fullness; to us it is given in moderation,[21] thus entailing the necessity of external instruction. The essential structural elements of the link between conscience and Church in the regiment of the new law thus seem clear: the primacy of inner inspiration on the part of the Spirit, but also the necessary verification and outward instruction on the part of the Church in its disciplinary, magisterial, and sacramental elements. The presence of the Spirit also permits the interiorization of this outward dimension: it no longer speaks to Christian conscience "from without," but is viewed rather with docility of faith as an aid to personal growth.

It seems, however, that not everything has yet been said, because the ecclesial element cannot enter only the "secondary and outward" factor of the new law. In his commentary on the Letter to the Romans, the Angelic Doctor comes to a more intimate understanding of the communion dimension proper to Christian moral conscience.[22] *Concordance* is one of the essential dimensions of ecclesial *caritas*. That there be disagreement on speculative questions does not deny concordance understood as friendship in charity. The case of a judgment on things to do is instead quite different: here dissent is opposed to friendship and destroys ecclesial concordance insofar as it entails a discordance of will, a rupture of the unity of hearts that is essential for the Church. Surprisingly, based on this necessary unity on moral questions, Saint Thomas argues that even showing dissent on faith destroys ecclesial unity: the faith is, in fact, not only a

21. See Saint Thomas Aquinas, *Super Ep. ad Romanos*, chap. XII, lect. I., no. 971 (Turin: Marietti, 1953).

22. Saint Thomas Aquinas, *Super Ep. ad Romanos*, chap. XII, lect. III, nos. 1005–6. On the theme of the Church on the *lex nova*, see J. Mahoney, *Seeking the Spirit: Essays in Moral and Pastoral Theology* (London: 1981), esp. 63–117, and S. Pinckaers, "L'Eglise dans la loi nouvelle: Esprit et institution," *Nova et Vetera* 4 (1987): 246–62.

speculative fact (it "works through charity," according to Gal 5.6). To dissent in matters of faith implies an opposition in charity. Thus, to overcome dissent in moral judgment the apostle recommends to his hearers: "Do not be wise in your own estimation" (Rom 12.16). Aquinas adds: "thus only he who seems to you to be so should be judged prudent." In this way, ecclesial concordance, the *communio* of hearts effected by the Spirit, becomes an ecclesial modality of discernment of moral judgment, not only an external, but also an internal, dimension of verification.

4. THE COMMUNION FORM OF "LISTENING"

Modern sensibility has placed the theme of the subject, and thus that of conscience, at the center of philosophical and theological attention. Confronted with the contemporary claims of an autonomous and foundational subjectivity, Saint Ignatius of Loyola in his *Exercises* expounds a rigorously Catholic definition of the subject at the core of the theological relations that connote its genesis. In his *Regulae ad sentiendum cum Ecclesia*,[23] the great Spanish saint proposes a series of practical indications for the formation of an ecclesial perceiving *(sentire cum Ecclesia)*, which are, however, also an expression of a dense theology of the Spirit and the Church in relation to subjective experience.

The mature Christian subject is born, according to Ignatius, from the election in which he responds with his whole self, without reservation, to the call of God, which is known through the hearing of the Spirit. The relation with the Spirit nonetheless enjoys an internal ecclesial dimension that is contrary to any individualistic tendency represented in Ignatius's time by the current of the *alumbrados*. Two titles are used to characterize the Church in the *Regulae:* that of Bride and that of Mother.

In relation to Christ, the Church is a *Spouse* with an immediate connection with the Spirit that is given to her so that she can authentically interpret the will of Christ the Spouse, his commandments,

---

23. For an original philosophical interpretation of the *Regulae,* see G. Fessard, *La dialectique des "Exercises Spirituels" de Saint Ignace de Loyola,* vol. 2 of *Fondement-Péché-Orthodoxie* (Paris: 1966), 167–222.

and his promptings. For Ignatius, therefore, the Spirit is given, first of all, to the Church who as a person stands before God in a stance of total acceptance and availability. The concrete figure of the Church, her full realization, is Mary as contemplated in the scene of the Annunciation. She receives the Spirit with a total openness that is itself made possible by an attitude of *vergüenza* or reverential fear for a gift against which one dreads giving offense. This, then, is a first indication: it is only in communion with the Church in her Marian form that Christian conscience partakes of the Spirit and can discern the will of the Spouse; any presumptuous autonomy is excluded in principle.

In second place, the Church is our *Mother* who generates us in the history of the new life of the sons of God. In this image, the immediate and internal connection with the Spirit of truth is no longer grasped, but rather a temporal and outward relation with teachings, provisions, and ecclesial institutions. In his Rule XIII, Ignatius affirms in a paradoxical way that "in order to think correctly in any matter it is necessary that one always be ready to hold that which one sees as white to be in fact black if the hierarchical Church says so. We believe in fact that the Spirit which governs us and directs us toward the salvation of our souls is in fact the same in Christ our Lord, who is *the* Spouse, and the same in the Church who is *his* Spouse." The relation with the Spirit passes through the historical mediation of the hierarchical Church, which is the Spouse of Christ who precedes me and generates me as a Christian. What is requested is no less than an intellectual conversion, a *metanoia* that consists in a willingness to place to the side the apparent evidence of our judgment (that which "I see" as white) in order to open myself up to the reality ("which is" black) as determined by ecclesial judgment. In analogy with Baptism, the birth of a Christian subject has a paschal character of death and resurrection; it is a losing of oneself in order to find oneself in which reason does not deny itself, but is ready to test its immediate beliefs. In truth, here we are not denying the capacity of the human spirit to accept truth, but we are recognizing the historical character of reason in its path of openness to the truth that precedes and transcends it. This means recognizing its creatureliness, the many affective conditions surrounding it, personal and communal sinfulness as factors within which the exercise of reason and knowledge of the truth, above all, moral truth, are carried out. The education of the affections necessarily involves the mediation of a community.

In this sense, Christian conscience is "ecclesial" conscience: it arises from a personal response to a common vocation *(ek-klesia)*, to a departing from oneself for an opening of oneself toward the truth that shines in Christ. It begins with a conversion: I cease to be an autonomous subject that has its own proper consistency, but enter into that new subject which is Christ, whose historical space is ecclesial *communio*.[24] Far from eliminating the primacy of the personal relation with the Spirit, which would reduce conscience to a passive obedience to the letter of the law, this framing of the question opens conscience up to a communion in which the spirit of the law is revealed. One thus grasps the methodological implication of the famous Augustinian affirmation: "We have the Spirit to the degree in which we love the Church."[25]

5. THE COMMUNION METHOD IN THE FORMATION OF MORAL CONSCIENCE

The link between conscience and *communio* is thus intrinsic and dynamic. What has been gained so far allows us to introduce the question of the formation of conscience, which is a rather neglected topic in contemporary theological moral reflection.[26] Already some of the presuppositions for an authentic formation of conscience have been hinted at: the recognition of the precedence of truth vis-à-vis the judgment of conscience, the ineliminable interiority of the call of morality, the predisposition in a subject to virtuous attitudes,

24. See J. Ratzinger, "Teologia e Chiesa," *Communio* [Italian ed.] 87 (1986): 92–111; English translation, "The Ecclesiology of the Second Vatican Council," *Communio* 13 (1986): 239–52.

25. Saint Augustine, *Commentary on the First Letter of St. John*, VI.10.

26. For a more detailed discussion of this, see my *Morale: Tra crisi e rinnovamento. Gli assoluti morali, l'opzione fodamentale, la formazione della coscienza* (Milan: Ares, 1993), chap. 4, 81–106.

the docility and openness to whomever might be our teacher on the road to morality, and the preparation for an encounter with truth in communion with those who sincerely seek it.[27]

Saint Augustine, for whom the Church is a *"morum regula,"* points to the way of "communion" as the method of moral growth: "He who wishes to live has where to live and has from which to live. One approaches, believes, enters into the body, and participates in the life. One does not escape union with the other members."[28] The realization of the way of formation of conscience certainly has some objective elements that are always assured by the sacramental character of the Church, but it also needs an adequate pedagogy which entails, as its condition, the authenticity of both communion reality and personal conscience. It seems to me that two theses are sufficient to express the conditions of this relation of formation.

1. *The person is born in "communio."* To be a person in the theological sense means to receive "in Christ" both a call and a task in the history of salvation.[29] This is the principle of Christian conscience that has its origins in the vocation of the Creator and Redeemer—a vocation that initially shines in the seal of the creaturely image and, then, definitively in the human face of the Son, the uncreated and perfect Image of the Father. Ecclesial *communio* is the place where the individual grasps his vocation in a dialogue with God and his brothers, the place where he is thus "personalized." Romano Guardini says that, for the individual, participation in communion is the "living presupposition for personal perfection: it is the way toward personality."[30] One becomes a Christian personality with a moral consciousness of one's proper task and of the steps adequate to gain it only to the degree that one is a member of the Church, to the degree that the Church consciously lives in him. The verification of *communio* (entailing all that may be not only visible and disciplinary,

---

27. For a stimulating and original contribution on this theme, see P. J. Wadell, *Friendship and the Moral Life* (Notre Dame, Ind.: University of Notre Dame Press, 1989).

28. Saint Augustine, *Commentary on the Gospel of John,* XXVI, 13.

29. Cf. Hans Urs von Balthasar, *Teodrammatica* (Milan: 1983), vol. 3, 191–206; English translation, *Theo-Drama* (San Francisco: Ignatius Press, 1992), 149–63.

30. R. Guardini, *La realtà della Chiesa* (Brescia: 1973), 63.

but also existential and familial) is the criterion for discerning the value of internal inspiration. But, more profoundly, Christian conscience is a call to assume an internal, ecclesial form in conformity with a Marian disponability to the Spirit.

2. *"Communio" is for persons.* If a person is not a person outside of *communio,* it is at the same time true that communal reality is authentic *communio* only as a *"communio personarum."*[31] There is no ecclesial communion without a respect and appreciation for every personal gift. As Balthasar puts it: "Charisms are not conferred to individuals through the mediation of the Church, but are rather given by God (Rom 12.3), by the glorified Christ (Eph 3.8–11), in view of the Church. An individual receives the absolute singularity of God and Christ as a gift a singularity that cannot be deduced from the community, nor conjectured in it, even though the community can count on this singularity as something that enriches it and has been thought out for it. Therefore, the individual, as someone entrusted by God with a special gift, is inserted into the community at his depths and is bound to it by a greater generosity."[32] In this sense, the Church can never bypass personal conscience, nor can it ever substitute for it. Individual ecclesial communities, far from being able to dispense with conscience in the name of obedience, must rather conceive themselves as a pedagogy for the growth of conscience and as a mystagogy to the personal and irreplaceable link of the person with the Spirit who speaks to it from within. The ideal to aim for will be not so much an outward conformity with precepts as the formation of mature personalities who know how to express themselves visibly in works, and in the unity of faith and charity in the dynamics of communion.

31. For a study of *"communio personarum"* as an ecclesiological category in the thought of K. Wojtyla (John Paul II), see my "La Chiesa come 'communio personarum' e la *Redemptor Hominis,*" *Synesis* 6, nos. 1–2 (1989): 143–63.

32. Hans Urs von Balthasar, *Teodrammatica* (Milan: 1982), vol. 2, 389; English translation, *Theo-Drama,* vol. 2 (San Francisco: Ignatius Press, 1990).

Bibliography

∞

AA. VV (= Various Authors). *Gesù Cristo, legge vivente e personale della Santa Chiesa.* Edited by G. Borgonovo. Casale Monferrato: Piemme, 1996.

AA. VV. *La virtù e il bene dell'uomo. Il pensiero tomista nella teologia post-moderna.* Edited by E. Kaczynski and F. Compagnoni. Bologna: EDB, 1993.

AA. VV. *Moraltheologie im Abseits? Antwort auf die Enzyklika "Veritatis splendor."* Edited by D. Mieth. Freiburg—Basel—Vienna: Herder, 1994.

AA. VV. *Understanding "Veritatis splendor."* Edited by J. Wilkins. London: SPCK, 1994.

AA. VV. *The Splendor of Accuracy: An Examination of the Assertions Made by "Veritatis splendor."* Edited by J. Selling and J. Janssens. Kampen, The Netherlands, and Grand Rapids, Mich.: Kok Pharos/Eerdmans, 1994.

AA. VV. *"Veritatis splendor" and the Renewal of Moral Theology.* Edited by J. A. Dinoia and R. Cessario. Chicago: Midwest Theological Forum, 1999.

AA. VV. *Virtue and Medicine: Explorations in the Character of Medicine.* Edited by E.E. Shelp. Dordrecht, The Netherlands—Boston, Mass.—Lancaster, U.K.: D. Reidel.

Abbá, G. *Felicità, vita buona e virtù: Saggio di filosofia morale.* Rome: LAS, 1989.

———. *Lex et virtus: Studi sull'evoluzione della dottrina morale di san Tommaso d'Aquino.* Rome: LAS, 1983.

———. *Quale impostazione per la filosofia morale? Ricerche di filosofia morale—1.* Rome: LAS, 1996.

———. *"Una filosofia morale per l'educazione alla vita buona." Salesianum* 53 (1991): 273–314.

Ambrose, Saint. *Expositio in psalmum CXVIII.* CSEL 62.

Anderson, C. *"Veritatis splendor* and the New Evangelization." *Anthropotes* 10, no. 1 (1994): 61–73.

Andrianopoli, L. *"Il Catechismo romano"* commentato: Con note di aggiornamento teologico-pastorale.* Milan: Ares, 1983.

Angelini, G. *Le virtù e la fede.* Milan: Glossa, 1994.

Ansaldo, A. *El primer principio del obrar moral y las normas morales específicas el el pensamiento de G. Grisez y J. Finnis.* Rome: Pontificia Università Lateranense, 1990.

Anscombe, G. E. M. *Intention.* 2nd ed. Oxford: Blackwell, 1963.

———. "Modern Moral Philosophy." *Philosophy* 33 (1958): 1–19.

Aristotle. *Ethica Nicomachea.* Edited by L. Bywater. Oxford: Oxford University Press, 1979.

———. *The Nicomachean Ethics.* Translated by H. Rackham. Cambridge, Mass.: Harvard University Press, 1958.

Augustine, Saint. *De Civitate Dei.* CCSL 48.

———. *De moribus ecclesiae catholicae.* Paris: Ed. Benedictine, 1949.

———. *De sermone Domini in monte.* CCSL 35.

———. *De Spiritu et littera.* CSEL 60.

———. *De Trinitate.* CCSL 50.

———. *Enarrationes In Psalmos.* CCSL 39–40.

———. *In Ioannis Evangelium Tractatus.* CCSL 36.

———. *Tractatus in epistolam Ioannis I.* SC 75.

Babini, E. *L'antropologia teologica di Hans Urs von Balthasar.* Milan: Jaca Book, 1988.

Balthasar, H. U., von. *Cordula ovverosia il caso serio.* Brescia: Queriniana, 1968.

———. *Elucidations.* London: Society for Promoting Christian Knowledge, 1975.

———. *The Glory of the Lord: A Theological Aesthestics,* vol. 7 of *Theology: The New Covenant.* San Francisco: Ignatius Press, 1989.

———. "Homo creatus est." In *Saggi teologici,* vol. 5. Brescia: Morcelliana, 1991.

———. *Love Alone.* New York: Herder & Herder, 1969.

———. "Nine Propositions on Christian Ethics." In J. Ratzinger, H. Schürmann, and H. U. von Balthasar, *Principles of Christian Morality,* pp. 77–102. San Francisco: Ignatius Press, 1981.

———. *The Persons of the Drama: Man in God,* vol. 2 of *Theodrama.* San Francisco: Ignatius Press, 1985.

———. *The Truth Is Symphonic: Aspects of Christian Pluralism.* San Francisco: Ignatius Press, 1987.

Bernard, C. A. *Vie morale et croissance dans le Christ.* Rome: PUG, 1973.

Bevenot, M. "Faith and Morals in Vatican I and the Council of Trent." *Heythrop Journal* 3 (1962): 15–30.

Biffi, G. *Alla destra del Padre: Nuova sintesi di teologia sistematica.* Milan: Vita e Pensiero, 1970.

———. *Approccio al cristocentrismo: Note storiche per un tema eterno.* Milan: Jaca Book, 1994.

———. *Tu solo il Signore Saggi teologici d'altri tempi.* Casale Montferrato: Piemme, 1987.

Biffi, I. "Il giudizio '*per quandan connaturalitatem*' o '*per modum inclinationis*' secondo S. Tommaso: Analisi e prospettive." *Rivista di Filosofia Neoscolastica* 61 (1974): 356–93.

———. "Integralità cristiana e fondazione morale." *La Scuola Cattolica* 115 (1987): 570–90.

———. "L'*auctoritas* di sant'Agostino nelle questioni sulla legge nuova della *Summa Theologiae* di San Tommaso d'Aquino." *La Scuola Cattolica* 115 (1987): 220–48.

Billy, D. J., and D. L. Orsuto, eds. *Spirituality and Morality: Integrating Prayer and Action.* New York: Paulist Press, 1996.

Blank, J. "Evangelium und Gesetz: Zur theologischen Relativierung und Begrundung ethischer Normen." *Diakonia* 5 (1974): 363–75.

Böckle, F. *Fundamental Moral Theology.* New York: Pueblo, 1980.

———. "Humanae vitae als Prüfstein des wahren Glaubens? Zur kirchenpolitischen Dimension moraltheologischen Fragen." *Stimmen der Zeit* 115 (1990): 3–16.

Boethius. *De persona et duabus naturis: Contra Eutichen et Nestorium.* PL 64, 1343.

Bonaventure, Saint. *Breviloquium.* Italian edition edited by L. Mauro. Milan: 1985.

———. *Collationes in Hexaëmeron.* Italian edition edited by V. C. Bigi. Milan: 1985.

———. *Commentaria in quatuor libros sententiarum Magistri Petri Lombardi.* Typ. Coll. S. Bonaventurae Ad Claras Aquas. 4 vols. Quaracchi: 1882–1889.

Boyle, J. "Freedom, the Human Person, and Human Action." In *Principles of Catholic Moral Life,* ed. W. E. May, 237–66. Chicago: Franciscan Herald Press, 1980.

Brunner, E. *The Divine Imperative.* New York: Harper & Row, 1953.

Bubner, R. *Handlung, Sprache, und Vernunft: Grundbegriffe praktischer Philosophie: Neuausgabe mit einem Anhang.* Frankfurt am Main: Suhrkamp, 1982.

Buttiglione, R. *La crisi della morale.* Rome: Dino, 1991.

Caffarra, C. "La competenza del magistero nell'insegnamento di norme morali determinate." *Anthropotes* 6, no. 1 (1988): 7–23.

———. *Living in Christ: Fundamental Principles of Catholic Moral Teaching.* San Francisco: Ignatius Press, 1987.

———. "'Primum quod cadit in apprehensione practicae rationis'. Variazioni su un tema tomista." In *Attualità della Teologia Morale: Punti fermi-problemi aperti,* Studies in Honor of the Rev. P. J. Visser, "Studia Urbaniana" no. 31. Rome: Urbaniana University Press, 1987.

Caldera, R. T. *Le jugement par inclination chez Saint Thomas d'Aquin.* Paris: Vrin, 1980.

Ceccarini, L. *La morale come Chiesa: Ricerca di una fondazione ontologica.* Naples: D'Auria, 1980.

Cessario, R. *Le virtù.* Milan: Jaca Book, 1994.

———. *The Moral Virtues and Theological Ethics.* Notre Dame, Ind.: University of Notre Dame Press, 1991.

Chantillon, J. "Le primat de la vertú de charité dans la théologie de Saint Bonaventure." In *San Bonaventura, maestro di vita francescana e di sapienza cristiana,* vol. 3, 217–38. Rome: 1976.

Chantraine, G., and A. Scola. "L'évenement Christ et la vie morale. *"Anthropotes* 3, no. 1 (1987): 5–23.

Chapelle, A. *Les fondements de l'éthique. La symbolique de l'action.* Brussels: IET, 1988.

Crosby, J. *The Selfhood of the Human Person.* Washington, D.C.: The Catholic University of America Press, 1996.

Crossin, J. *What Are They Saying about Virtue?* New York: Paulist Press, 1985.

Curran, Ch. E., and R. A. McCormick, eds. *Readings in Moral Theology,* Vol. 2: *The Distinctiveness of Christian Ethics.* New York: Paulist Press, 1980.

Danto, A. C. "Basis Handlungen." In *Analytische Handlungstheorie,* ed. G. Meggle, vol. 1. Frankfurt am Main: 1985.

Delhaye, Ph. "Les conditions generales de l'agir chrétien selon Saint Bonaventure." In *San Bonaventura, maestro di vita francescana e di sapienza cristiana,* vol. 3, 184–215. Rome: 1976.

Dinan, S. A. "The Particularity of Moral Knowledge." *The Thomist* 50 (1986): 66–84.

Fessard,G. *La dialectique des "Exercises Spirituels" de Saint Ignace de Loyola,* Vol. 2: *Fondement-Péché-Orthodoxie.* Paris: Aubier, 1966.

Finance, J. de. *Être et agir dans la philosophie de Saint Thomas.* 3rd ed. Rome: PUG, 1965.

————. *L'ouverture et la norme: Questions sur l'agir humain.* Vatican City: Libreria Editrice Vaticana, 1989.

Foot, P. *Virtues and Vices and Other Essays in Moral Philosophy.* Oxford: Blackwell, 1981.

Fraling, B. "Hypertropie lehramtlicher Autorität in Dingen der Moral." In *Lehramt und Sexualmoral,* ed. P. Hünermann, 95–129. Düsseldorf: Patmos, 1990.

Fuchs, J. *Christian Ethics in a Secular Arena.* Washington, D.C.: Georgetown University Press, 1984.

————. "Christian Morality: Biblical Orientation and Human Evaluation." *Gregorianum* 67 (1986): 745–63.

————. *Essere del Signore. Un corso di teologia morale fondamentale.* Rome: PUG, 1981.

————. "Moraltheologie und Dogmatik." *Gregorianum* 50 (1969): 689–718.

Gadamer, H. G. *Il problema della conoscenza storica.* Naples: Guida, 1974.

Haro, R. Garcia de. "I concetti fondamentale della morale." *Anthropos* 1, no. 1 (1985): 95–108.

————. "La esencia y organizacion de las virtudes en la antropologia revelada." *Anthropotes* 7, no. 2 (1992): 137–52.

Geach, P. T. *The Virtues: The Stanton Lectures, 1973–1974.* New York: Cambridge University Press, 1977.

Gerosa, L. "Santità e diritto canonico." *La Scuola Cattolica* 125 (1997): 661–74.

Gilleman, G. *The Primacy of Charity in Moral Theology.* Westminster, Md.: Newman Press, 1959.

Gilson, E. *La philosophie de Saint Bonaventure.* 3rd ed. Paris: Vrin, 1953.

Giussani, L. "La Chiesa come luogo di moralità." *Communio* (Italian ed.) 34 (1977): 13–18; republished in *Moralità: Memoria e desiderio* (Milan: Jaca Book, 1980).

Golser, K. "Das Gewissen als 'verborgenste' Mitte in Menschen." In *Grundlagen und Probleme der heutigen Moraltheologie,* ed. W. Ernst, 113–37. Leipzig: 1989.

Grisez, G. "Dualism and the New Morality." In *Atti del Congresso Internazionale su San Tommaso d'Aquino nel suo settimo centenario,* Vol. 5: *L'agire morale.* Naples: Ed. Domenicane, 1977.

————. "The First Principle of Practical Reason: A Commentary on *Summa Theologiae,* I–II, q. 94, a. 2." *Natural Law Forum* 10 (1965): 168–96.

————. "Legalism, Moral Truth, and Pastoral Practice." In *The Catholic Priest as Moral Teacher and Guide,* ed. T. J. Herron, 97–113. San Francisco: Ignatius Press, 1990.

————. "Moral Absolutes: A Critique of the View of Joseph Fuchs, SJ." *Anthropos* 1, no. 2 (1985): 155–201.

————. *The Way of the Lord Jesus,* vol. 1 of *Christian Moral Principles.* Chicago: Franciscan Herald Press, 1983.

Grotius, H. *De iure belli ac pacis.*

Guardini, R. *The End of the Modern World.* Chicago: Regnery, 1984.

————. *La realtà della Chiesa.* Brescia: Morcelliana, 1973.

————. *Welt und Person.* Würzburg: 1962.

Guindon, A. "La liberté transcendentale à la lumiére d'une explication constructiviste de l'option fondamentale." In *Questions de liberté,* ed. J. C. Petit and J. C. Breton, 197–230. Montreal: Desclée / Novalis, 1991.

Habermas, J. *The Theory of Communicative Action.* New York: Oxford University Press, 1986.

Hamel, E. "La legge nuova per una comunità nuova." *La Civiltà Cattolica* 3 (1973): 351–60.

————. "La scelta morale tra coscienza e legge." *Rassegna di Teologia* 17 (1976): 121–36.

————. *Les dix paroles: Perspectives bibliques.* Montreal: Desclée de Brouwer, 1969.

————. *Loi naturelle et Loi du Christ.* Bruges and Paris: Desclée de Brouwer, 1964.

Hauerwas, S. *A Community of Character: Toward a Constructive Christian Social Ethic.* Notre Dame, Ind.: University of Notre Dame Press, 1981.

Hedwig, K. "Circa particularia, Kontingenz, Klugheit und Notwendigkeit im Aufbau des ethischen Aktes bei Thomas von Aquin." In *The Ethics of St. Thomas Aquinas,* ed. L. J. Elders and K. Hedwig. Vatican City: Libreria Editrice Vaticana, 1984.

Heidegger, M. "Die Frage nach der Technik." In *Vortraege und Aufsaetze,* 29–31. Pfullingen: Neske, 1954.

————. *Lettera sull'umanesimo.* Turin: 1975.

Herms, E. "Virtue: A Neglected Concept in Protestant Ethics." *Scottish Journal of Theology* 35 (1983): 481–95.

Hilary of Poitiers, Saint. *Commentarium in Mattheum.* PL 9.

————. *De Trinitate.* CCSL 62.

Hildebrand, D. von. *Ethics.* Chicago: Franciscan Herald Press, 1972.

Hoose, B. *Proportionalism: The American Debate and Its Europeans Roots.* Washington, D.C.: Georgetown University Press, 1987.

Hume, D. *A Treatise on Human Nature.* In *British Moralists, 1650–1800,* ed. D. D. Raphael, vol. 2. Oxford: Oxford University Press, 1969.

Hünermann, P. "Die Kompetenz des Lehramtes in Fragen der Sitte." In *Lehramt und Sexualmoral,* 130–56. Düsseldorf: Patmos, 1990.

John Chrysostom, Saint. *In I Corinthios Homiliae.* PG 61.

———. *In II Corinthios Homiliae.* PG 62.

Jonas, H. *Dalla fede antica all'uomo tecnologico.* Bologna: Il Mulino, 1991.

Jerumanis, A. M. *Le Christ, fondement ultime de l'agir moral. Etude du rapport christologie—morale dans l'oeuvre de Hans Urs von Balthasar.* Rome: Alfonsiana, 1988.

Juvenal (D. Iuni Iuvenalis). *Saturarum libri.*

Kaczynski. "Abbandono e ritorno alla virtù. Ma quale?" In *Sanctus Thomas de Aquino, Doctor hodiernae humanitatis,* 635–59. Rome: Libreria Editrice Vaticana, 1995.

———. "Il momento della verità nella riflessione di K. Wojtyla." *Angelicum* 56 (1979): 273–96.

———. *La legge nuova: L'elemento esterno della legge nuova secondo San Tommaso.* Rome and Vicenza: 1974.

———. "Verità sul bene nei diversi elementi della morale." *Rivista di Teologia Morale* 49 (1981): 419–31.

Kant, I. *Foundations for a Metaphysics of Morals.*

Keenan, J. F. "Distinguishing Charity as Goodness and Prudence as Rightness: A Key to Thomas's *Secunda Pars.*" *The Thomist* 56 (1992): 407–26.

———. *Goodness and Rightness in Thomas Aquinas's "Summa Theologiae."* Washington, D.C.: Georgetown University Press, 1992.

Kluxen, W. *Philosophische Ethik bei Thomas von Aquin.* 2nd ed. Hamburg: F. Meiner Verlag, 1980.

Lewis, C. S. *The Four Loves.* New York: Harcourt, Brace, & World, 1960.

L'Hour, J. *La morale de l'Alliance.* Paris: 1985.

Lopez Rodriguez, T. "Fides et mores en Trento." *Scripta theologica* 5, no. 1 (1973): 175–221.

Lubac, H. de. "Credo Sanctorum communionem." *Communio* (Italian ed.) 1 (1972): 22–31.

———. *The Splendor of the Church.* Glenlock, N.J.: Deus Books of Paulist Press, 1963.

Luther, Martin. *A Treatise on Christian Liberty.* In *Three Treatises.* Philadelphia: Muhlenburg Press, 1943.

MacIntyre, A. *After Virtue: A Study in Moral Theory.* Notre Dame, Ind.: University of Notre Dame Press, 1981.

May, W. E. *An Introduction to Moral Theology.* Rev. ed. Huntington, Ind.: Our Sunday Visitor Press, 1994.

―――. "The Sacredness of Life: An Overview of the Beginning." *Linacre Quarterly* 63 (1996): 87–96.

―――. "*The Splendor of Accuracy:* How Accurate?" *The Thomist* 59 (1995): 465–84.

―――. "*Veritatis splendor* and the Natural Law: From First Principles to Moral Absolutes." *Rivista teologica di Lugano* 2 (1996): 193–215.

Mahoney, J. *The Making of Moral Theology: A Study of the Roman Catholic Tradition.* Oxford: Clarendon Press, 1987.

―――. *Seeking the Spirit: Essays in Moral and Pastoral Theology.* London: Sheed & Ward, 1981.

Maritain, J. "De la connaissance par connaturalité." *Nova et Vetera* 55 (1980): 181–87.

McCormick, R. "Some Early Reactions to *Veritatis splendor.*" *Theological Studies* 55 (1994): 481–506.

Mehl, R. *Catholic Ethics and Protestant Ethics.* Philadelphia: Westminster Press, 1971.

Meilaender, G. *The Theory and Practice of Virtue.* Notre Dame, Ind.: University of Notre Dame Press, 1984.

Melina, L. "Coscienza, libertà e Magistero." *La Scuola Cattolica* 120 (1992): 152–71.

―――. "La Chiesa come *communio personarum* e la *Redemptor Hominis.*" *Synesis* 6, nos.1–2 (1989): 143–63.

―――. *La conoscenza morale: Linee di riflessione sul commento di San Tommaso all'Etica Nicomachea.* Rome: Città Nuova, 1987.

―――. *Morale: Tra crisi e rinnovamento: Gli assoluti morali, l'opzione fondamentale, la formazione della coscienza.* Milan: Ares, 1993.

Moore, G. E. *Principia Ethica.* Cambridge: Cambridge University Press, 1903.

Mühlen, H. *Una Mystica Persona. La Chiesa come il mistero dello Spirito Santo in Cristo e nei cristiani una persona in molte persone.* Rome: Città Nuova, 1968.

Nadeau-Lacour, T. "Le martyre comme 'celebration al plus solennelle de l'Evangile de la Vie.'" *Anthropotes* 13, no. 2 (1997): 297–316.

Nelson, D. M. *The Priority of Prudence, Virtue, and Natural Law in Thomas Aqiuinas and the Implications for Modern Ethics.* State Park: Pennsylvania State University, 1992.

Origen. *In Exodum Homiliae.* Edited by W. A. Baerhrens. Leipzig: 1920.

Pannenberg, W. *Ethics.* Philadelphia: Westminster Press, 1981.

―――. *Ethik und Ekklesiologie: Gesammelte Aufsaetze.* Göttingen: Vandenhoeck & Ruprecht, 1977.

————. *Grundlagen der Ethik: Philosophisch-theologische Perspektiven.* Göttingen: Vanderhoeck & Ruprecht, 1996.

Perez-Soba Diez del Corral, J. J. *La interpersonalidad en el amor? La respuesta de Santo Tomas.* Ph.D. diss., Istituto Giovanni Paolo II per studi su Matrimonio e Famiglia. (Published in part under this title in Rome in 1997).

Perini, G. "Il 'trattato' di teologia morale fondamentale." In *Divus Thomas* 14. Bologna: Ed. Studio Domenicano, 1996.

Pero-Sanz Elorz, J. M. *El conocimiento por connaturalidad: La afectividad en la gnoseologia tomista.* Pamplona: Eunsa, 1964.

Pinckaers, S. *La morale catholique.* Paris: Cerf, 1991.

————. "La vertu est toute autre chose qu'une habitude." In *Le renouveau de la morale,* 144–61. Paris: Téqui, 1979.

————. "L'Eglise dans la loi nouvelle: Esprit et institution." *Nova et Vetera* 4 (1987): 246–62.

————. *L'evangile et la morale.* Paris and Fribourg: Cerf/Presses Universitaires de Fribourg, 1990.

————. "Linee per un rinnovamento evangelico della morale." *Annales Theologici* 10 (1996): 3–68.

————. "Qu' est-ce que la spiritualité? 1. Morale: Ascétique, mystique, spiritualité." *Nova et Vetera* 1 (1990): 8–19.

————. "Rediscovering Virtue." *The Thomist* 60, no. 3 (1996): 361–78.

————. *The Sources of Christian Ethics.* Washington, D.C.: The Catholic University of America Press, 1995.

Pieper, J. *Auskunft über die Tugenden.* Zurich: Verlag der Arche, 1970.

————. *The Four Cardinal Virtues.* Notre Dame, Ind.: University of Notre Dame Press, 1965.

————. *Uber die Schwierigkeit, heute zu glauben.* Munich: 1974.

Plato. *The Republic.*

Pompei, A. "Influssi di Francesco sul pensiero bonaventurano circa il rapporto tra cristologia e morale." *Miscellanea Francescana* 82 (1982): 534–68.

Poppi, A. *Studi sull'etica della prima scuola francescana.* Padua: Centro Studi Antoniani, 1996.

Porter, J. *The Recovery of Virtue: The Relevance of Aquinas for Christian Ethics.* Louisville, Ky.: Westminster/John Knox Press, 1990.

Pouchet, R. *La rectitudo chez Saint Anselme: Un itinéraire augustinien de l'âme à Dieu.* Paris: Ed. Augustiniennes, 1964.

Poupard, P. *La morale chrétienne demain.* Paris: Desclée, 1985.

Prümmer, D. M. *Manuale Theologiae Moralis secundum principia S. Thomae Aquinatis.* Freiburg im Breisgau: Herder, 1935.

Rahner, K. *Foundations of Christian Faith: An Introduction to the Idea of Christianity.* New York: Seabury Press, 1978.

———. "The Theological Concept of Concupiscence." In *Theological Investigations,* 1: 385–420. Baltimore: Helicon, 1962.

———. "Theology of Freedom." In *Theological Investigations,* Vol. 6: *Concerning Vatican Council II,* 190–93. Baltimore: Helicon, 1969.

Ratzinger, J. *"The Catechism of the Catholic Church* and the Optimism of the Redeemed." *Communio* 20 (1993): 469–84.

———. *Church, Ecumenism, and Politics: New Essays in Ecclesiology.* New York: Crossroad, 1988.

———. "The Ecclesiology of the Second Vatican Council." *Communio* 13 (1986): 239–52.

———. *Guardare Cristo: Esercizi di fede, speranza e carità.* Milan: Jaca Book, 1989.

———. *Il nuovo popolo di Dio: Questioni ecclesiologiche.* 3rd ed. Brescia: Queriniana, 1984.

———. *La Chiesa: Una comunità sempre in cammino.* Alba: Paoline, 1991.

———. *La via della fede: Le ragione dell'etica nell'epoca presente.* Milan: Ares, 1996.

———. *Popolo e casa di Dio in S. Agostino.* Milan: Jaca Book, 1971.

———. *San Bonaventura: La teologia della storia.* Firenze: Nardini, 1991.

Rhonheimer, M. "Ethics of Norms and the Lost Virtues: Searching the Roots of the Crisis of Ethical Reasoning." *Anthropotes* 9, no. 2 (1993): 231–47.

———. *Gut und Böse oder Richtig und Falsch: Was unterscheidet das Sittliche?* In *Ethik der Leistung,* ed. H. Thomas, 47–75. Herford: 1988.

———. "Intentional Actions and the Meaning of Object: A Reply to Richard McCormick." *The Thomist* 59 (1995): 279–311.

———. "'Intrinsically Evil Acts' and the Moral Viewpoint: Clarifying a Central Teaching of *Veritatis splendor.*" *The Thomist* 58 (1994): 1–39.

———. *La prospettiva della morale: Fondamenti dell'etica filosofica.* Rome: Armando, 1994.

———. "Morale cristiana e ragionevolezza morale. Di che cosa è il compimento la legge del Vangelo?" In *Gesù Cristo legge vivente e personale della Santa Chiesa,* ed. G. Borgonovo, 147–68.

———. *Natural Law and Practical Reason.* New York: Fordham University Press, 2000.

———. *Praktische Vernunft und Vernunftigkeit der Praxis: Handklungstheorie bei Thomas von Aquin in ihrer Entstehung aus dem Problemkontext der aristotelischen Ethik.* Berlin: Akademie Verlag, 1994.

Richard of St. Victor. *De Trinitate*. PL 196.

Rodriguez Luño, A. *Etica*. Firenze: Le Monnier, 1992.

————. *La scelta etica. Il rapporto tra libertà e virtù*. Milan: Ares, 1988.

————. "'*Veritatis splendor*' un anno dopo. Appunti per un bilancio, 1."*Acta Philosophica* 4, no. 2 (1995): 223–60.

Ross, W. D. *The Right and the Good*. Oxford: Oxford University Press, 1930.

Ruggieri, G. "Ecclesiologia ed etica." *Cristianesimo nella Storia* 9 (1988): 1–22.

Santoro, F. *La comunità condizione della fede*. Milan: Jaca Book, 1976.

Scarpelli, U. *Etica senza verita*. Bologna: Mulino, 1982.

Scheeben, M. J. *The Mysteries of Christianity*. St. Louis: Herder, 1946.

Scheffczyk, L. "*Sensus Fidelium*: Witness on the Part of the Community." *Communio* 15, no. 2 (1988): 182–98.

Schlögel, H. *Kirche und sittliches Handeln. Zur Ekklesiologie in der Grundlagenddiscussion der deutschsprachigen katholischen Moraltheologie seit der Jahrhundertwende*. Mainz: Mathias Grünewald Verlag, 1981.

Schmitz, P. "Ein Glaube-kontroverse Gewissensentscheidung." In *Gewissen: Aspekte eine vieldiskutierten Sachverhaltes*, ed. J. Horstmann, 60–76. Schwerte: Katholische Akademie, 1983.

Schockenhoff, E. *Bonum hominis. Die anthropologischen und theologischen Grundlagen der Tugendethik des Thomas von Aquin*. Mainz: Mathias Grünewald Verlag, 1987.

Schönborn, C. "Breve introduzione alle quattro parti del Catechismo." In J. Ratzinger and C. Schönborn, *Breve introduzione al "Catechismo della Chiesa cattolica*." Rome: Città Nuova, 1994.

Schüller, B. "Zu den Schwierigkeiten, die Tugend zu Rehabilitieren." *Theologie und Philosophie* 58 (1983): 535–55.

Schürmann, H. "Die Gemeinde des Neuen Bundes als der Quellort des sittlichen Erkennens nach Paulus." *Catholica* 26 (1972): 15–37.

————. "Du caractère obligatoire des normes et directives morales du Nouveau Testament." In *Principes d'éthique chrétienne*, ed. J. Ratzinger and Ph. Delhaye, 37–71. Paris and Namur: Lethiélleux, 1979.

Scola, A. "Christologie et morale." *Nouvelle Revue Théologique* 109 (1987): 382–410.

————. "Gesù Cristo legge vivente e personale." In *"Veritatis splendor"*: *Testo e commenti*, Quaderni de "L'Osservatore Romano," 153–57. Vatican City: Libreria Editrice Vaticana, 1994.

————. *Identidad y diferencia: La relacion hombre-mujer*. Madrid: Encuentro, 1989.

————. *La fondazione teologica della legge naturale nello "Scriptum supra Senten-*

tiis" di San Tommaso d'Aquino. Freiburg im Schweiz: Universitaetsverlag, 1982.

———. *Questioni di antropologia teologica.* 2nd ed. Rome: PUL-Mursia, 1997.

Segalla, G. "L'etica di Gesù da Dodd a Dillman (1951–1984)." *Teologia* 1 (1986): 24–67.

Spaemann, R. "La responsabilità personale e il suo fondamento." In *Etica teleologica o etica deontologica. Un dibattito al centro della teologia morale odierna,* Quaderni CRIS nos. 49-50. Rome: 1983.

———. *Moralische Grundbegriffe.* Munich: Beck, 1983.

Stelzenberger, J. *Conscientia bei Augustinus.* Paderborn: 1959.

Styczen, T. *L'amore come comunione con gli altri e il senso della vita.* Rome: Pro manuscripto, 1985.

Szostek, A. *Natur, Vernunft, Freiheit. Philosophische Analyse der Konzeption "schöpferisher Vernunft" in der zeitgenössischen Moraltheologie.* Frankfurt am Main: Peter Lang, 1992.

Tatarkiewicz, W. *Analysis of Happiness.* The Hague and Warsaw: 1976.

Tertullian. *De Baptismo.* PL 1.

———. *De carnis resurrectione.* PL 2.

Theiner, M. *Die Entwicklung der Moraltheologie zur eigenständige Disziplin.* Regensburg: 1970.

Thomas Aquinas, Saint. *De Veritate.* Ed. Leonina, vol. 22. Rome: 1975–1976.

———. *In Joannem Lectura.* Turin: Marietti, 1972.

———. *Quaestiones disputatae (De Malo).* Ed. Leonina, vol. 23. Rome: 1982.

———. *Sententia Libri Ethicorum.* Ed. Leonina, vol. 47. Rome: 1969.

———. *Summa contra gentiles.* Turin: Marietti, 1961–1967.

———. *Summa theologiae.* Ed. Leonina, vols 6–11. Rome: 1888–1903.

———. *Super Ep. ad Corinthios.* Turin: Marietti, 1964.

———. *Super Ep. ad Galatas.* Turin: Marietti, 1964.

———. *Super Ep. ad Romanos.* Turin: Marietti, 1964.

Tremblay, R. *Cristo e la morale in alcuni documenti del Magistero. "Catechismo della Chiesa Cattolica," "Veritatis splendor," "Evangelium vitae."* Rome: Ed. Dehoniane, 1996.

———. *L'"homme" qui divinise. Pour une interpretation christocentrique de l'existence.* Montreal: Ed. Paulines, 1993.

Van Si, A. Nguyen. *Seguire e imitare Cristo secondo San Bonaventura.* Milan: Ed. Bibl. Francescana, 1995.

Vereecke, L. *Da Guglielmo d'Ockham a Sant'Alfonso de Ligouri: Saggi di storia della teologia morale moderna (1300–1787).* Rome: Alfonsiana, 1990.

Vigna, C. "La verità del desiderio come fondazione della norma morale." In

Problemi di etica: Fondazione, norme, orientamenti, ed. E. Berti. Padua: Fondazione Lanza, Gregoriana Editrice, 1990.

Wadell, P. J. *Friendship and the Moral Life.* Notre Dame, Ind.: University of Notre Dame Press, 1989.

———. *The Primacy of Love: An Introduction to the Ethics of Thomas Aquinas.* New York: Paulist Press, 1992.

Wald, B. *Genitrix virtutum: Zum Wandel des aristotelischen Begriffs praktischer Vernunft.* Munster: 1986.

Westberg, D. *Right Practical Reason: Aristotle, Action, and Prudence in Aquinas.* Oxford: Clarendon Press, 1994.

Wojtyla, K. *The Acting Person.* Boston: D. Riedel/Dordrecht, 1979.

———. *Czlowiek w polu odpowiedzilnosci.* Rome and Lublin: 1991.

———. *Love and Responsibility.* New York: Farrar-Straus-Giroux, 1981.

———. "Subjectivity and the Irreducible Element in Man." *Analecta Husserliana* 7 (1978): 107–16.

Yannaras, C. *La libertà dell'ethos: Alle radici della crisi morale in occidente.* Bologna: Ed. Dehoniane, 1984.

———."La morale della libertà: Presupposti per una visione ortodossa della morale." In C. Yannaras, R. Mehl, and J. Aubert, *La legge della libertà: Evangelo e morale.* Milan: Jaca Book, 1973.

Ziegler, J. G. "Christozentrische Sittlichkeit—christusförmige Tugenden." *Trierische Theologische Zeitschrift* 96 (1987): 290–312.

Index

∞

Index of Subjects

Index of Authors and Documents

Sharing in Christ's Virtues: For a Renewal of Moral Theology in Light of Veritatis Splendor
was designed and composed in Monotype Dante with Poetica Chancery display type
by Kachergis Book Design, Pittsboro, North Carolina, and printed on
60-pound Glatfelter Natural and bound by Cushing-Malloy, Inc.,
Ann Arbor, Michigan.